THE MASTER MUSICIANS

SCHÜTZ

Series edited by Stanley Sadie

THE MASTER MUSICIANS

SCHÜTZ

Basil Smallman

OXFORD

UNIVERSITY PRESS

OXFORD
UNIVERSITY PRESS

Great Clarendon Street, Oxford OX2 6DP

Oxford University Press is a department of the University of Oxford.
It furthers the University's objective of excellence in research, scholarship,
and education by publishing worldwide in

Oxford New York

Athens Auckland Bangkok Bogotá Buenos Aires Calcutta
Cape Town Chennai Dar es Salaam Delhi Florence Hong Kong Istanbul
Karachi Kuala Lumpur Madrid Melbourne Mexico City Mumbai
Nairobi Paris São Paulo Singapore Taipei Tokyo Toronto Warsaw

with associated companies in Berlin Ibadan

Oxford is a registered trade mark of Oxford University Press
in the UK and in certain other countries

Published in the United States
by Oxford University Press Inc., New York

British Library Cataloguing in Publication Data

Data available

Library of Congress Cataloging in Publication Data

Smallman, Basil.
Schütz / Basil Smallman.
p. cm. (The master musicians)
Includes bibliographical references and index.
1. Schütz, Heinrich, 1585–1672—Criticism and interpretation.
I. Title. II. Series: Master musicians series.
ML410.S35S6 2000 782.2'2'092—dc21 99–42131
ISBN 0–19–816674–5

1 3 5 7 9 10 8 6 4 2

Typeset by Hope Services (Abingdon) Ltd.
Printed in Great Britain
on acid-free paper by
Biddles Ltd.,
Guildford and King's Lynn

To Tony, Chris, and Ros, with love

Preface

It may seem an act of great daring, even of considerable folly, to provide at the end of the twentieth century an account for English-speaking readers of the life and work of a German composer who died over three hundred years ago after a long career, and whose surviving output consists almost entirely of sacred music. In justification, however, there are important considerations which should be taken into account: that music, even when allied to a specific, unfamiliar language, is not easily constrained by national frontiers; that 'early music' (a term taken to embrace all which predates that of Bach and Handel) has nowadays a large following and continually attracts further adherents; and, most crucially, that Schütz is by any criteria a seminal figure in European cultural history, one of a constellation of seventeenth-century creative artists and thinkers which, in addition to other major composers, includes Bernini, Descartes, Milton, Newton, Rembrandt, and Vermeer. It is on these grounds that I hope to find some vindication for my work; for the rest, the composer and his music can be relied upon to provide the most persuasive advocacy. The prefatory observations which follow, though not unimportant, are few and relatively simple. It must be acknowledged, however, in all humility, that they display little of the magisterial skill with which Schütz's introductions to his published collections are unfailingly endowed.

Attention may be called first to the way in which the book is organized. Rather than providing for a survey of Schütz's compositions, separately by genre, my policy has been to focus in chronological succession on the large collections of works published during his lifetime, together with the most important of those which were left in manuscript, and to interpolate accounts of these between chapters devoted to biography. By this means it has been possible to trace a clear path from the ardent, often experimental, writing of the composer's earliest period to the serene, more abstract manner characteristic of his maturity; and at the same time to identify instances where momentous external events appear to have impinged upon his music—for example in his setting of Psalm 2, 'Why do the heathen rage and the people imagine a vain thing?' (SWV 23), published in 1619 shortly after the start of the Thirty Years War, and his heartfelt version of 'Now thank we all our God' (SWV 418) which followed upon the signing of the Peace of Westphalia in 1648.

Secondly, since most of Schütz's major publications contain a great many individual items (no less than fifty-six in the two sets of small sacred concertos of 1636 and 1639) it has been thought advisable, in this moderately sized volume, to focus on those relatively few (listed in the Index under the composer's name) which have seemed to me to provide in particular contexts the most valuable insights into the composer's style and technique. The reader is nevertheless advised to extend his range of study to include as many as possible of the 'neglected' works (all of which can be traced through the list of works in Appendix B), and wherever feasible to consult the scores in order to reach a fuller grasp of the issues under discussion.

Some special mental agility may be required of the reader (as it has been of the author) with regard to the religious convictions and usages of the Schütz era. Although there is no reason to suppose that the composer was deeply immersed in theology, there is evidence, both in his writings and in his relations with his contemporaries, that even in the unstable times in which he lived, when religious differences were a prime cause of war, and revelation was beginning to yield place to reason, he held unwaveringly to the doctrines of his Lutheran faith and lived, to all outward appearances, in a state of constant religious awareness, apparently untroubled by inner doubts. From a present-day standpoint, where free-thinking is more the norm than the exception, an imaginative penetration of Schütz's historical circumstances may well be necessary if a true understanding is to be reached of his approach to his work—and, by pertinent association, of my attempts to place it securely in its appropriate religious context. In this general connection it may be prudent to remark also that the term 'Catholic', unqualified by the epithet 'Roman', is used throughout the book—erroneously, of course, but as a useful means of simplifying the text—in reference both to the ancient Church of Rome and its adherents.

As a glance at my bibliography will show, the vast majority of writings about Schütz are the work of German scholars (not surprisingly, since the composer holds such a prominent place in their national history and culture), and parallel contributions in English are regrettably few. The main exception is the classic study *Heinrich Schütz: sein Leben und Werk* by H. J. Moser which, following its original publication in 1936, was translated into English in 1959 by the American scholar Carl F. Pfatteicher. Immensely detailed, and at the same time richly discursive, this work, in both its German and English forms, has served as a basis for virtually all later Schütz study. Inevitably, however, some of the information it contains has been superseded by later research findings—such as those relating to the composer's life, which are well summarized by Wolfram Steude in a recent article, 'Zum gegenwärtigen Stand der Schütz-Biographik' (On the present state of Schütz biography), details of which, and of the Moser/Pfatteicher book, are to be found in the bibliography. It is therefore with the needs of the English-speaking reader in mind that, as a general introduction to the composer and his work, which nevertheless incorporates several aspects of the most recent research, the present book has been devised. It has not, of course, proved possible (nor in many cases proper) to eliminate all German- and Latin-related information; but wherever feasible English translations have been appended. And as further compensation, some readers may find (as I have, repeatedly) that a study of Schütz's texts and music can provide a wholly enjoyable way of gaining an increased knowledge of the language involved—at least in its biblical manifestation.

I am much indebted to the Devon County Library at Kingsbridge, and in particular to the librarian, Wendy Read, and the senior library assistant, Yvonne Doidge, for assistance, readily and efficiently given, in obtaining essential source material for me; also to Bettina Erlenkamp of the State and University Library of Dresden for help in securing illustrations for the book; and to W. H. Fox for advice on matters of German history. Finally I am delighted to express my deep gratitude to Bruce Phillips and Helen Foster of the Oxford University Press for first encouraging me to write the book; to Stanley Sadie for the continuing confidence he has shown in my work; and to Julia Kellerman, without whose meticulous editorial attentions the whole enterprise would have been immeasurably the poorer.

Basil Smallman
Thurlestone, Devon, 1998

Contents

Schütz

Illustrations

Schütz

15 The Electoral Palace at Dresden: engraving from *Wechsen Chronik*, Nuremberg, 1679
16 St John Passion, title-page and opening of Introit in manuscript of Zacharias Grundig (Leipzig Musikbibliothek of S. Becker II 2 15)

Bibliographical abbreviations

AV   Authorized Version: the King James Bible of 1611

GBS   *Heinrich Schütz: Gesammelte Briefe und Schriften* (collected letters and writings), ed. E. H. Müller (Regensburg, 1931)

MGG   *Die Musik in Geschichte und Gegenwart*

Mos/Pf.   H. J. Moser, *Heinrich Schütz: sein Leben und Werk* (Kassel, 1936/54). Eng. trans., Carl F. Pfatteicher, *Heinrich Schütz: His Life and Works* (St Louis, Concordia, 1959)

NSA   *Heinrich Schütz: Neue Ausgabe Sämtlicher Werke*, ed. W. Bittinger, W. Breig, W. Ehmann, *et al.* (Kassel, 1955–)

SGA   *Heinrich Schütz: Sämtliche Werke*, ed. P. Spitta *et al.* (Leipzig, 1885–94, 1909, 1927; repr. 1968–73)

SJb   Schütz-Jahrbuch, ed. W. Breig (Kassel, 1979–)

Spagn.   *Letters and Documents of Heinrich Schütz 1656–72*, ed. Gina Spagnoli (Rochester, N.Y., 1990)
    (The two page references given in the footnotes refer, respectively, to the German and English versions of the text.)

SSA   *Stuttgarter Schütz-Ausgabe*, ed. G. Graulich *et al.* (1971–)

SWV   *Schütz-Werke-Verzeichnis. Kleine Ausgabe* (numbered catalogue of works), ed. W. Bittinger (Kassel, 1960)

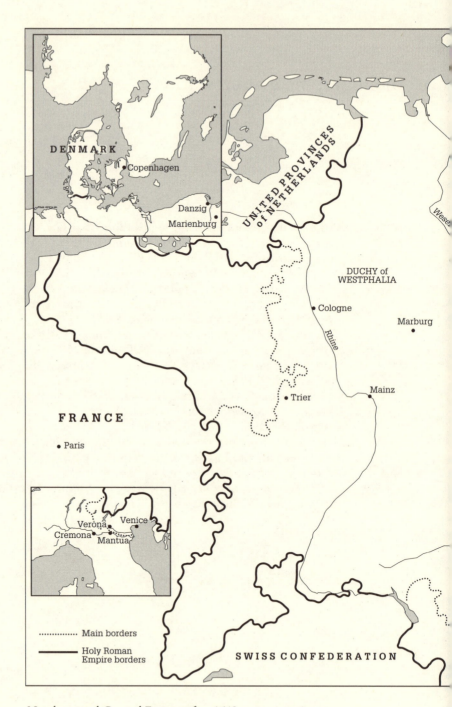

Northern and Central Europe after 1648

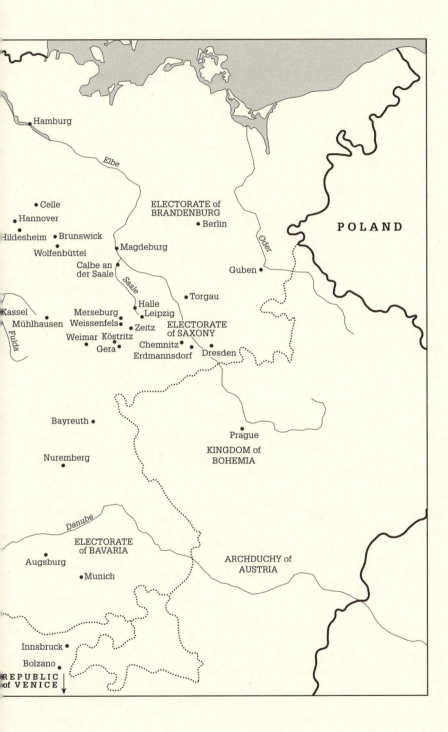

Introduction

Inscribed in 1672 on the composer's memorial tablet in the old Frauenkirche in Dresden (now lost through rebuilding), the Latin phrase 'Heinricus Schützius Seculi sui Musicus excellentissimus' (Heinrich Schütz the most excellent musician of his age), grandly epitomizes the honour in which the composer was held in Lutheran Germany throughout the greater part of the seventeenth century, and which has since been echoed, at first faintly, and then ever more robustly and more widely over the centuries to the present day. His route to fame and great achievement was not always an easy one. In his youth his obvious bent towards music was at first stifled by self-doubt and parental opposition; and at crucial stages in his development it was only by the support of the patrons and mentors best able to serve his interests—whom he later saw as fulfilling the 'will of God'—that he was set firmly on his course towards the heights of his profession. During the middle years of his career still further severe tests were made of his resolution as the ravages of the Thirty Years War undermined his scope for musical performance, and limited many of his chances of gaining publication. During the late 1660s, in his eighth decade, and with his zest for original work unquenched, he continued to write works of outstanding vitality, comparable in imaginative vigour to those of the octogenarian Verdi two hundred years later. But like many another creator of genius, his reputation was soon eclipsed after his death, as the tide of history swept on, and for the time being passed him by. And it was not until the early decades of the nineteenth century that the German nation, prompted by the Romantic spirit of the age to seek out its cultural roots, undertook the systematic review of its musical past which was to lead to the earliest of the great collected editions of modern times—initially, from 1851 and 1859, of the music of J. S. Bach and Handel, respectively, and in 1885, on the tercentenary of his birth, that of Schütz.

Together with the rediscovery of his music, there has been assembled over the last hundred years, partly by chance, but more particularly by the dedicated efforts of numerous scholars, a valuable body of source material—comprising portraits, letters, prefaces, memorials, and sundry other printed and manuscript documents—by means of which it has been possible to create a remarkably rounded picture of the composer and the milieux in which he worked.[1] From the portraits there emerges an immediately arresting impression, of a man of exemplary character, keen intellect, and a profound sense of duty and self-denial—an impression amply confirmed by the documentary material, which constantly discloses the composer's integrity and strength of purpose in the context of his prodigiously industrious career. The surviving letters (couched always in the courteous, but often excessively florid, style of the age) provide vivid glimpses of Schütz's multifarious activities, not only his regular ones with the Dresden Kapelle but, more widely, those involving such tasks as the procuring of Italian musicians for service at the Saxon court (a move which was eventually to involve him in unjustified censure), the tactful arbitration between musical disputants, and the constant provision of new compositions, as much for private events such as the birthdays, weddings, and funerals of relations and friends, as for impressive state occasions, with colourful musico-dramatic performances, at the royal courts of Germany and Denmark. From the letters we learn how greatly admired he was by the successive electors he served at Dresden—an esteem too rarely matched by a regard for their financial obligations; and at the opposite extreme, how little notice the court dignitaries took of his urgent pleas for the relief from desperate monetary problems of the chapel musicians under his care. Further evidence of the warmth of his personality (an aspect which is perhaps less immediately apparent in the portraits) is provided by the close ties he maintained continually with the members of his family; and by the aid—in terms of advice, music, and money—which, in the aftermath of the Thirty Years War, he freely gave to those courts whose musical establishments had suffered the most serious degradation. The sort of counsel he was prepared to offer is well demonstrated in a letter which he addressed, in September 1663, to Duke Moritz (the youngest brother of the Dresden Elector) about the rebuilding, then in progress, of the court chapel at Zeitz. 'The new choir lofts', he declared, 'should be moved forward by one-and-a-half ells [since otherwise] the musicians are hidden . . . and their resonance will thus carry much less effectively into the church'[2]—hardly the words of a remote visionary, but of a pragmatist for whom attention to detail was clearly of prime importance. Finally, as evidence of the respect in which Schütz was held by other musicians, even from his earliest days at Dresden, one may point to the many pupils who were drawn to study with him, and who remained loyal to him throughout their careers. Prominent among them were his cousin, Heinrich Albert, later to be acclaimed for his continuo-accompanied songs, sacred and secular; Christoph Bernhard who, after service as a Kantor in Hamburg, returned to Dresden and was

---

[1] Important printed sources, listed under their authors' names (for details see bibliography) are as follows. (a) Documents and letters: Müller; Spagnoli. (b) Catalogue of Works: Bittinger/Breig. (c) Biography: Geier; Leaver (2); Moser; Pirro; Steude. (d) Research: Skei. (e) History (non-musical): Parker; Wedgwood.

[2] Spagn., Doc. 43, 339 and 341.

appointed Kapellmeister there in 1681; the composer Caspar Kittel and his son Christoph; Johann Klemm, an organist who later prospered in music publishing, and his cousin Anton Colander; Matthias Weckmann, who became organist at the Jacobikirche in Hamburg and a leading composer of his time; and Johann Theile who was appointed Kapellmeister at Gottorf and achieved recognition both in opera and church music, and as a theorist. As André Pirro observed, in his delightful early study of the composer, 'the Dresden Kapelle [in those days] became a veritable school of music'.[3]

In most modern editions of the source material outlined above, the original, often somewhat convoluted, German is retained, a natural enough procedure in the interests of scholarship, but one likely to be problematic for the non-German reader. Help is available, however, in the prefaces to many recent volumes of Schütz's works which include English translations of several of the more important passages; and in the existence of a richly informative collection of writings from the last sixteen years of the composer's life, edited by the American scholar Gina Spagnoli, which provides, side by side, both the original German texts and excellent modern English translations. In the present study, an attempt is made to trace a median line between the cognoscenti and the non-linguists (and thus, it is hoped, to avoid giving offence to either) by providing—as a general but not invariable principle—the quoted material in English translation, with the original German placed in parentheses for the shorter excerpts, and in footnotes for the longer ones. Although language difficulties (extending to Italian and Latin as well as German) can also impede the study of Schütz's compositions, these should prove generally less severe. In the great majority of his works, Schütz draws his texts from the Lutheran bible, and for these a familiar and readily accessible English counterpart exists in the King James Authorized Version of 1611. The problems, therefore, are unlikely to be much greater than those presented by (and in general comfortably accepted for) the best known of nineteenth-century lieder. For Schütz, it may be argued, the Lutheran bible, with its noble language and rich imagery, became as much a literary quarry to be mined as did the poetry of Goethe, Mayrhofer, and Schiller for Schubert, or that of Heine, Rückert, and Eichendorff for Schumann. That one genre deals with sacred and the other with profane themes is hardly likely to inconvenience the 'gracious reader' (günstiger Leser—as Schütz would have put it).

Information about the nature of the services specified for the principal days of the Church's Year at the Dresden court, during the later part of Schütz's career, can be gained from a Chapel Order, which was compiled under the command of the Elector Johann Georg II, after the renovation of the palace church in c.1662.[4] Of the two main services, *Gottesdienst* (including Mass) seems usually to have been celebrated early in the

---

[3] A. Pirro, *Schütz*, 50.   [4] Spagn., Doc. 13, 175 and 193.

morning, since it is noted that on feast days, such as Christmas, Easter, and Whitsun, it was customarily preceded by cannon shots from the Kreuzturm and bell-ringing throughout the city, intermittently between 4.00 a.m. and 7.30 a.m.; and *Vesper* (invariably with a Latin or German Magnificat) to have started early in the afternoon, from about 2.00 p.m., possibly to take advantage of the winter daylight. The items of music to which Schütz would chiefly have been expected to contribute are the concertos and motets (exhibiting *moderno* and *antico* styles, respectively) which are listed for both types of service. It is noteworthy that in the morning services the 'concerto or motet' is normally placed just after the sermon, almost certainly as a way of enhancing the preacher's biblical exegesis by cross-relating it to a musical work on the same (usually biblical) topic. It may be indicative of such a practice that the first rule of the Chapel Order requires that 'the texts, in Latin as well as in German, provided for the composition of concertos and motets, should always be shown to [the senior court preacher] by the Kapellmeister'. In the Order the only compositions actually identified are the 'Histories' for Christmas and Easter, each allocated to its relevant *Vesper* service; and the only mention of Schütz by name occurs in the lists for certain weekday services, where in place of the usual Latin Introit, 'A Psalm of Dr. Becker set to the melodies by the Kapellmeister Heinrich Schütz [shall be sung]'.[5]

The important role of the organist, and various of the particular demands made upon him, are the subject of comment in many of Schütz's prefaces. Usually, at Dresden, at least two organists were employed, who would undertake between them the duties required by the daily services.[6] The special skills expected of them would include the improvisation of accompaniments from a figured bass (often, no doubt, only in manuscript), the ability to transpose to suit the pitch requirements of particular groups of singers, and to put together organ scores in support of the choral voice-parts, and the provision of preludes and other short pieces, improvised or pre-composed, for performance at fixed points during services. There remains, however, no indication of what independent organ music was actually performed; and there is nothing to suggest that, during Schütz's lifetime, any significant school of organ composition, equivalent to that of Heinrich Scheidemann (*c*.1595–1663) and his pupil Johann Adam Reincken (1623–1722) at Hamburg, was established at Dresden. Matthias Weckmann, the only organist, and Schütz pupil, who contributed at all significantly to the repertory, did so after leaving Dresden and taking up his appointment, from 1655, to the Jacobikirche in Hamburg. And Schütz himself, who gained a considerable reputation as an organist, particularly in his younger days, appears, regrettably enough, to have left no independent music for the instrument.

[5] Spagn., Doc. 13, 190 and 208.
[6] See Eberhard Schmidt, *Der Gottesdienst am kurfürstlichen Hofe zu Dresden*; Vol. 12 of *Veröffentlichungen der Evangelischen Gesellschaft für Liturgieforschung* (Göttingen, 1961).

In order to elucidate discussion of the music in later chapters, some preliminary observations may prove helpful about one special aspect of Schütz's musical language: his management of 'keys', 'scales', and 'tonality'. Based on ancient modal traditions, those codified by Glarean in his *Dodecachordon* of 1547, the system used by Schütz involves six main 'keycentres'—D, E, F, G, A, and C, which correspond, respectively, to the modefinals of the Dorian, Phrygian, Lydian, Mixolydian, Aeolian, and Ionian modes,—and provides (apart from a few exceptional cases to be noted separately in their later contexts) for a pattern of three major 'keys' (on F, G, and C) and three minor ones (on D, E, and A). Also in keeping with tradition is his adoption (apart again from some minor exceptions) of the plain 'key-signatures' typical of modal practice: an open one (without flats or sharps) for all settings related to the basic modes, and one involving a single B flat to indicate a transposition down a fifth (or up a fourth) of the modal note-sequence, to provide, for example, the commonly found G minor version of the Dorian mode or F major one of the Ionian mode. Changes emanated, however, from an increasingly frequent introduction of accidentals during the course of the music (primarily, but by no means solely, to ensure a sharpened leading-note at cadences), whereby the individuality of the modes, both as a melodic and harmonic force, was naturally diminished. As a result the major and minor modes (apart from the Phrygian mode which did not readily shed its special characteristics) tended to lean, respectively, towards Ionian (C major) and Aeolian (A minor) scalepatterns, and thus increasingly closer to the modern diatonic system. Schütz's methods represent an effective compromise. While there is growing evidence in his music of proto-diatonic elements at work, there are at the same time clear indications of the special appeal which certain typically modal shades of melodic and harmonic colouring continued to hold for him. In some of his works, indeed, there is still preserved modal writing of a remarkable purity—in the St Luke and St John Passions, for example, in which, respectively, basic features of the Lydian and Phrygian modes are retained, as a means of imparting to them special expressive qualities. In the light of all these considerations the policy in this book has been to adopt, wherever most reasonable, such modern terms as 'tonality', 'keycentre', and 'modulation' (in the sense of the 'key-changes' inherent in the placing of the main and subsidiary cadences), while acknowledging, by setting them in inverted commas, their somewhat anachronistic character. In the case of the music examples, however, the preferred principle has been to keep Schütz's plain key-signatures, partly to retain an important historical feature and partly to provide a clear, uncluttered 'feel' for the customs of the period. In several modern editions of Schütz's works the practice has been to include transpositions of some settings, in order to furnish comfortable pitch-ranges for present-day singers. Although perfectly reasonable as a practical device, this can in some cases provide key-signatures with as many as three or four sharps or flats, or such confusing patterns as

D minor with two flats (Phrygian, a tone lower) or E minor with two sharps (Dorian, a tone higher), with results which, for purposes of study, are unsuitably at variance with the overall character of the music.

Before leaving the subject of modes it may be added that, although the Italian composers of the period, by their relatively swift abandonment of modal practices in favour of the new diatonicism, were arguably more advanced technically than their German counterparts, it does not necessarily follow that by his fidelity to supposedly 'old-fashioned' methods Schütz was adopting a reactionary stance. Although he sought inspiration throughout his career from the work of his great Italian contemporaries, his eagerness to adapt for his own purposes many of their basic genres and techniques was not paralleled by a desire to follow them equally closely in the treatment of 'keys' and 'tonality'. His attitude, based on a confident assessment of the value to his personal, essentially Teutonic, artistic aims, of the rich melodic and harmonic colouring still to be found in modal writing, appears substantiated by an observation he made in the Latin dedicatory preface of his first set of *Symphoniae sacrae* of 1629, to the effect that the Italians were neglecting the ancient church modes in favour of 'new delights' (recenti titillatione) with which they sought to 'charm modern ears',[7] a remark which seems to imply as much disapproval as surprise. It is noteworthy that the modal traits which served Schütz so well, as an integral part of his Protestant cultural inheritance from the time of Luther, were rarely entirely absent from later German music: obvious examples include various of J. S. Bach's organ works (his so-called 'Dorian' toccata and, most naturally, some of his preludes based on Lutheran chorale melodies); Beethoven's 'Heilige Dankgesang . . . in der Lydische Tonart' from his A minor Quartet Op. 132, and his calculated 'archaisms' in some parts of the *Missa solemnis*; and, most strikingly, the first of Brahms's three motets, Op. 110, 'Ich aber bin elend', in which the modalisms appear to have flowed directly from the close study he is known to have made of Schütz's music. In all these cases the national thread which links them may be identified as having spiritual rather than exclusively religious attributes.

Schütz's surviving output of works is very large, running in total to over five hundred authenticated compositions; and these between them manifest a truly remarkable range of genres and styles, from solo vocal concertos with continuo accompaniment to grandly structured choral compositions for multiple choruses with extensive instrumental support. It is noteworthy that each of the fourteen great collections of his music, published in succession during his lifetime, represents (apart from the final expanded version of the *Becker Psalter*) an exploration by the composer of an almost entirely new genre. This applies even to the three sets of *Symphoniae sacrae* which, despite their shared title, have each at least as many differences in structure and scoring (and language in the case of the first set) as they have

---

[7] *GBS*, No. 31, 103.

features in common. This not only provides graphic evidence of the creative drive by which Schütz was motivated, but suggests also that, however pressing may have been his regular obligations to the electoral chapel, it was mainly for his own personal artistic satisfaction that he continued to compose so tirelessly. Furthermore it strongly intimates that his publication strategy was designed as much to provide an epitome of the German music of his age—and, indeed, for himself a lasting personal memorial—as to achieve transitory kudos for his court and its royal master.

Publication, however, was not always easily achieved during the perilous times in which he lived, and a number of his finest works—the three Passions, the *Christmas History*, the *Seven Words of Christ from the Cross*, and his final great setting of Psalm 119, amongst others—survived only in autograph manuscripts, handwritten copies, or in some cases with essential parts missing. And totally lost, in many reported instances by fire, is the music which Schütz is known to have provided for a variety of theatrical productions, given in celebration of royal marriages and other great occasions at the courts of Germany and Denmark. Such music, pin-pointed to special events, was possibly regarded at the time as too ephemeral to be worthy of careful preservation; but its loss has robbed posterity of the chance to savour, no doubt in a highly picturesque form, some part of the otherwise poorly represented secular aspect of the composer's output.

The Schütz revival in the nineteenth century brought about the first attempt, by Philipp Spitta, to publish a complete modern edition of Schütz's works. Issued initially between 1885 and 1894 (by the Leipzig firm of Breitkopf und Härtel), it was enlarged in 1909 and 1927 and reprinted between 1968 and 1973.[8] A beautiful example of the music printer's craft, and remarkably complete for its time, this version contains all the composer's original notation—including clefs, note-values, and time-signatures—and has thus become a continuing source of much value to scholars. More recently two further editions have appeared. The first, initiated in 1955 by the International Schütz Society, has provided, under the supervision of Werner Bittinger and a number of other editors, thirty-nine volumes designed to embrace the entire range of the composer's currently authenticated works, each given in consistently modernized notation, including G and F clefs, halved note-values, transpositions, and straightforward continuo realizations.[9] The second recent edition, which started publication (by Hänssler of Stuttgart) in 1971 under the principal editorship of Günter Graulich and is as yet some way from being complete, provides a handsomely produced alternative, richly annotated in German and English and similarly modernized in notation.[10] From the greatly increased

---

[8] *H. Schütz: Sämtliche Werke*, ed. Philipp Spitta *et al.* (Leipzig, 1885–94, 1909, 1927; repr. 1968–73). Hereafter *SGA*.

[9] *H. Schütz: Neue Ausgabe sämtlicher Werke*, ed. W. Bittinger, W. Breig, W. Ehmann, *et al.* (Kassel, 1955–). Hereafter *NSA*.

[10] *Stuttgarter Schütz-Ausgabe*, ed. G. Graulich *et al.* (Stuttgart, 1971–). Hereafter *SSA*.

availability of his music which these new editions have provided, and from the numerous scholarly writings which have appeared (particularly in the annually published volumes, from 1979, of the *Schütz-Jahrbuch*[11]) regarding many aspects of his work and historical circumstances, Schütz has in recent times acquired altogether wider international recognition. And in happy consequence there has resulted a marked resurgence in the idiomatic live performance and recordings of his music by which, increasingly, it has once again been brought vividly to life.

[11] *Schütz-Jahrbuch*, ed. Werner Breig, 1979– , published on behalf of the International Schütz Society by Bärenreiter, Kassel, Basle, London, New York, Prague. The leading periodical for Schütz research. Hereafter *SJb*.

1

The early years, 1585–1612; the first visit to Venice

The most reliable information about Schütz's early life and upbringing is provided by two seventeenth-century sources; the celebrated 'Memorial', addressed by the composer to the Elector Johann Georg I of Saxony in January 1651, in which he contributed an invaluable survey of the initial part of his career; and the short biography which Dr Martin Geier, the senior court chaplain in Dresden, attached to his funeral oration for the composer in November 1672. Although the two accounts do not agree in every respect, they none the less provide together the most secure foundation upon which to base an outline of the composer's early development. It is important to recognize, however, that the findings of modern research have in a number of cases cast doubt on 'facts' which were previously considered unassailable, and will no doubt continue to do so. And consequently various features of the following account have to be acknowledged as conjectural and thus open to possible modification in the light of later discoveries.[1]

Heinrich (or Henrich, as he commonly signed himself) Schütz was born at Köstritz (now Bad Köstritz), a small town near Gera, the capital of the principality of Reuss in Saxony. A Schütz family of Franconian origin, generally believed to have been the composer's forebears, can be traced in Saxony in the mid-fifteenth century, where over the years they gained a modest degree of wealth, together with a position of some prominence amongst the bourgeoisie of the area. Although the composer in his 'Memorial' makes no reference to his ancestry, Geier appears confident in describing his father as Christoph Schütz (*c.*1550–1631) and his mother as Euphrosyne, daughter of Johann Bieger, a noted lawyer and burgomaster of Gera. Also he identifies his paternal grandfather as Albrecht Schütz 'the council chamberlain in Weissenfels' and his maternal grandmother as Dorothea, who, he says, was 'born in Gera into the well-known family named Schreiber'.[2] There remains, however, the further possibility (more remote and largely conjectural) that some part in the composer's ancestry may be traced back to another Schütz family which removed from

[1] See Wolfram Steude, 'Zum gegenwärtigen Stand der Schütz-Biographie', *SJb*, 12 (1990), 7–30.
[2] Ibid., 15.

Nürnberg to Chemnitz in the fifteenth century, and that his grandfather may conceivably have been Georg Christoph Schütz, the elder (*c*.1505–85), of Erdmannsdorf and Marienburg. If this were the case, Albrecht Schütz, who certainly played an important role in the family affairs, would necessarily have been more distantly related to the composer—possibly as a great uncle on his father's side.[3]

In 1571, fourteen years before Heinrich's birth, Albrecht, who owned a hostelry in Köstritz, 'Zum goldenen Kranich' (At the Golden Crane), moved to Weissenfels to manage another inn there, called 'Zum güldenen Ring' (At the Golden Ring); and during the later 1570s, Christoph, the composer's father, took over the management of the inn in Köstritz. At this period he is known to have served as town clerk in Gera, but whether this was before or after he became the owner of the inn at Köstritz is uncertain.[4] Following the death, in 1583, of his first wife, Margaretha Weidemann, by whom he had three children, Christoph married Euphrosyne Bieger and subsequently fathered a further eight children, five sons and three daughters, of whom Heinrich was the second-born, and eldest son. Of his brothers, it was with two in particular, Georg (1587–1637) and Benjamin (1596–1666), both of whom had successful careers as jurists, that the composer maintained the closest contact in later life. Albrecht died in July 1590, and Christoph, having inherited the inn in Weissenfels, moved there with his family in the late summer of that year. Situated on the right bank of the river Saale, some twenty-five miles south of Halle, the charming 'white rock' town of Weissenfels (probably so named because of its connections with salt mining) soon gained particular significance for the composer, becoming for him, for virtually the whole of his life, an enduring type of spiritual home. Not only did he pay frequent visits to his sister, Justina, there, but eventually spent a large part of his retirement in the town, apart from some months at Dresden at the very end of his life.

Some confusion surrounds the date of Heinrich's birth. In their separate accounts, Geier gives 8 October 1585 'in the evening at seven o'clock', while the composer himself simply states that he was 'born into this world on St Burkhard's Day, 1585'. It seems probable that Geier's version is the correct one, since the parish records at Köstritz show that his baptism took place on 9 October. Schütz, in his 'Memorial' of 1651, gives no precise date, and it is possible that his reference to St Burkhard's Day was intended to indicate 4 October, in 'old style' dating, rather than 14 October in ' new style'. However, if this earlier date were to be accepted, it would indicate a gap between his birth and baptism of unusual length for that period.

Christoph Schütz, it is natural to assume, obtained for Heinrich and his brothers the best education available in Weissenfels, particularly in religion and in classical and modern languages. Those responsible for Heinrich's

---

[3] See Wolfram Steude, 'Zum gegenwärtigen Stand der Schütz-Biographie', *SJb*, 12 (1990), 15.

[4] Ibid., 15.

musical education are not positively known, though they are most likely to have been the local cantor, Georg Weber, together with the town organist, Heinrich Colander. Weber, a musician of some standing, had held his post at Weissenfels since 1572, and earned a considerable reputation for his church compositions, especially his 'German sacred songs and psalms' of 1588 (second edition, 1596). According to one authority his duties at the local Latin school included the instruction of the choirboys of the three top forms in figural (contrapuntal) music, from twelve noon to one on most school days, and in plainchant on Wednesday.[5] If he was in fact the boy's tutor, it is to his credit that, as Geier reported, the young Heinrich 'developed in a short time' a fine soprano voice and learned 'to sing securely and well, and with particular grace'.

In 1598 the family inn in Weissenfels was visited, for an overnight stay, by the Landgrave Moritz of Hessen-Kassel who expressed great pleasure on hearing Heinrich sing. Although it is sometimes assumed that this fateful meeting occurred purely by chance, it seems more likely that word of the boy's prowess may have reached the Landgrave either through Georg Weber or through his own Kapellmeister at Kassel, Georg Otto, and that he had come in person specifically to form his own opinion. Justly known as 'Moritz the Learned', the Landgrave, at this time a Lutheran, was renowned for his active cultivation of art, literature, and music. A generous patron of musicians, he was closely connected with several prominent composers of the time, including Michael Praetorius, who made prolonged visits to the Kassel court in 1605 and 1609, and Hans Leo Hassler, who in 1596 dedicated to him his set of large-scale Italian madrigals for five to eight voices, based on texts by some of the greatest poets of the genre, including Petrarch, Tasso, and Guarini. In 1594/5 he welcomed Alessandro Orologio and John Dowland to his court and, himself an accomplished lutenist, composed a short piece for the latter, described as a 'Pavane *in honorem J. Dowlandi Anglorum Orphei*'. In 1605 he established the first permanent theatre in Germany, the *Ottoneum* (named after Georg Otto), and encouraged visits from a number of English theatre companies; and from 1617, as a founder member of the famous literary society, the *Fruchtbringende Gesellschaft* (Fruit-bearing society), he published writings on poetry, philology, and theology, and made translations of several classical dramas. His achievements as a composer of sacred music include two twelve-voice psalm settings with supporting instruments, Magnificats in all the twelve modes, and, in 1607, melodies and settings for the Lobwasser Psalter, this last a reflection of his growing interest in, and eventual conversion to, Calvinism.

As a result of the meeting in 1598, Moritz expressed a strong desire to take Heinrich with him to Kassel to serve as a choirboy in the court

---

[5] Arno Werner, *Städtlische und fürstliche Musikpflege in Weissenfels bis zum Ende des 18. Jahrhunderts* (Leipzig, 1911), 11.

Kapelle, and to undertake further study at the *Collegium Mauritianum*, an institution founded by the Landgrave to provide superior educational facilities for the children of the members of his court. The boy's parents appear at first to have been resistant to the idea, but after further correspondence with the Landgrave they eventually acceded to his wishes; and in August 1599 Heinrich was taken by his father to the Kassel court. The opposition from his parents was no doubt prompted mainly by unhappiness at the prospect of a long separation from their eldest son. But it is equally likely, in the light of later events, that they feared the enthusiastic Moritz might too readily press their son into a career as a musician, one which they regarded, not without reason, as too uncertain in outcome.

The liberal studies which Heinrich pursued at the *Collegium Mauritianum* are certain to have embraced classics, some modern languages, including French, and theology. His abilities as a classicist, comparable to that of most educated people of his time, are evidenced by the many Latin poems and other writings he provided throughout his life for special occasions, such as the weddings of friends and relatives, funeral condolences, and as texts for ceremonial motets. One early example is an elegiac Latin poem beginning 'Conquerar, an taceam? ponam sine nomine nostrae/Tristitiae causam quae vorat ossa mea?' (Shall I bewail or remain silent? Shall I show without [revealing] a name the cause of our grief which consumes my bones?), which was composed in 1602 (at the age of sixteen) on the death of a fellow pupil at the *Collegium Mauritianum* and is now preserved in the State archive at Detmold.[6] In the same year, it is recorded that the pupils of the college (astonishingly, if not unbelievably) performed a 'Comedy' written in Latin, German, Greek, Italian, French, and Slavonic languages. The bemused audience were likely, one must assume, to have been more impressed than enlightened.[7] For his musical instruction he must certainly have come under the care of Georg Otto, whose renown as a composer rested largely on his three-volume *Opus musicum novum* (Kassel, 1604), containing motets on Latin gospel texts for each Sunday and Festival of the Church's Year. Although no compositions of substance by Schütz have survived from his schooldays at Kassel, it is likely that Otto's guidance was directed at least as much to creative endeavour as to purely technical study. The earliest extant work by Schütz is generally believed to be the concerto 'Ach wie soll ich doch in Freuden leben' (Ah how shall I still live in joy), SWV 474; a composition of considerable elaboration, it is scored for three 'choruses', each of which involves a soprano (original parts lost) and three instruments—respectively, three lutes, three violas, and three trombones—together with a separate capella comprising alto, tenor, and bass, with violin, cornett, and continuo. Formerly the work was thought to have been

[6] See Hans-Peter Fink, 'Ein bisher unbekanntes Gedicht von Heinrich Schütz in einer Schrift der Hofschule zu Kassel', *SJb*, 11 (1989), 15.

[7] See Albert Duncker, 'Landgraf Moritz von Hessen und die Englischen Komödianten', *Deutsche Rundschau*, 48 (1886), 262.

composed around 1615–18; but it has recently become apparent, from the rescue of some hitherto unknown manuscript sources, that its origins may have been considerably earlier.[8] The sources comprise a lute-book at Kassel and a song-collection at Aurich, which contain settings of the same text and, in general melodic and harmonic terms, the same music as the concerto, and thus can be clearly seen as the basis on which Schütz's more elaborate work was constructed. The date of the lute-song is uncertain, but could quite well have been as early as 1608, since there are references in the text to 'separation from my beloved' ('den dass ich muss geschieden sein von der Herzliebsten mein') and the 'loss of joy' ('Lust ist fern von meinen Herzen') which suggest that it may have been written to mark the composer's sad final leave-taking from the *Collegium Mauritianum*, and very possibly from some lady in whom he had developed a particular interest. On these grounds this date (or perhaps early 1609) can be taken as the most likely one for the creation also of the concerto. The discovery of the lute-song material, it may be added, has made possible the restoration of the three soprano lines of the concerto, formerly thought to have been mislaid beyond recall.

In September 1608, in deference to his parents' wishes, Heinrich, at the age of twenty-three, enrolled at the University of Marburg with the intention of studying law; and, according to Geier, rapidly won good opinions for his academic ability. However, in Schütz's own words, 'this plan was soon altered (undoubtedly by the will of God), in that my lord the Landgrave Moritz came to Marburg . . . and made me the following proposal: [that] since at that time a truly celebrated but quite old musician and composer was still living in Italy, I should not miss the chance to hear him and learn from him'.[9] The 'quite old' musician was Giovanni Gabrieli (then aged about fifty-five) who was organist at St Mark's, Venice, and renowned particularly for his sacred compositions in the colourful polychoral and concertato styles of the period. So generous was the Landgrave's offer—not least because he had agreed to provide a supporting stipend of 200 thalers a year—that it could hardly be refused; and 'as a youth eager to see the world' Schütz departed for Venice during 1609—still in opposition, however, to his parents' desires.

'On my arrival in Venice', he was later to record, 'I soon realized the importance and difficulty of the study of composition which I had undertaken, and what a poor start I had so far made in it'.[10] The self-deprecatory style of expression commonly used by Schütz (and indeed by the majority of his educated contemporaries) can in particular cases rather easily confuse the facts; but in this instance it seems very likely that the composer, having come from a relatively sheltered, even somewhat reactionary, background, was genuinely disturbed by the lively, thoroughly 'modern'

[8] A. Watty, 'Zu Heinrich Schütz' weltlichem Konzert "Ach wie soll ich doch in Freuden leben" (SWV 474)', *SJb*, 9 (1987), 85.

[9] *GBS*, No. 77, 208–9.   [10] *GBS*, No. 77, 209.

musical styles of his new Italian environment and the strenuous demands made on him by his new teacher. It is clear (from later comments by Schütz himself) that Gabrieli's teaching methods sprang very largely from his belief that a firm grounding in composition could only be achieved by a close study of the self-sufficient textures of Renaissance-style polyphony, unaided by continuo support; and that only on such a secure technical basis could work in the more advanced styles of the period—those involving solo voices, the concertato use of instruments, and continuo accompaniments— be successfully attempted. Schütz's programme of study is likely therefore to have involved the close analysis of compositions by such major church composers of the time (or of the recent past) as Lassus, with whom Gabrieli had served for several years as organist in the court chapel at Munich, Palestrina, Victoria, de Monte, and Hassler; and amongst the madrigalists, Marenzio, de Wert, Striggio, Ruffo, and Porta. An indication of the type of study he undertook may well be provided by a version he made of a Christmas motet, 'Angelus ad pastores ait' (The angel spake to the shepherds), by Andrea, the elder Gabrieli, which, with an adapted German text, 'Der Engel sprach zu den Hirten', he included, perhaps forgetful of the fact that it was not his own composition, in his published *Geistliche Chor-Music* of 1648. Furthermore there is provided in the same collection an apparent example of 'style composition' (possibly also an Andrea Gabrieli parody) which may well date from the composer's first Venice period: a chorale-based motet, 'Was mein Gott will, das g'scheh allzeit', the six contrapuntal lines of which are set, in a decidedly archaic manner, for alto and tenor voices together with four unspecified instrumental parts. Probably the most significant outcome of this type of early training was the value which Schütz, throughout his career, and in opposition to many contemporary trends, attached equally to both the traditional polyphonic and modern concertato styles, not infrequently grafting the two together to form over-all musical concepts of great power, which were to exert influence of prime importance to the future of German music.

In 1611, after two years of study with Gabrieli, Schütz published his first major work, *Il Primo libro / de madrigali, di Henrico Sagittario / Allemano / in Venetia MDCXI*, and recorded subsequently that it had been 'warmly received by 'the most distinguished musicians then in Venice'.[11] The composition of a set of Italian madrigals appears to have been a standard 'graduation' requirement imposed on his students by Gabrieli. Other pupils of his who undertook similar assignments include the Danes, Melchior Borchgrevinck (in 1606/08), Hans Nielsen, known in Venice as Giovanni Fonteio (in 1608), and Mogens Pedersøn, known as Magno Petreo, (in

---

[11] *GBS*, No. 77, 209–10. The 'distinguished musicians' Schütz is most likely to have encountered in Venice include: Giulio Cesare Martinengo (the maestro di cappella at S. Marco), Gioven Francesco Venetia, Gabriel Usper, Guglielmo Minischalchi (the maestro di cappella of S. Stefano, Gabrieli's parish and funeral church), and, very importantly, Giovanni Bassano (head of the instrumental ensemble at S. Marco and singing teacher at the Venice seminary).

1608); the Germans, Johann Grabbe (in 1609) and Christoph Klemsee (in 1613); and the Italian Giovanni Priuli (in 1612/13).[12] It is worth remarking that for the German and Danish musicians study in Venice may have proved particularly attractive, not only because of the tuition offered by Gabrieli, but also because of the tolerance shown by Venetians at this time towards Protestants—a reaction in some measure to the papal interdict imposed on the republic during 1605–7 for its religious 'irregularities'. It is noteworthy that two of the poems in Schütz's collection were set also by other Gabrieli protégés: 'Alma afflitta, che fai' by Grabbe and 'Feritevi, ferite viperette mordacci' by Priuli. This suggests that Gabrieli may himself have selected some of the verse for his pupils.[13] In each case the madrigals were written, in contrast to the growing trend of the time, for voices alone, without continuo support, and thus underlined, in an ideal fashion, Gabrieli's emphatic teaching of the importance of acquiring skill in pure polyphony as a basis of technique. Schütz's work, however, is no mere student exercise, but a formidably accomplished, highly polished, collection, an astonishing 'opus one' which has few rivals in musical history. As a young man flexing his creative muscles, he shows a natural sense of adventure; but, in contrast to the jejune experiments with dissonance and chromaticism found in the work of some of his contemporaries, he does so with an astonishing sureness of touch. Despite the expression 'first book' (*Primo libro*), a conventional printed description common at the time, this was Schütz's only volume of madrigals, his only setting of Italian texts, and by far the most substantial of his surviving secular works.

Towards the end of 1610, Sigismund, Margrave of Brandenburg, wrote to the Landgrave Moritz, on behalf of Gabrieli, asking that he should support Heinrich for a further year of study in Venice, a request that appears to have been readily granted. And from May 1612, at the insistence of Gabrieli, G. C. Martinengo, and other prominent musicians, Schütz decided, with the support of his parents, to remain for one more year in Venice. In August, however, Gabrieli died and, according to Geier, his pupil left Venice shortly afterwards and returned to Germany. Schütz's account in his 'Memorial' is less clear about the various dates involved. He says, for example, that 'after three years (and one year before I returned from Italy)' [that is, early in 1612] he published his 'first little musical work in the Italian language';[14] but this, of course, is contradicted by the date, April 1611, on the Venetian print of his madrigals. Also, contrary to Geier, he states that he 'returned to Germany from Italy for the first time in 1613'.[15] Apart from the fact that his memory of the events may have been somewhat unreliable, forty-eight years later, the most likely explanation is that he may

---

[12] See Mos/Pf., 70 and 72.

[13] Madrigals by three of Gabrieli's northern European pupils, Johann Grabbe, Hans Nielsen, and Mogens Pedersøn, are published in *Das Chorwerk*, 35, ed. R. Gerber (Möseler Verlag, Wolfenbüttel).

[14] *GBS*, No. 77, 209–10.   [15] *GBS*, No. 77, 210.

15

have been counting the period, from May 1609 to May 1611, as three years. However, the matter is further confused by a statement in the preface to his first set of *Symphoniae sacrae* of 1629, that on his first visit to Venice he was 'quadriennio toto illius contubernio' (for four years his [Gabrieli's] house-companion).[16] This appears to conflict with Geier's assertion that he returned to Germany immediately after Gabrieli's death. If Schütz did in fact remain in Venice for four years, only three of them could have been spent at the home of Gabrieli; during any additional one, subsidized no doubt by his father, it may (as has been conjectured) have been the hospitality of his brother Georg that he enjoyed. But, if that were the case, it is remarkable that, in a newly-discovered 'biographical account', which he submitted in 1623 with his application for an advocate's post at the high court of justice in Leipzig, Georg made no mention of any such past arrangement. The question of the date of Schütz's return journey must therefore remain an open one.[17]

The mutual respect and devotion which existed between Gabrieli and Schütz becomes plainly evident at the time of the former's demise. On his death-bed the Italian master bequeathed to his pupil a ring, 'out of special affection, and in his blessed memory', a gift which was delivered later by Gabrieli's father confessor, 'an Augustinian monk (from the cloister where Dr Luther once stayed)'.[18] And following his great mentor's decease, on 12 August, 1612, the young German composer attended his funeral at the church of S. Stefano and thereafter accompanied him faithfully to his last resting-place.

[16] Preface to *Symphoniae sacrae* I. [17] See W. Steude, op. cit., 16–17.
[18] *GBS*, No. 77, 210.

2

The Italian Madrigals of 1611

For the principal literary basis of his madrigal collection Schütz turned to stanzas by two of the finest Italian poets of the period, Giambattista Marino (1569–1625) and Giovanni Battista Guarini (1537–1612), with whose work he had doubtless become familiar through settings, some very numerous, by such leading madrigalists of the time as Marenzio, Giaches de Wert, Philippe de Monte, Luzzaschi, and Monteverdi. Of the nineteen verses he chose there are ten by Marino, the poet of whom it was said that he could 'create music with words', and six by the renowned poet-dramatist, Guarini; and in each of these there is expounded, as a consistent 'theme', the despair of the rejected lover.[1] To complete his amatory design he included stanzas of equal relevance by two lesser-known poets: Alessandro Aligieri, whose 'D'orrida selce alpina, cred'io, Donna, nasceti' (Of the fearful Alpine rocks I believe you to have been born, lady) is a lover's bitter outcry against the stony indifference of his beloved; and Alessandro Gatti, whose 'Fiamma ch'allaccia e laccio sei tu ch'infiamma, o caro' (An encircling flame and trap are you, dear one, who kindles the sweet charm of love), provides a sad but often tender portrayal of the lover's conflicting hopes and fears in the pursuit of his mistress. Finally, to round off his collection, he included, as a dedicatory tribute to his admired patron, Moritz, a single poem, 'Vasto mar, nel cui seno fan soave armonia d'altezza e di virtu, concordi venti' (Vast sea, in whose breast the sweet harmonies of majesty and virtue create peaceable winds), of which, it can hardly be doubted, he himself was the author.[2] At the end he entreats the Landgrave to look kindly on his humble efforts and 'make from his rough endeavours, harmonious song' (e in tanto farai di rozzo armonioso 'l canto)—a typical piece of mock modesty, since, as he well knew, his patron would be the first to recognize the excellence of his work.

The six Guarini texts (madrigals 1, 2, 3, 5, 11, and 15) form an integrated group, linked by their origin in the poet's renowned Arcadian drama, *Il*

---

[1] See Paolo Emilio Carapezza, 'Schützens Italienische Madrigale: Textwahl und stilistische Beziehungen', *SJb*, 1 (1979), 44.

[2] If the poem is in fact by Schütz, it is likely to have been inspired by the young German's astonishment at his first encounter, in 1609, with the immensity of the Adriatic sea ('Vasto mar'), off Venice.

pastor fido. Completed in 1583, (second edition, Venice 1601), this influential work continued for more than a century to inspire composers, among them Handel, whose lightweight three-act opera based freely on it, with each act's final scene adorned by a ballet, first appeared in 1712.[3] In place of its set-piece 'choral' lyrics—the parts most obviously suitable for setting to music— Schütz, the innate dramatist, selects from the play passages of dialogue or soliloquy of a vividly emotional nature, each of which is readily identifiable with a specific character: Mirtillo, a shepherd in love with Amafilli, in SWV 1 and 2 (a single text divided into two *partes*), and No. 3; Amarilli, the object of Mirtillo's passion, who is condemned to death for her refusal to marry Silvio, in SWV 5 and 15, both from the same scene where she laments her impend- ing fate; and Dorinda, who pines throughout for the love of Silvio, in SWV 11. An understanding of the play's somewhat convoluted plot, it may be added, is not essential to an appreciation of Schütz's settings, but can help neverthe- less to uncover some otherwise hidden meanings in various of the characters' utterances, especially those of the sadly wronged Amarilli.

With the exception of the final dedicatory piece, which is set for double- choir (SATB/SATB), the madrigals are all scored for five voices, with the 'additional' voice (the 'Quinto') varying between a second soprano, a sec- ond tenor, or (in one slightly debatable case, in No. 6, which is conditional on the placing of the clef) a mezzo-soprano or another alto. The contrasted ranges used appear to have been chosen to accord with the shades of emo- tion at which, independently, the poet and composer were aiming, the dou- bling of the inner voices in the texture, for example, often providing colouring of a deeper hue for the profounder levels of sorrow. An associated problem concerns the clefs provided in the original print, and the extremes of compass which result in a number of cases. Special difficulty is presented by seven madrigals, SWV 7–8, 12–15, and 17, where the two top lines are supplied with treble g clefs, and No. 18 which has treble g and soprano c clefs. In these cases all the voice-parts have a wide compass, usually of an eleventh or twelfth, together with such extreme high notes as a'' or b'' in each of the treble parts, and need, in terms of present-day pitch, to be trans- posed down a tone, or even a minor third. In the other settings with divided sopranos (SWV 1–3, 9–10, 11, and 16), soprano c clefs are used and the upper extremes of compass are avoided. In one case, however, (No. 10) the depth of the lower voice-ranges—B in the tenor and E in the bass—suggests that an upward transposition may well be necessary. In light of our earlier discussion of modal notation (see p. 5), it will be clear that written-down transpositions were not available in Schütz's day; the practice at that time would have been for any necessary adjustments of pitch to be left to the musician in charge of the performance.[4]

[3] See Arnold Hartmann, Jnr., 'Battista Guarini and *Il Pastor Fido*', *Musical Quarterly*, 29 (1953), 415.

[4] One supposition, promoted particularly by H. J. Moser as editor of *NSA*, 22 (Italian Madrigals), is that in various instances changes of pitch are indicated by the choice and positioning

The madrigal collection is clearly designed as an anthology, without any connecting narrative to justify the sequence of its items. But there are, none the less, clues to suggest that their placing may reflect in some degree a planned pattern. This is revealed particularly by the first ten madrigals. The opening three, involving soliloquies by Mirtillo from Acts 3 and 5 of *Il pastor fido*, and scored for divided sopranos, provide with their transposed Dorian (G minor) colouring, a type of 'median' position in emotional expression, best described as one of 'melancholy resignation'. The mood is well defined in the second work, which enshrines the concept that it is 'better never to have loved at all than to have loved and lost' (quanto e più duro perdevi, che mai / non v'aver o provate o possedute!)—a notion which, in its delicately inverted form in canto 27 of Tennyson's *In Memoriam*, was destined to become not unfamiliar. The next three settings (SWV 4, 5, and 6) then move to a position below the 'median' emotional line, one of an altogether deeper mood of rejection and despair, typified by such lines as Marino's 'Tormented soul, what are you doing? Who gives you more life, when the one for whom you live has gone today? (Alma afflitta, che fai? Chi ti darà più vita, se colei, per cui vivi, oggi è partita?). The mode in these three settings is Phrygian, the 'Quinto' line is given to a second tenor, and the style of the music is often cold and dissonant. And lastly, in two pairs of madrigals (SWV 7–8, and 9–10) the mood changes once again, lifted now above the original 'median' line to achieve an expression of gentle reproach, not unmixed with a pleasant degree of self-mockery—for example in No. 8, 'Fuggi, fuggi, o mio core' (Flee, flee, O my heart), again by Marino, where 'she with the lovely eyes conspires to take you captive: but alas, a sigh . . . issues from the breast and says: What use is it to fly? He is already taken and must die!' (Che congiurata co' begli occhi anch'ella, perfarti prigioni: ma lasso, ecco un sospir . . . ch'esce del petto e dice: Che più giova il fuggire? Egli è già preso e gli convien morire!). The original scoring with divided sopranos returns for each of these last four settings, and major modes are introduced for the first time—Mixolydian for SWV 7 and 8 and Ionian for 9 and 10. The effect created by this initial sequence of items is of a carefully balanced design, in which contrasted moods, between deep distress and relative insouciance, are vividly pitched against each other. It is possible that the choice of modes involved may hold a significance beyond the simple

of clefs, the use, for example, of two g clefs in the canto lines, and 'high' clefs in each of the other parts, signifying a downward transposition of a whole tone. More recently, however, the further view has been expressed that different clefs (the c clefs in soprano, mezzo-soprano, alto, and tenor placings, and the F clef in its baritone position) were used, in accordance with an established custom, so as to avoid as far as possible the use of leger-lines (both above and below the stave) and thus save extra printing costs. Furthermore, it appears that where the plagal, as opposed to the authentic, form of the mode is used it normally coincides with a change of clef, in a manner which provides a valuable clue to tonal interpretation. See S. Schmalzriedt, *Heinrich Schütz und ander Zeitgenossische Musiker in der Lehre Giovanni Gabrielis, Studien zu ihren Madrigale*, Tübinger Beitrage zur Musikwissenschaft I, ed. Georg von Dadelsen (Hänssler-Verlag, Neuhausen-Stuttgart, 1972), 48; and *idem, SSA*, 1 (Italienische Madrigale), English preface, xvi.

distinction between major and minor. At this period, following theories outlined many years earlier by Nicola Vicentino (in his *L'antica musica ridotta alla moderna prattica*, Rome, 1555), it remained not unusual to assign particular forms of expression to the various modes, but from a largely subjective viewpoint and certainly with no more than a very general application. Thus the Phrygian mode was taken typically to signify 'sadness', the Ionian 'joy', the Aeolian 'seriousness', the Mixolydian 'gentleness' or 'exuberance', and the Dorian (often with much ambivalence) 'earnestness'.

The masterly reconciliation which Schütz achieves between the demands of music and poetry is testimony to the thoroughness of his studies in Venice, especially since he was working with a language other than his native one. In typically madrigalian fashion, particular words and phrases are 'painted' musically, often with vocal figuration demanding great virtuosity in performance. But at the same time the requirements of sound musical structure—the formation of integrated sections, the placing of 'keys' and cadences, the use of striking chord changes, and the inventive treatment of contrapuntal imitation—are carefully observed, in a manner typical of Venetian practice at the time. The composer's methods are well demonstrated by his setting of No. 7, 'Ride la primavera', one of the loveliest of the Marino stanzas. The brilliant opening in c time, descriptive of the joys of springtime, leads from a Mixolydian G major to a full close in C major at bar 9. Then an immediate (third-related) chord of A major on 'Ma' (but) heralds the new idea that Cloris, though more lovely 'in the new season' ('nella stagion novella'), keeps old Winter alive in her heart. This second section which moves over fifteen bars to a cadence on E major, contains a short triple-time passage to give added dash to the idea of the 'stagion novella'. At bar 25, a further third-related chord-change, from E major to C major, this time for the exclamation 'Deh' (Ah), introduces a 26-bar final section in which the 'cruel but gentle' nymph is asked, reproachfully, why she buries her heart in 'eternal ice', while 'carrying the sun in her eyes and April in her face'. Precisely interpreting the swiftly changing ideas in the text, a 'frozen' passage in five different note-values (longs, breves, semibreves, minims, and crotchets) in separate voice-parts (bars 28 to 34) represents the 'eternal ice', tripla patterns (recalling those used for 'nella stagion', but set here within the overall c time), gracefully underline the nymph's 'gentleness' (bars 37–9), and delicately poised imitative writing, with upward leaps at each reference to the sun (sol), imparts to the lover's final rhetorical question a none-too-serious tone of lofty indignation.

Following common practice, Schütz's word-painting takes two principal forms, active and passive, according to the sense of the text. Active types, which normally involve melismas of varying length, are applied to such highlighted objects as 'flowers' (in No. 1 and No. 7), 'leaves' (in No. 3), 'vipers' and 'arrows' (in No. 9), and 'winds' (in No. 19); or to descriptive epithets, such as 'smiling' (in No. 3), 'laughing' (in No. 7), 'fleeing' (in No.

8), and 'stinging' (in no. 9). A typical example is the setting of 'e 'l bel volto divino' (and [her] beautiful divine face) from No. 12, 'Mi saluta costei' (She greets me)—see Ex. 1. Passive word-painting, on the other hand, underlines

Ex. 1

emotions rather than actions and is achieved mainly by the use of striking harmonies, including suspended dissonances, false relations, augmented triads, and chromatic chord progressions. From the numerous examples to be found, attention may be called to No. 6, 'D'orrida selce alpina', the most bitterly reproachful poem in the collection, the setting of which is entirely syllabic and involves some of the most vividly experimental harmony used by the composer. The passage from bar 8, in which the lover reacts emotionally to his lady's flint-heartedness by believing her to have drunk, from birth, 'the milk of wild tigers' (e dalle tigri ircane il latte avesti) contains, successively, false relations, augmented triads, a sudden move from the dominant of A minor to the dominant of F sharp minor, and a relentless postponement of anticipated cadences (see Ex. 2).

By no means all the characteristic subtleties of madrigal poetry can be illustrated in music; there are, for example, no realistic equivalents for the puns, ironies, and paradoxes so typical of the genre. One interesting exception, however is the 'bitter-sweet' oxymoron which, having apparently originated with Petrarch, features in many later pieces of madrigal verse, and can quite readily be paralleled in music.[5] One example in Schütz's collection occurs at the start of No. 2, 'O dolcezze amarissime' (literally, O sweetnesses most bitter), where the 'sweet' G minor/B flat major harmonies of the opening two-and-a-half bars are followed by a succession of 'bitter' dissonances: successively, a major seventh between alto and bass, a minor seventh between soprano and alto, a major second between the two sopranos, together with a sudden plethora of sharps ('Kreuze' in German, symbols of suffering), see Ex. 3. More intense still is the treatment found in No. 16, 'Tornate, o cari baci' (Come back, O dear kisses), where, at the start of bar 15, an augmented triad on ' dolce amaro' (bitter sweetness) graphically

[5] A German version occurs in one of Leonhard Lechner's *Neue teutsche Lieder* of 1577, his 'O Lieb, wie süss und bitter', the text of which (probably the composer's own) contains a graceful allusion to Petrarch's definition of love: 'Ein Anfang aller Freud und Leid . . . ein süsse Bittrigkeit' (a beginning of all joy and sorrow . . . a sweet bitterness).

Ex. 2

underlines the lover's longing for his lady's kisses, 'poisonous nectar' though they are. In this case the expressive impact is compounded by the composer's treatment of the ensuing line—'To long for you is precious to me' (per cui languir m'è caro)—where contradictory accidentals produce some of the most unstable harmony in the entire collection, with an anguished repetition in bars 18 and 19 to give ever increased poignancy to the lover's conflicting emotions (see Ex. 4).

One illustrative resource often used by Schütz, which has no counterpart in verse alone, is the combination of two musical patterns, and their associated poetic ideas, in simultaneous or overlapping strands of counterpoint. An ingenious example is provided by No. 14, a setting of Marino's 'Sospiro della sua donna'. The opening line, 'Sospir, che del bel petto di Madonna esci fore' (A sigh from the lady's lovely breast breaks out') is set, imitatively and in short note-values, for two sopranos and alto, with the sigh vividly coloured by a rapid ascending figure. Then, in bar 3, against a three-voice working of the first idea with extended melismas on the word 'fore', the lover's question in line three about the cause of the sigh, 'dimmi, che fa quel core? (tell me, what is her heart doing?), is set in long notes, initially for the tenor, and subsequently in imitation for the first soprano, and thus provides an immediate reaction to his lady's apparent distress (see outline in Ex. 5). From bar 15, new imitative entries, based on a version of the opening 'sospiro' figure, are evolved, as the lover asks urgently whether the sigh is for him or for some new love: 'Serba l'antico affetto oppur messo se' tu di novo amore?' (Does it maintain the old affection or have you found a new love?). These engender short but vivid ascending melismas, and the final lines, 'Deh no, piuttosto sia sospirata da lei la morte mia!' (Ah no, may it rather be that she sighs at my death!), augmented triads, cross relations, and, before the final cadence, a 'despairing' scale for the tenor, descending a minor ninth (g' to f#) in semiquavers. Equally striking is the use of paired ideas in the setting of No. 8, Marino's 'Fuggi, fuggi, o mio core' (Flee, flee, O my heart), where close imitation between the four lowest voices, with excited upward-running phrases to signify 'flight', is set against a descending pattern in longer note-values in the first soprano line which imparts

Ex. 3

Ex. 4

deeper feeling to the phrase 'o mio core'. In the process both 'active' and 'passive' word-painting are heard simultaneously—the urge to flee, on the one hand, and to quell the heart's emotional response, on the other—each giving added point to the other and bringing extra vividness to the situation portrayed.

In general, it is in his settings of the Guarini stanzas that Schütz achieves his most overtly dramatic treatment. Finest among them is No. 15, 'Dunque addio, care selve' (So farewell, beloved woods), the text of which comes from the fourth act of *Il pastor fido*. Amarilli, who loves Mirtillo, has been sentenced to death for spurning her decreed marriage with Silvio (arranged to appease the goddess Diana), and in this scene is found roaming her 'beloved woods' and bewailing her sad fate. Wonderfully apt expression of the shepherdess's cruel dilemma is to be found in Sir Richard Fanshawe's free but admirably poetic translation (from 1647) of Guarini's pastoral drama:

> Deer woods adieu then, my deer woods adieu;
> Receive these sighs (my last ones) into you,
> Till my cold shade, forc'd from her seat by dire
> And unjust steel, to your lov'd shades retire.
> For sink to hell it can't, being innocent;
> Nor soar to heav'n, laden with discontent.

While retaining a consistent imitative treatment of melodic patterns in the normal madrigalian manner, Schütz at times underlines the drama by means of brief patterns of two or three notes, broken by rests, to colour such phrases as 'addio' (farewell) and 'questi ultimi sospiri' (these last sighs), and in the process comes closer to operatic recitative than to any of the more usual modes of madrigalian writing. In the last paragraph, august and sombre in expression, the penultimate line of the text 'nè può star tra' beati' (nor to stand among the blessed) is set to short notes against a drooping chromatic pattern in longer ones for the concluding words 'disperata e dolente' (despairing and sorrowful) which gradually permeates all five voice-parts with starkly emotional effect (see Ex. 6). Amarilli's situation, and its musical setting, may well be compared to that of Dido in Purcell's miniature opera. Each heroine believes herself to have been robbed of the

Ex. 5

Ex. 6

one she loves by a deity's cruel decree, and each decides upon suicide as the noblest path to take.[6] Furthermore each composer, by way of a chromatic descent, a familiar symbol of grief, provides effective colour to his texture, Purcell with his ostinato bass and Schütz with his final expressive melodic line. Artificial though Guarini's basic concept may be, Schütz in his setting manages to imbue it with a singular degree of human feeling. It no longer matters that Amarilli is merely a pastoral puppet set in a make-believe Arcadian scene; the result remains high art.

[6] In Guarini's play Amarilli does not in fact have to share the fate of Dido, since Mirtillo offers to die in her stead, the officiating priest announces that the goddess is appeased and a sacrifice is no longer necessary, and a happy ending is achieved.

3

The Move to Dresden in 1617

On his return to Germany in 1613, Schütz decided to conceal for the time being the progress he had made in composition until, as he remarked in his 'Memorial' of 1651, 'he could distinguish himself with the publication of a worthy piece of work'.[1] One should not infer from this that he was unwilling to acknowledge his *Italian Madrigals* as a 'worthy' publication, particularly since they had been so warmly praised in Venice. The madrigals were the culminating product of his Italian apprenticeship, and held for him deep personal significance as a tribute to his friend and benefactor the Landgrave Moritz. It was therefore only natural that, when writing to the Dresden Elector, forty years later, he should have left them out of consideration and emphasized instead his desire, on returning home, to produce a wholly German work in the Lutheran tradition, one which he might then have hoped would eventually grace an electoral chapel.

In 1613 he settled back into his former place with the Kassel court, and from September held appointment there as second organist, with a modest salary. His parents, though pleased by the progress he had made as a musician, continued to urge him to seek some other profession and keep music only as a sideline; and in duty bound he agreed to resume his neglected legal studies. Providence, however, intervened once again. 'God Almighty', he recollected in 1651, '(who had no doubt singled me out in the womb for the profession of music),[2] ordained that, in 1614, I should be called to service in Dresden for the then impending royal christening of my lord the Duke August, now administrator of the archbishopric of Magdeburg—I know not whether through the advice of Christoph von Loss, then privy councillor, or of Chamber Counsellor Wolffersdorff, also appointed commander of Weissenfels. After I had arrived and been auditioned, the directorship of your music was soon offered to me, [which] with humble thanks and a vow to fulfil it with my best efforts, I was persuaded . . . to accept.'[3]

---

[1] *GBS*, No. 77, 210.

[2] André Pirro, *Schütz* (Paris 1924), 2: 'Il aurait accepté plus volontiers de trouver, dans le nom de sa mère, les signes de son avenir. Elle s'appelait Euphrosyne, comme l'une des Graces: "Euphrosyne", écrit Pontus de Tyard, "est la joie que nous cause la pure délectation de la voix musicale et harmonieuse" [*Les discours philosophiques*, dans le *Solitaire premier*; "c'est d'elle que dépend la beauté de la voix" (1587 edit:, folio 15, verso)].'

[3] *GBS*, No. 77, 211.

In fact the procedure was not as simple as this might suggest, but involved a series of not altogether seemly interchanges (evident in the surviving correspondence) between Johann Georg and the Landgrave Moritz. Some eight months after the elector's original request, of August 1614, that he might 'borrow' Schütz temporarily to assist the semi-retired Kapellmeister, Rogier Michael, and the 'visiting director', Michael Praetorius, at his son's baptism, he sent a further demand to Moritz that he be allowed Schütz's services for a further two years, his stated reason being that two of his most promising musicians, Johann Nauwach and Johann Klemm, had gone to Italy for study and had not yet returned. Moritz was understandably dismayed at the idea of losing Schütz for so long a period; but no doubt acutely conscious of the elector's superior status and immense political influence, he eventually agreed to the plan, and some four months later, after putting his affairs at Kassel in order, the composer left for Dresden. In December 1616, Moritz wrote to Johann Georg asking that Schütz should be returned to him as soon as possible, since his help was urgently needed to counter falling musical standards in the Kapelle at Kassel. However, the elector (prompted once again by Christoph von Loss) made it plain, in a further letter, that he wished to secure Schütz's services permanently. After further pleading by Moritz, and various suggested compromises, all unavailing, the Landgrave eventually agreed, in January 1617, to Schütz's permanent transfer, and in March, his final move to Dresden took place. Even so, Moritz made one last attempt, in November 1618, to win the composer back; but on that occasion his request was spurned by the elector, almost disdainfully. Although one can hardly fail to see the composer as a somewhat helpless pawn in a power game between two rulers of great, though unequal, influence, it is entirely likely that, once he had experienced the altogether grander status and facilities which would be available to him at Dresden, Schütz was drawn there irresistibly for the fulfilment of his career ambitions. His removal from Kassel must, however, have proved a considerable wrench, both for him and for Moritz, and it is a remarkable testimony to the warmth of both their characters that he appears to have made the transition without harming, on a personal level, his longstanding relationship with his former patron. It was clearly as a token of the admiration and respect he felt for him that, at the time of his departure (as reported by Geier), Moritz gave him a gold chain as a memento.

During the first six months after his arrival in Dresden, Schütz was called upon to make provision for two major events at the court: a state visit, from 15 July, by the Emperor Matthias and the Archduke Ferdinand of Austria, together with a large retinue, the intention of which was to gain Johann Georg's support for the succession of Ferdinand to the imperial throne; and from 31 October, a celebration lasting three days, to mark the centenary of the start of the Reformation. For the first of these he provided the text[4] and

[4] See *GBS*, No. 3, 41; and Geoffrey Parker (ed.), *The Thirty Years War* (London, 1984), 43.

probably also the music (though none has for certain survived) for a ballet entitled *Wunderlich translocation des weitberümbten und fürtrefflichen Berges Parnassi* (Wondrous translocation [in the sense of a re-enactment in modern times] of the marvellous and widely renowned Parnassus), which was performed on 25 July, in honour of the visitors, and with its personification of Apollo and the nine Muses, provided scope for flattering parallels to be drawn with several of those present. One composition which may have belonged originally to this work is a setting for two sopranos of a part of Schütz's text 'for the entry of Apollo', beginning 'Damit, dass diese Gsellschaft wert'; but its authenticity is uncertain. For the second occasion, Schütz was given the chance to provide a series of church compositions, mainly of psalm texts, in the polychoral concertato style he had studied so assiduously in Venice. In a detailed description of the services, the senior court chaplain, Matthias Hoë von Hoënegg,[5] refers to five works by Schütz—richly scored settings of Psalms 98, 100, 103, 115, and 136 involving several choirs, both vocal and instrumental, the latter including cornetts, trumpets, trombones, and timpani—which were performed over the three days of the celebration, and which must certainly have created an impression of great splendour. Also specified, for 31 of October, but now apparently lost, was a Magnificat for six choruses with trumpets and drums, between each verse of which (probably at section endings marked by fermatas) there was said to be inserted a stanza from Luther's hymn 'Erhalt uns, Herr, bei deinen Wort (Lord, keep us steadfast in thy word). Each of the five psalm settings, it is now generally accepted, were subsequently incorporated, after revision, into Schütz's first major publication of sacred music, the *Psalmen Davids* of 1619, under the numbered headings SWV 35 (Ps. 98), SWV 36 (Ps. 100), SWV 41 (Ps. 103, a chorale paraphrase), SWV 43 (Ps. 115), and SWV 45 (Ps. 136). However, various other items recorded in the accounts of the services—among them a 'Kyrie and Gloria for seven choirs, with trumpets and timpani'—cannot now be related to any surviving compositions by Schütz.

On 22 May, 1618 a Protestant uprising in Prague, during which the royal castle of Hradschin was attacked and the city's oppressive Catholic regents, William Slavata and Jaroslav Martinitz, together with their secretary, were thrown from the castle window (and astonishingly survived), marked the beginning of the Thirty Years War, a conflict that was to cause immense suffering and devastation throughout central Europe, and in the long run to have a severely adverse effect upon Schütz's career and that of numerous other musicians of the time. The struggle started as a religious war, in which powerful Catholic forces, headed by the Holy Roman Emperor Ferdinand II and Duke Maximilian of Bavaria, sought to subdue the princelings of the Protestant states and restore the Catholic persuasion in their lands. But later it widened out into a politically inspired struggle, in

[5] See Chr. Mahrenholz, 'Heinrich Schütz und das erste Reformations-Jubiläum 1617', *Musik und Kirche*, 3 (1931), 149; repr. in *Musicologica et liturgica* (Kassel, 1960), 196.

which the majority of European nations, including Denmark, Sweden, and eventually France and England became involved. Saxony, surprisingly in view of her longstanding Protestant traditions, remained at first loyal to the imperial cause; and it fell to Johann Georg to act as a neutral intermediary between the warring sides at several successive treaties, in attempts, albeit unavailing, to bring the hostilities to an early conclusion.

During the first stages of the war, because of the largely settled neutrality of Dresden, Schütz was spared any special problems with his career. During 1618, in recognition of the increasing fame he was beginning to enjoy, he was invited, together with Michael Praetorius and Samuel Scheidt, to oversee a major reorganization of the Kapelle at Magdeburg cathedral. No doubt his recent experience of the latest types of Italian church music made his advice particularly valuable to the authorities there. His compositions during this year, apart from additional psalm settings for eventual inclusion in the *Psalmen Davids*, consist mainly of the concertos, 'Wohl dem, der ein tugendsam Weib hat' (Happy is he who has a virtuous wife), SWV 20, and 'Haus und Güter erbet man von Eltern' (Home and property are from one's parents inherited), SWV 21, provided for the weddings, held in April and June, respectively, of Joseph Avenarius and Anna Dorothea Görlitz, at Dresden, and Michael Thomas and Anna Schultes, at Leipzig. At this stage, despite his growing reputation, his position at Dresden was simply that of 'organist and musical director'; it was not until January 1619 that Johann Georg finally accorded him the full title of 'Electoral Kapellmeister', and thus set him officially at the head of one of the most important musical establishments in Lutheran Germany. His forerunners in the post, of varying repute, included Johann Walter (1548–54), Luther's principal musical adviser from the earliest Reformation times; Matthäus le Maistre (1554–68), remembered particularly for his sacred and secular German songs of 1566; Antonio Scandello (1568–80), an Italian convert to Lutheranism, renowned for his German *St John Passion* (1561) and *Resurrection History* (before 1573); Giovanni Battista Pinello de Ghirardi (1580–84), whose appointment was terminated after only four years because of friction with his German colleagues; G. Förster (1584–87), whose tenure, for some unknown reason, was equally brief; and finally, his immediate predecessor, the long-serving Rogier Michael (1587–1617) a prolific composer of sacred music, including Passions, motets, and chorale arrangements.[6]

A number of special events marked the year 1619. In May the *Psalmen Davids* were published with a dedication to Johann Georg, and Schütz's long-held ambition to bring out 'a truly worthy piece of work' was at last realized. The foreword was, by design, postdated 1 June 1619, since this was the day on which he was to marry Magdalena Wildeck, the eighteen-

---

[6] A work of particular interest by Rogier Michael is his *Die Geburt unsers Herren Jesu Christi nach dem Evangelisten Lukas und Matthaeus*, dated 1602. A modern edition, ed. W. Ostoff, is published in *Chor Archiv*, Vol. 1 (Bärenreiter, Kassel).

year-old daughter of a Dresden court official. By enclosing with the wedding invitations copies of his newly-published work, the composer and his young bride became the recipients of splendid gifts from many parts of Saxony and beyond. Early in August, Schütz travelled to Leipzig for the wedding of his brother Georg to Anna Gross, and enhanced the occasion with the specially written concerto, SWV 48, 'Siehe, wie fein und lieblich ists' (Behold, how fine and lovely a thing it is for brothers to dwell together in unity), from Psalm 133; and six days later he joined Praetorius, Scheidt, and Johann Staden on a visit to Bayreuth for the inauguration of a new organ in the Stadtkirche. In a poem of later date, the Bayreuth organist, Elias Unmüssig, recorded that 'all four visitors played splendidly' on the new instrument. And in a further reference to the occasion—in the foreword to his *Pars prima concertuum sacrorum* (1622) (the dedicatee of which, Heinrich Posthumus, was also present in Bayreuth for the event)—the Halle organist and composer, Samuel Scheidt, wrote: 'I hope you will always recall with what pleasure you listened to the late Michael Praetorius, Heinrich Schütz and me . . . as we sang the praise of almighty God at the assembly of princes and potentates in the illustrious courts of Bayreuth.'

In 1620, following victory by the imperial forces at the Battle of White Mountain, near Prague, Johann Georg was called upon to negotiate a treaty between the Silesian states and the newly-crowned Emperor, Ferdinand II; and on 3 November of the following year, at Breslau, acting on behalf of the Emperor, he received from the various minor rulers, whether graciously or not is unclear, their customary oath of allegiance to the Holy Roman Empire. For this occasion Schütz, who was present with eighteen members of his Kapelle, composed the *Syncharma musicum*, 'En novus Elysiis succedit sedibus hospes', SWV 49, a richly coloured setting for three contrasted ensembles comprising: two tenors accompanied by three cornetts (the third replaceable by a trombone); three bassoons; and three sopranos, a bass, and basso continuo (organ and string bass), marked 'coro aggiunto'. In translation, the Latin text (probably the work of Schütz himself) begins: 'Behold, to the seats in Elysium there approaches again, as guest and friend, / the Saxon duke and sword-bearer of the Roman Empire, / that to the welcoming land he may bring the gifts of peace, / and preserve the loyal people in the emperor's favour'. The 'gifts of peace' were, however, very far from being universally achieved, and the war continued to break out, with increased savagery, for a further seventeen years, creating widespread ruin and desolation. Another political work which may very possibly have been performed on the same occasion is 'Teutoniam dudum belli atra pericola molestant' (Latterly dark dangers of war have oppressed Germany), SWV 338, which provided yet another fervent plea for the restoration of peace. Set in short sections for contrasting groups of solo singers (SSATTB), the work has obbligato parts for two violins; and these, taken together with the forces required for SWV 49, significantly match the number of Kapelle performers who are reputed to have accompanied the composer on the visit to Breslau.

For the celebration of the elector's birthday, on 5 March 1621, Schütz returned to the classical theme he had adopted for the imperial visit to Dresden in 1617 and provided a laudatory ballet entitled *Glückwunschung des Apollinis und der neun Musen* (The good wishes of Apollo and the nine Muses). Sung by 'the Collegium musicum, with twelve cornetts and as many living voices / besides trumpets and drums', it opens with the words 'Wilkomm / wilkomm / O schön Auror / Dein hellen glanzes sich Apollo freuet' (Welcome, beauteous Aurora, Apollo rejoices in thy bright radiance).[7] As with the great majority of Schütz's secular works, the score has not survived, but in view of the composer's recent studies in Venice, it is likely to have contained sections of music for dancing in the latest Italian styles. At an unspecified date towards the end of 1621, Schütz's eldest child, Anna Justina, was born; and some two years later, in November 1623, her sister, Euphrosina, arrived. His joy at these events was, however, cruelly shattered in 1625, first by the death of his sister-in-law, Anna Maria Wildeck, and six weeks later by the decease, 'after a short illness' (believed to have been small-pox), of his beloved wife, Magdalena, aged twenty-four. His grief at her loss is movingly expressed in the aria 'Mit dem Amphion zwar mein Orgel und mein Harfe', SWV 501, for tenor and continuo, to a text very probably of his own composition. Since, contrary to the custom of the times, he did not remarry, he regarded the upbringing of his two daughters without help in the home as too great a burden for him to support; and he therefore committed them, eventually with happy results, to the care of Magdalena's mother.

His chief compositions of this period were: the *Resurrection History* [Op. 3] SWV 50, the first of his *Historia*-style works, published in Dresden in 1623; a vividly pictorial five-voice setting of Psalm 116 'Das ist mir lieb' (I love the Lord because He hath heard my voice and my supplication), SWV 51, which, though probably composed originally as early as 1616, was published only in 1623 in Burkhard Grossman's *Angst der Höllen* (Fear of Hell) collection, together with fifteen other settings, including ones by Schein, Demantius, and Praetorius;[8] the *Cantiones sacrae* [Op. 4], SWV 53–93, comprising twenty-two Latin motets (some in several *partes*), which were published in Freiburg in 1625; and the first version of the *Becker Psalter* [Op. 5], issued in Dresden in 1628. This latter work (to be discussed in more detail on pp. 60–2) involved settings 'in the normal contrapuntal style' of 103 church melodies (ninety-two new ones and eleven old, as stated in the original title) to German rhyming texts for the entire psalter, published originally in 1602 by Cornelius Becker.[9] The concentrated work

---

[7] *GBS*, No. 4, 52.

[8] The settings of Psalm 116 by Schein and Demantius, included in Burkhard Grossman's *Angst der Höllen und Friede der Seelen* (1623), are available in a modern edition in *Das Chorwerk*, 36.

[9] A modern edition of the *Becker Psalter* is published in *NSA*, 6.

demanded by its preparation seems to have provided the composer with a powerful means of distracting his thoughts, and to some extent assuaging his grief, in the aftermath of his wife's decease. In the first published edition the foreword was dated 6 September 1627, the second anniversary of Magdalena's death.

Two particularly notable events marked the year 1627. In April there was produced at Hartenfels castle in Torgau, for the wedding of Johann Georg's daughter Sophia Eleanora to the Landgrave Georg II of Hessen-Darmstadt, the opera-ballet *Dafne*. Though often claimed as the first German opera, the work's precise nature is uncertain, since only the text has survived;[10] quite possibly it may have involved only spoken dialogue with interpolated songs and ballet sequences.[11] The text is a free German adaptation by Martin Opitz of the renowned Italian libretto (of 1597) by Ottavio Rinuccini, which was set, probably as the first opera in history, by Jacopo Peri, and performed in Florence in 1598. A second setting, which Peri is said to have regarded as superior to his own, was made in 1607 by Marco da Gagliano, and premiered at Mantua in 1608. The plot, drawn from the first book of Ovid's *Metamorphoses*, recounts the story of the demi-god Apollo who, after slaying a dragon, boasts of his bravery to Venus and Cupid. In order to punish him for his vainglory, Cupid causes him to fall in love— sadly unrequited—with the nymph Dafne. He pursues her ardently, but is foiled when she is transformed into a laurel; and the opera ends with a chorus of mourning and a vow by Apollo to devote himself in future to the pursuit of art and the poet's laurel wreath. Opitz's version includes a pro- logue in which Ovid appears from the Elysian fields to speak of the power and cruelty of love; and his text is so fashioned as to allow the audience to recognize, from time to time, graceful allusions to the royal marriage part- ners. Also, by adding some mocking references to Cupid as the 'little archer' (Schütze), he was able to introduce some gentle shafts of wit at the composer's expense.[12] It is not known whether Schütz's contribution was wholly original or in part an adaptation of Peri's (or even Gagliano's) music to the new German text; but the general course of the plot remained largely unaltered.

The second event took place during the autumn of 1627 when Schütz, with members of his Kapelle, accompanied Johann Georg to Mühlhausen for an electoral meeting, held between 4 October and 3 November. For this occasion he composed the ceremonial motet 'Da pacem, Domine, in diebus nostris', SWV 465.[13] This remarkable composition is scored for two chor- uses: (i) SSATB, the parts of which may, according to the composer's

---

[10] See Jörg-Ulrich Fechner, 'Zur literaturgeschichtlichen Situation in Dresden 1627. Überlegungen im Hinblick auf die "Dafne"-Oper von Schütz und Opitz', *SJb*, 11 (1989), 15.
[11] See Wolfram Steude, 'Zum gegenwärtigen Stand der Schütz-Biographik', *SJb*, 12 (1990), 20.
[12] The role of Cupid, it should be noted, was added by Opitz to Rinuccini's original work.
[13] A modern edition of 'Da pacem, Domine', SWV 465, is published in *NSA*, 38.

instructions, 'be played by five viols, with one or two doubling voices singing *submisse* [softly], and (ii) 'four [solo] singers [SATB] who must pronounce the words clearly and sing strongly, and who may be set apart from the first chorus'. Each chorus has its own text: the first, the medieval antiphon 'Da pacem, Domine, in diebus nostris' (Grant peace in our time, O lord, for there is none other than fightest for us but only thou, our God); and the second, a specially written Latin text containing the acclamations of the assembled electors: Moguntinus (Mainz), Treverensis (Trier), and (the more easily identified) Coloniensis, Saxo, Bavarus, and Brandenburgicus. In the course of a three-verse structure, the emperor is extolled three times with the words 'vivat Ferdinandus, Caesar invictissimus', while the first chorus continues quietly with its heartfelt pleas for peace. The composer's skill in linking the conventional salutations with his deeply thoughtful setting of the antiphon text makes this the most effective of his political motets; and it is therefore the more regrettable that he failed to enhance its later performance prospects by providing an alternative, less specific, text—as he did for example in the case of his *Syncharma musicum*). In its existing form, however, the work provides interesting historical evidence about the current war situation, and makes abundantly clear the extent of the Saxon elector's commitment to peace and, at this period at least, to the imperial Catholic cause.

4

The Music of 1619–23: the *Psalmen Davids* and the *Resurrection History*

In 1619, following a lengthy period of gestation, during which he explored ways of adapting to the demands of his native language and Lutheran ritual the polychoral and concertato techniques he had studied in Venice, Schütz finally published his first major collection of German church works, the *Psalmen Davids sampt etlichen Moteten und Concerten*[1] (the Psalms of David, together with some motets and concertos) [Op. 2] for eight or more voices and instruments. Imposing in style and structure, these were amongst the most richly scored of all his works, designed to fill with maximum sonority the resonant expanses of Dresden's electoral chapel. Chief amongst his models was Giovanni Gabrieli's first set of *Symphoniae sacrae* of 1593, from which he had clearly absorbed such techniques as the balanced integration of choral and instrumental forces, the ways of achieving structural symmetry (not least by the use of rondo-like structures), and the importance to word-setting of metrical and rhythmic variety. Equally valuable, however, was the skill he had acquired in vocal polyphony, and the poised management of German texts, from his study of the Italianate works of such of his leading compatriots as Hans Leo Hassler, Philipp Dulichius, Adam Gumpelzhaimer, and in particular his close associate, Michael Praetorius, whose *Musae Sionae* (1605–10) and crowning masterpiece entitled *Polyhymnia Caduceatrix et Panegyrica*, also published in 1619, yielded for analysis an immense and historically significant compendium of German sacred music in the Venetian manner.[2]

In his new post at Dresden, Schütz was afforded singularly favourable facilities for his exploration of the lavish Italian styles he so greatly admired. Not only did the royal chapel, with its lofty grandeur and ample space for the placing of separate choral and instrumental groups, afford him a first-rate venue for polychoral music; but also the court, with its (at this time) plentiful resources, provided him in abundance with the vocal and instrumental performers he needed. The feasibility of some of his large-scale psalm-settings had, as we have seen earlier (on p. 29), already been tested in 1617 during the celebrations for the centenary of the Reformation; and since on these occasions it had been possible for him to

---

[1] *Psalmen Davids* (1619), NSA, 23–6.
[2] See Friedrich Blume, *Protestant Church Music: A History* (London, 1975), 201.

give personal guidance to his musicians into the intricacies of the Italian style, it is safe to assume that he was reasonably well satisfied with the results. However, when he came to publish his full range of psalm-settings in 1619, concern that his work might fare poorly at the hands of less experienced German musicians led him to provide a lengthy preface (the first of the many he furnished so abundantly for practically all of his printed collections) in which he gave precise instructions about the size and nature of the forces to be assembled, the surest means of achieving balance and integration between them, the best way to position them in the performance area, and the most appropriate tempos to adopt for verbal clarity—instructions which, it may be added, are no less valuable for present-day performers.[3]

Fundamental is the distinction he draws between two types of chorus, the 'Coro favorito' and 'Coro capella', which are designed to fulfil roles somewhat akin to the concertino and ripieno groups in the instrumental concertos of the later part of the century. The Cori favoriti, he says, should comprise 'those singers whose voices the Capellmeister most esteems, and should be situated in the most favourable position [in the performing area]'; as an obbligato group, their function, either in consort or as individual soloists, is to present the most elaborate music, and in the process to be entrusted with the whole of the text. The Capelle, on the other hand, should be larger and relatively less skilled bodies of performers, either singers or instrumentalists, or more often a combination of each, whose function it is to add sonority and splendour to the music at section endings and points of climax, and to give instrumental support to the voices at the extreme limits of their compass. Their contribution is necessarily intermittent, and as a result they are likely to be assigned only certain parts of the text. Where pairs of each type of chorus are used, each Capella, he recommends, should normally be linked with one specific Favorito group, placed diagonally opposite it in a 'cross-wise' (Kreuzweiss) arrangement, so that the sound can emanate ('stereophonically') from all four corners of the performing area. Equal care is required in the formation and function of the continuo. The instruments specified on the title page include organ, lute, and chitarrone; it is, however, clear from the composer's preface that, while the stringed instruments can usefully supply additional colour and variety, his choice lies mainly with the organ—partly because of its ability to provide sonorous reinforcement to the bass, and partly because of its capacity to make rapid dynamic changes in support of the contrasted choral groups. 'The organist', as he puts it, 'should pay careful attention to the terms

---

[3] The inclusion of an explanatory preface clearly fulfilled a pressing need during the adventurous, even experimental, era in which Schütz was working. Not dissimilar is the usage found in many avant-garde works of the present century. A characteristic example is the *Requiem* (1963–5) by György Ligeti which in its published form requires, in addition to a single prefatory sheet, a 23-page booklet of instructions (in both German and English) to convey precise details of the composer's recommended performance practice.

['Favorito' and 'Capella'] in the basso continuo partbook and register the organ appropriately'.

Of the twenty-six works in the collection twenty are based on complete psalms (normally short ones of some eight or nine verses), three on selected verses drawn from the psalms, one each on passages from Jeremiah and Isaiah, and one (designated a 'Canzon') on chorale stanzas by Johann Poliander, which provide a paraphrase of Psalm 103: 1–6. Two items marked 'Moteto' on their title-pages—SWV 40, 'Is not Ephraim my dear son?' (Ist nicht Ephraim mein teurer Sohn?), on Jeremiah 31: 20, and SWV 42 'They that sow in tears' (Die mit Tränen säen) on Psalm 126: 5–6—involve, because of their funereal associations and very short texts, relatively restrained scoring and a larger than usual amount of Renaissance-style polyphony and melismatic treatment. Whereas the great psalms of praise and exultation—such as Psalm 136, 'O give thanks unto the Lord' (Danket dem Herren, denn er ist freundlich), SWV 45, and Psalm 100, 'Make a joyful noise unto the Lord' (Jauchzet dem Herren, alle Welt), SWV 47—for their proper effect require a full panoply of voices and instruments, with two or more Favorito ensembles and their supporting Capelle, plus a large array of instruments, including, in varying numbers, flutes, bassoons, cornetts, trumpets, and trombones, as a wind band, and violins, violas, viols, and basses, as a string ensemble. Aware, however, that few German courts apart from Dresden would be able to muster the full forces necessary for the grandly scored works, Schütz provides continually for flexibility in his recommendations, a flexibility somewhat at odds with more recent ideas about the need for 'ideal' concepts in artistic creation and performance, but one wholly consonant (particularly in relation to instrumental participation) with early seventeenth-century practice. The Capelle, for example, are in many cases marked *ad libitum*, and much freedom is allowed in the choice and deployment of the instruments.

Certain works, such as Psalm 121, 'I will lift up mine eyes unto the hills' (Ich hebe meine Augen auf), SWV 31, and Psalm 23, 'The Lord is my shepherd' (Der Herr ist mein Hirt), SWV 33, may, he suggests, be performed simply as eight-voice, double-choir settings, and with the continuo as the only instrumental support, provided that an essential weak/strong (favorito/capella) degree of tonal contrast is preserved between the vocal groups involved. And for settings with high- and low-voice choruses, such as Psalm 8, 'O Lord our God, how excellent is thy name' (Herr, unser Herrscher), SWV 27, and Psalm 128, 'Blessed is every one that feareth the Lord' (Wohl dem, der den Herren fürchtet), SWV 30, each with SSAT and ATBB choruses, he declares it to be 'not inelegant' (nicht übel schicken), if cornetts or violins are used in the upper chorus and trombones or other suitable instruments in the lower one' (wann der höhere Chor mit Zincken/Geigen, der nidrige mit Posaunen oder andern Instrumenten gemacht), provided there is one voice (and preferably the topmost one in each chorus) to sing the text.

37

The texts, it may be added, have no clear liturgical application. They were doubtless chosen mainly for their brevity—fewer than ten verses in the majority of cases—and for the rich imagery of their language. Brevity was important because of the amount of text repetition which polychoral writing, with its concomitant leaning towards antiphony, almost inevitably incurs; and imagery because of the scope it provided for the characteristic 'word- and sentence-painting' which is such a consistent feature of Schütz's style.

Some insight into Schütz's procedures may be gained by surveying several pairs of works of similar length and scoring. It is far from certain that the composer regarded these as matching pairs, but it may well be significant that many of them share the same modal 'key-centre' and, indeed, occupy adjacent positions in the published collection. One such 'coupling' involves the settings of Psalm 1 (SWV 28), 'Blessed is the man that walketh not in the counsel of the ungodly' (Wohl dem, der nicht wandelt in Rat der Gottlosen) and Psalm 84 (SWV 29), 'How lovely are thy dwelling-places, O Lord of Hosts' (Wie lieblich sind deine Wohnungen). Both works are scored for two four-part chorus, high- and low-voice, and both are set in the transposed Dorian (G minor) mode. In SWV 28 overall contrast is created between the sections referring to the 'godly' and 'ungodly' (verses 1–3 and 4–6 respectively), a contrast marked by a clear change of musical expression from bar 73, a notional halfway point. At the start, in an extended triple-time passage, the top three voices (SSA) of Coro 1 depict 'blessedness' with repeated utterances of 'Wohl dem', set in calm trochaic patterns, while Coro 2 remains silent until bar 20, where it supplies only short antiphonal interventions before joining in an eight-voice section-ending. At the centre point, the full ensemble in 'stern' homophony assert that 'the ungodly are not so [blessed]' and proceeds to liken them to 'the chaff which the wind driveth away', graphically depicted by swift antiphonal exchanges between the choruses, originally of three-and-a-half bars but, with increasing intensity, reduced to short 'gusts' of only a single bar's length (see Ex. 7).

Similarly, SWV 29, perhaps the most immediately attractive of all the settings, begins with a radiant section in long note-values for the high-voice Coro 1 in which a sense of 'loveliness' is conveyed by means of an ascending pattern in five chromatic steps, underpinned by seven major chords in root position (see Ex. 8a). As in the previous work a change of mood is apparent at the midpoint (bar 101), where the basses of Coro 2 initiate a darkly coloured imitative pattern for the words 'as they pass through the vale of tears', using long note-values and a partially chromatic ascent subtly reminiscent of the opening passage of the whole work, though greatly different in expression (see Ex. 8b). Contrasted sections of word-painting bring vigorous life to the first half of the setting: at bar 39, for verse 3, 'Even the bird [sparrow, in AV] finds a home and the swallow a nest', where the swooping flight of the birds is charmingly depicted by a dipping fourteen-

Ex. 7

bar melisma, with cambiata-like figuration; and from bar 87, for the last phrase of verse 5, '[blessed are those] whose hearts follow after thee', where long note-values and mirror imitations between the voices of both choruses achieve a sudden transformation of the scene into one of solemn dedication. During the final section of the work (from bar 136), added splendour is created by a tutti setting of verses 8, 9, and 10 in *falsobordone*, a type of unmeasured chanting (for chorus or a solo voice) with an ancestry traceable back at least as far as the early sixteenth century. Employed sparingly, as it is here by Schütz, its effect is twofold: to absorb, for structural reasons, a large amount of text within a small musical space; and more particularly, to provide special emphasis to a series of commanding ideas, related in this case to 'mercy', 'truth', and 'salvation'. The three passages are set to different root-position chords, rising stepwise, in pitch and brightness, from D minor through E minor to F major; and each ends impressively with a measured cadence two or three bars in length.

Linked by their penitential texts are the settings of Psalm 6 (SWV 24), 'O Lord, rebuke me not in thine anger' (Ach, Herr, straf mich nicht) and Psalm 130 (SWV 25) 'Out of the deep have I cried unto thee, O Lord' (Aus der Tiefe ruf ich). Each work is scored for a pair of equal (SATB) choruses, each is set in a freely treated (E minor) form of the Phrygian mode (the one traditionally associated with sorrow and contrition), and each discloses a pattern of powerful antiphonal echoes, with 'waves' of overlapping choral entries. At the beginning of SWV 25 (for Coro 1 alone) a sustained augmented triad (in bar 3) provides expressive colouring to the word 'Tiefe';

Schütz

Ex. 8

(a)

Coro 1   Wie   lieb - lich,   wie   lieb - lich   sind dei - ne

Woh - nun - gen

(b)

and subsequently an imaginative use is made of silent bars, tellingly placed so as to suggest the petitioner's anxious wait for a response to his words of supplication—at bar 9, for example, immediately after the opening phrase, and at bar 43, following the urgent plea from both choruses, in eight-voice scoring, of 'my soul waits, and in his word do I trust' (meine Seele harret, und ich hofe auf sein Wort).

More exultant settings, appropriate to the nature of their texts, are accorded to Psalm 98 (SWV 35), 'O sing unto the Lord a new song' (Singet dem Herrn ein neues Lied) and Psalm 100 (SWV 36), 'Make a joyful noise unto the Lord' (Jauchzet dem Herren alle Welt), both scored for two equal (SATB) choruses and set in the transposed Ionian (F major) mode. In SWV 35, in response to its colourful text, the composer employs sweeping melismatic patterns in quavers to depict in verses 6, 7, and 8 the 'trumpets and trombones' (Drommeten und Posaunen (cornetts in AV)), the 'roaring of the sea' (das Meer brause), and the 'rejoicing of the floods and the hills' (die Wasserströme frohlocken, und alle Berge sind frölich), after which the 'judgement of the world with righteousness' (der Erdboden richten mit Gerechtigkeit) is given impressive weight by a solemn procession of root-position chords, set in passages of overlapping antiphony. The lesser doxology (Glory be to the Father) is appended, the opening section of which, unusually for Schütz, recalls almost exactly the music of the first eighteen bars of the work.

The distinctive character of SWV 36 results from the use of immediate echoes by the second chorus, one, two, or four bars later and mainly at the same pitch, of each phrase sung by Coro 1, with those of the longest phrases often confined, in a realistic manner, to the final two bars. In performance the echo effect can be greatly enhanced by using a second chorus of reduced size, accompanied (as the composer indicates) by a *coro di liuti* (lute chorus) and placed at some considerable distance behind the first; and by adding cornetts and trombones to the first choral group for extra brilliance. It is noteworthy that an earlier version of this work (SWV Deest) has survived in which a system of double echoes is produced by the use of three choruses. This may well have been another of the settings composed in 1617 for one of the services at Dresden in celebration of the centenary of the Reformation; and it was possibly Schütz's experience, on that occasion, of the slackening effect which an extended pattern of double echoes can produce on the music's forward drive that convinced him of the need to create his later, more tightly organized version.

A solitary example of independent instrumental writing occurs in the setting of Psalm 111 (SWV 34), 'I [will] thank the Lord with my whole heart' (Ich danke dem Herrn von ganzen Herzen), where a sinfonia based on the madrigal 'Lieto godea' by Giovanni Gabrieli ('imitatione sopra: Lieto godea Canzone di Gio[vanni] Gabrieli', to use the composer's phrase) is inserted at the end of the psalm, before the doxology setting. The twelve-bar sinfonia is scored for two four-part Capelle with initial sections of overlapping antiphony leading to a stable eight-part texture. No precise instrumentation is specified, but an effective arrangement, which conforms to Schütz's recommendation about preserving homogeneity in instrumental groups, would involve cornetts and trombones for Coro 2 and a contrasted ensemble of stringed instruments at the appropriate (SATB) pitches for Coro 1. At the start of the ensuing doxology the same material from Gabrieli is allotted to the Capelle, and the texture increased to sixteen parts by the addition of both Favorito choruses. Thereafter, in a free setting, the remaining text, from 'wie es war im Anfang' (as it was in the beginning), proceeds majestically to a final plagal cadence.

Two other settings which include instrumental contributions of particular interest are SWV 45, the second of two versions of Psalm 136, 'O give thanks unto the Lord, for he is good' (Danket dem Herren, denn er ist freundlich) and Psalm 150, 'Alleluja! Praise the Lord in his sanctuary' (Alleluja! Lobet den Herren in seinen Heiligtum), SWV 38. The text of SWV 45 provides the only example of an antiphonal 'refrain' psalm, the twenty-six verses of which each have an identical second half, comprising the words 'For his goodness endureth for ever' (Denn seine Güte währet ewiglich). The basic scoring is for two choruses—SSAT, and A with TTB trombones—plus a Capella a 5, and a trumpet and timpani ensemble, the size of which is not precisely specified, but may originally have included as many as six performers.[4] The text is divided by Schütz into five sections, each of five to ten verses, and during each section the first half-verse is set throughout for the second and first chorus in rotation, with Capella support added in the third and final sections. The second half-verse (the refrain) is in each case given extra weight by the Capella, and at the end of sections 2, 4, and 5 dramatic interventions by the trumpet chorus create an overall tripartite effect.[5] Yet another of the works which Hoe von Honegg recorded as having been performed at the Reformation commemorative services in Dresden in 1617, SWV 45, or an earlier version of it, was described on that occasion as '136. Psalm mit Trommeten und Heerpauken'.

The scoring of Psalm 150 is remarkable for its use of obbligato instruments—flute, violin, and a pair each of cornetts, bassoons, and trombones—in support of the vocal duets which alternate with tutti passages during the first four verses. The references to instruments in verses 3 and 4—'the sound of the trombone [trumpet in AV]', 'the psaltery and harp', 'stringed instruments and organs'—are each related, as nearly as possible, to the actual instrumental sounds employed. An effective example occurs in verse 3, where, at the words 'lobet ihn mit Posaunen' (praise him with sackbuts), a short canonic passage for the tenor soloists of Favoriti 1 and 2 is accompanied, and given additional warmth, by independent lines for three trombones (see Ex. 9). Finally, in order perhaps to place a personal

---

[4] See M. H. Schmid, 'Trompetenchor und Sprachvertonung bei Heinrich Schütz', *SJb*, 13 (1991), 28–55.
[5] See Schmid, op. cit., 45.

Ex. 9

imprint on his version of the last of the psalms, Schütz provides a wonderfully radiant tutti setting of the words, 'Alles was Atem hat, lobe den Herr' (Let everything that hath breath praise the Lord), and in the process articulates most imaginatively one fundamental aspect of his religious and musical philosophy.

Four years later, in 1623, there appeared the *Resurrection History*, the first of Schütz's biblical dramas in the traditional *Historia* form.[6] The text is drawn from a work entitled *Die Historia des Leidens und der Auferstehung unsers Herrn Jesu Christi aus den vier Evangelisten* (The story of the Passion and Resurrection of our Lord Jesus Christ from the four gospels), published in Wittenberg in 1526 by Johann Bugenhagen, a friend of Luther and a noted theologian. The earliest known musical setting of the Resurrection account from this source dates from *c*.1550. Based on a mock plainchant 'Easter tone' it is monodic throughout, apart from some simple chordal passages for the utterances of the high priests and the

---

[6] *The Resurrection History* (1623), NSA, 3.

disciples, and in style it resembles the Passion settings, from the same period, attributed to Johann Walter, but like them is almost certainly not by him. Subsequently, during the second half of the century, but before 1573, a more elaborate version was produced by Antonio Scandello, an Italian from Bergamo, noted for his skill as a cornett and sackbut player, who after conversion to Protestantism joined the Kapelle at Dresden, *c*.1550, and became Kapellmeister there from 1568. The particular novelty of his setting lies in its use of polyphony in a varying number of parts, not only for the crowd (*turba*) utterances but also for those of all the 'speaking' characters including Jesus. Only the Evangelist narrator continues to employ the traditional 'Easter tone'. Thus, duet sections are provided for the words of Mary Magdalene (S.1 and S.2), the two angels at the sepulchre (A and T), and Cleophas (T and B); a trio section for those of the Three Marys (SST); and a four-part (SATB) ensemble for those of Christ. The application of mixed-form (chant and polyphony) writing to a biblical story was a practice which Scandello had almost certainly learnt from his mentor, Gaspar de Albertis, at Santa Maria Maggiore, Bergamo, who, before 1541, had composed three Passions using this method. The influence of Scandello's *Historia* is shown by a work of similar structure, from 1598, by the Altenberg Kapellmeister Nikolaus Rosthius, and its continuing popularity by the many reprints which it later enjoyed, including one in a Czech translation from the mid seventeenth century.[7]

Schütz may well have encountered Scandello's setting when he first arrived in Dresden, and it is not unlikely that he was responsible for mounting several Eastertide performances of it during his first years with the royal chapel. The respect which he had gained for the older work, and for the ancient tradition it represented, is clear when one considers the extent to which he used it as the basis of his own setting. Not only did he keep the traditional texts of the opening and concluding choruses (a title statement and a final act of thanksgiving), but also preserved largely intact the original mosaic of bible texts, drawn from all four gospels, and its ingenious layout of the Easter story in five main scenes: the discovery by Mary Magdalene and her companions of the empty tomb and their encounter with angels who declare that Jesus has risen from the dead; Mary's meeting with the risen Christ; the bribing of the watch by the chief priests, to claim that the disciples have removed Jesus's body during the night; the encounter with Jesus by Cleophas and his companion on the road to Emmaus; and finally the meeting between Jesus and the eleven disciples in Jerusalem. Also, he not only retained many features of the traditional 'Easter tone', but in an entirely novel manner adapted for his own purposes, the principle of setting the sayings of the individual characters for small solo groups of varying size. The main features of what may be called his 'modernization' include the provision of a continuo part throughout, the

[7] Scandello's Easter *Historia* and the similar setting by Rosthius are published in the *Handbuch der deutschen evangelischen Kirchenmusik*, 1, 3, and 4 (Göttingen, 1937).

addition of occasional descriptive vocal figuration to the basic plainchant narration, the intensification of the character utterances by means of rich harmony and imitative counterpoint, and the optional use of four viole da gamba to provide a colourful accompaniment to the Evangelist's narration. The eventual outcome is a work of startling originality, the increased fervency of expression of which is specifically designed to imprint its message most powerfully on the minds of those who hear it.

In his preface[8] the composer calls for a separation of the singers and instrumentalists into two groups, described as the 'Evangelist's Chorus' and the 'Chorus of the speaking characters' (*personen colloquenten*). While the former should, he says, be placed at some distance from the main organ, the others must necessarily be situated close by the organ, so that the conductor can provide for them, in the interests of verbal clarity, a 'slow and carefully measured beat—in which, as he delightfully observes, 'the soul of all music resides'. Amongst several detailed instructions he recommends that the mock-plainsong recitation of the tenor Evangelist should, for the best effect, be accompanied by an ensemble of four viole da gamba (three with independent ATT parts and the fourth supplying the continuo bass); but, that failing this, an organ, lute, or pandora (a metal-strung instrument of deep pitch, plucked with the fingers or a plectrum) may be used. Whichever medium is adopted, however, the accompaniment, he says, should be decorated, in the Italian manner of the time, by ornamental *passaggi* (simple scales and flourishes), a practice which he acknowledges is more easily accomplished by a single player—organist or lutanist—than by a group of violists, who would need, in advance, to practice assiduously with the singer. Lastly, he recommends that, in performance, only the Evangelist should be visible, while the other characters remain hidden, a remarkable, quasi-theatrical (and perhaps not entirely practical) suggestion, designed, it would seem, to surround the narrator with an altogether unusual aura of mystery, and thus give greater emphasis to his central evangelical role.

The second ensemble embraces each of the voice-groups representing the individual characters: the three women (SSS), the two men at the sepulchre (TT), Mary Magdalene (SS), the two angels (TT), Jesus (AT), the young man in the sepulchre (AA), Cleophas (T), Cleophas and his companion (TT), the chief priests (TTB), and the eleven disciples at Jerusalem (SSATTB). Where the individual characterizations involve upper voices only, the continuo bass consistently enlarges their textures, the duets and trios becoming three- and four-part ensembles respectively; only in the case of the chief priests' trio and the disciples' six-voice chorus does the continuo line function solely in support of the lowest voice-part. The contribution of the continuo bass is, however, invariably more static than those of the voices it accompanies, and there are no instances where it enriches the texture with

---

[8] *GBS*, No. 12, 69.

independent imitative patterns. In one curious observation, the composer suggests that in the duet sections where a single character is represented—such as those for Jesus and Mary Magdalene—one of the voices might be replaced by an instrument or omitted entirely. It is not easy to see the purpose of this. Without a full complement of singers (essential for the six-part setting of the words of the disciples at Jerusalem) a performance would scarcely be feasible, so that the use of an instrument in place of one of the voices, though likely to provide (in the case of a stringed instrument at least) a satisfactory blend, would be no more than a makeshift arrangement; and presentation by a single voice, though arguably more lifelike, would entail the sacrifice of the contrapuntal resource so uniformly characteristic of the composer's style.

The dominant note *a*, in the prevailing Dorian 'tonality', provides a basic level for the Evangelist's recitation; but repeatedly small variations in pitch give emphasis to particular words, or underline, through a lightening or darkening of the voice colouring, the meaning of special passages in the text. The method can be seen in the opening section where the tenor soloist, against a held D minor chord, begins with the distinctive plainchant pattern *d a a c' a* (a recurrent one throughout the work[9]), and proceeds, after narration on the note *a*, to a measured cadence on *f*, the normal plainsong note of inflection. Then after similar treatment of the second phrase, which refers to the women's purchase of spices to anoint the body of Jesus, the reciting-note moves down to *f*, with *d* as its note of inflection, to provide the darker colouring appropriate to the words 'For they rested on the Sabbath, according to the commandment'. Subsequently, after two further sections, using successively the *a–f* and *f–d* intonations to describe the arrival of the women at the sepulchre, the pitch is raised excitedly to *c'* in order to colour the words 'and behold there was a great earthquake'. More extravagant examples of word-painting are rare in the Evangelist's part; but a notable exception is provided (in the passage which follows on immediately after that just described) for the words 'the angel of the Lord descended from heaven, and came and rolled back the stone from the door' (from Matthew 28: 2), where the angel's descent is represented by a scale falling stepwise over an octave and the removal of the stone by a 'rolling' figure as remarkable for its visual as its audible realism of effect (see Ex. 10).

It is, however, in his settings of the utterances of the *personen colloquenten* that Schütz finds greatest scope for text interpretation. Capitalizing on the varied resources inherent in his multi-voice ensembles, he uses imitative counterpoint to lengthen his sections and give substance to his musical arguments, melodic sequences to convey excitement or a sense of stressful anxiety, and rich harmony to give emphasis to words of particular emotional significance. In Mary Magdalene's first utterance at

[9] The opening chant pattern is one commonly found in Gregorian melodies for psalms, antiphons, and responsories. See O. Kade, *Die ältere Passionskomposition bis zum Jahre 1631* (Gütersloh, 1893), 206.

Ex. 10

the sepulchre, for example, a vivid sense of fear and unease is created in the first six bars by a repeated chromatic chord progression for the words, 'They have taken the Lord out of the grave', and by the imitative passages which ensue, rising sequentially over an octave for the phrase 'and we know not where they have laid him' (see Ex. 11). And in the scene where Mary Magdalene first encounters the risen Christ, a tranquil drama of equal emotional weight, is unfolded. By means of a solemn three-part chord progression, *echt*-Schützian with its internal 'Dorian' B natural, the composer creates a remarkable aura of mystery and wonder for the Saviour's gentle greeting, 'Maria!'; and by the use of a precisely placed augmented triad on the stressed syllable of the word 'Rabbuni' (Master), provides for Mary's awestruck response a setting of entirely parallel beauty and intensity of expression (see Ex. 12).

Ex. 11

The final chorus, on a text from I Corinthians 15: 57, 'But thanks be to God, which giveth us the victory through our Lord Jesus Christ', is scored for two SATB choruses (the first supported, optionally, by the four viole da gamba) which engage in antiphonal responses of ever increasing vigour. Very possibly extra Capella resources would have been incorporated to strengthen the choral sonority, but it is noteworthy that the soloists needed for the main body of the work could alone have provided all the necessary voice-parts. Threaded through the chorus is the voice of the tenor Evangelist who, abandoning his role as narrator, contributes one further part (marked 'Nona vox Evangelistae') with the single word 'Victoria' sung to repeated-note patterns, each based, at their first appearance, on the six pitches *a g c′ d′ e′ a*. This concept, a strikingly dramatic one, used also by Scandello and Rosthius, subtly relates the whole work to a woodcut printed on the cover of the original continuo partbook, showing the risen Christ trampling Satan underfoot, with the verse 'Ubi tuus, Mors, aculeus? ubi tua, inferne, victoria?' ('O death, where is thy sting? O grave, where is thy

Ex. 12

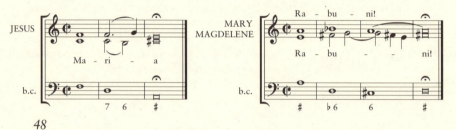

victory?) from I Corinthians 15: 55, set beneath it. Satan, whose right leg appears buried in a grave, from which a skull and the upper part of a skeleton protrude, has the wings of a fallen angel and the breasts of a woman; and around his/her right arm there is entwined a snake, the serpent tempter of the Garden of Eden.

In an interesting survey of the varied fortunes of the *Resurrection History* during the later seventeenth century, resulting from gradual changes in style and taste, Matthias Herrmann has called attention to four manuscripts, held in the former municipal library in Breslau, which reveal how, in a series of increasingly radical revisions (in these sources alone), Schütz's work was gradually altered out of all recognition.[10] The earliest of the manuscripts (Ms. mus. 201 a, No. 1) provides a more or less exact copy of Schütz's original 1623 print; but of the later ones, the first two include wholly new sections, or ones which are free adaptations of Schütz, while the third is virtually a newly-composed setting in which only faint traces of Schütz's original ideas remain. The discovery of these sources provides valuable evidence of the extent to which musical settings of the Resurrection story continued to hold their place in Lutheran worship; and, at the same time, shows that Schütz's version, itself a modification of his predecessors' work, provided a transitional link, though one of the greatest significance, in a lengthy, albeit intermittent historical process.[11]

[10] See Matthias Herrmann, 'Bemerkungen zur Schütz-Rezeption im 17. Jahrhunderts am Beispiel der "Breslauer Variante" der Auferstehungs-Historie, SWV 50', *SJb*, 12 (1990), 83–111.

[11] The only Resurrection Histories of the later 17th century to have survived are those of Thomas Selle (a 8 and a 14) *c.*1660, and Christian A. Schultze, his *Historia resurrectionis* of 1686, based on the Bugenhagen text.

5

The Music of 1625–8: the *Cantiones sacrae* and the *Becker Psalter*

The diversity of genres evident in the first group of Schütz's major publications is extended still further by the *Cantiones sacrae* [Op. 4] of 1625, a collection of Latin motets for four voices, usually SATB but with variants, such as SSST, SSAB, and SAABar, indicated by the positioning of the clefs. The collection, comprising forty works (many linked in sets of two or more *partes*), is dedicated to Prince Hans Ulrich von Eggenberg, a former Protestant aristocrat from Styria, who had converted to Catholicism and taken up a position as imperial chancellor in Vienna at the court of the Emperor Matthias (d. 1619). By dedicating the work to a man whom he knew to be deeply interested in music, and whom he may well have met in 1617 on the occasion of the imperial visit to Dresden, Schütz no doubt hoped to increase the dissemination of his work well beyond the borders of Saxony; and by flattering, at the same time, one of high rank in the imperial service, to provide on behalf of the Dresden Elector an effective means of maintaining amicable relations with Matthias's successor, Ferdinand II, despite the ever-increasing pressures of the religious war.

The use of Latin texts, and the colourful devotional style of many of the settings, should not be taken to indicate any covert Catholic leanings on the part of the composer. His lengthy stay in Venice from 1609 to 1611 would doubtless have given him more insight into the Catholic ritual of the day, and the music in which it was clothed, than was usual amongst his colleagues in Lutheran Saxony; but there is abundant evidence to show that he never wavered from his Protestant allegiance. Confirmation is provided by a letter he wrote in April 1632 to Philipp Hainhofer, the ducal agent at Wolfenbüttel, in which he expressed his immense joy on learning (from a sermon delivered by Hoe von Hoenegg) of the 'newly-gained freedom of the Lutheran Church from great Catholic oppression, which had gladdened many thousand, indeed hundred-thousand, human hearts in northern Germany and especially in Augsburg'.[1] It would nevertheless be right to describe the collection, because of its texts, as offering wider denomina-

---

[1] '. . . was massen bishero die Evangelischen Kirchen, wegen grosser unterdrucken der Catholischen, auch viel traurigkeiterduldet, an itzo aber der h. Christus in Oberteutschlandt und namentlich auch zu Augspurg viele 1000, ja hunderttausendt menschenhertzen wiederumb zu erfreuen . . .'

tional scope than any other of his works, and because of the 'chamber' character of its music, as more appropriate for private performance at princely courts, both Catholic and Protestant, than for public worship.

The principal source of the texts is a volume entitled *Precandi formulae piae et selectae ex veterum ecclesiae sanctorum doctorum scriptis* (Prayers of a pious nature, chosen from the writings of the holy doctors of the ancient Church) which was published in 1553 by the Lutheran theologian, Andreas Musculus, a professor at Frankfurt-am-Oder, whose credentials may be regarded as impeccably Protestant. In total, the anthology embraces biblical passages from the Psalms[2] and the Song of Solomon, together with a responsory from the Roman Office for the Dead, and a number of extracts from what Musculus apparently believed were the writings of St Augustine (d. 430), but which are now known to have been taken from various eleventh- and twelfth-century sources: the *Meditationes* of St Anselm of Canterbury, the *Soliloquia* from the *Archa animae* of Hugo of St Victor, and a *Manuale* of sermons on the Song of Solomon by Bernard of Clairvaux. By choosing some of his texts from works of a heightened fervency of expression by the 'holy doctors', Musculus contributed to some extent to a strain of German mysticism, traceable from the *Theologia Germanica* (1516), which Luther edited and attributed to Tauler, through the works of Jacob Boehme (1575–1624) to the Pietist poets of the seventeenth century; and by incorporating what he supposed were Augustinian texts, he may well have hoped to win particular favour within contemporary Lutheran circles, where, in view of Luther's fundamental training as an Augustinian monk, the authority of the saint's writings was strongly upheld.

Some insights into the character and organization of the collection may be gained both from its dedicatory epistle to Prince Eggenberg[3] and its preface to the 'gracious reader' (Benevolum lectorem),[4] each couched in elegant Latin. In the former the composer refers to some of the motets as having been 'long since finished' (pridem inchoatas)—meaning, perhaps, written before he had chosen Musculus as his principal text source—and contrasts them with others which reveal a more up-to-date style of vocal composition ('novam canendi rationem'). And in the preface he declares that his publisher had 'wrested from him' a continuo line ('Bassum istum Generalem mibi extorsit'), which, though unnecessary for the majority of the works, was nevertheless essential for a number of settings in a more modern style, included towards the end of the volume. Taken together these remarks suggest that the motets were probably composed over a lengthy period of time, and thus involve a wide spectrum of changing styles, from

---

[2] Psalms between 10 and 147 in the Vulgate, it should be noted, are numbered one digit lower than their vernacular equivalents in Protestant sources. This results from the combination of nos. 9 and 10 to form the single Latin psalm 9 and the division of no. 147 to provide Latin psalms 146 and 147.

[3] *GBS*, No. 15, 75.   [4] *GBS*, No. 16, 77.

traditional choral polyphony, found, for example, in 'Deus misereatur nostri', No. 3, and 'Heu mihi, domine', No. 13, at one extreme, to the monodic concerto style with obbligato continuo, such as the Monteverdian 'Turbabor, sed non perturbabor', No. 18, and 'Domine, ne in furore tuo', Nos. 33–5, at the other. Such intermediate stages as occurred no doubt did so gradually, and are therefore less easy to identify; but recently attempts have been made to allot various of the works to three central categories in which (i) only minor modifications of the older vocal style are found; (ii) contrapuntal writing is combined with concerto-style diction: and (iii) a more radical manner is revealed, close to that of the monodic madrigal.[5] It can hardly be claimed, however, that such changes in style necessarily correspond closely to the chronological order of composition, since, throughout his career, Schütz was continually committed to a parallel development of both older and newer styles, and in many instances to a combination of both.

Typical of settings in the older polyphonic style are Nos. 9 and 10, the paired motets 'Verba mea auribus percipe' (Give ear to my words, O Lord) and 'Quoniam ad te clamabo' (For I will cry to thee, O Lord), SWV 61–2, based on a version of Psalm 5: 1–3, a text which is associated with the Roman Office for the Dead. In No. 9 traditional features include the use of largely conjunct melodic lines, and a division of the initial theme into two compatible phrases for immediate combination in double counterpoint during the opening paragraph; and in No. 10, lengthy melismas in descending sequential patterns to colour the words 'vocem meam' (from bar 24), together with a setting, for all four voices in closely woven canonic imitation, of the single word 'videbo' (I will look up), which provides a final climax of a quality worthy of Lassus.

Also cast in the older manner, but allied to more colourful texts, are Nos. 11 and 12, the linked settings 'Ego dormio et cor meum vigilat' and 'Vulnerasti cor meum', SWV 63–4, based on chapters 5: 2 and 4: 9 of the Song of Solomon. Acceptance, within the overall canon of church texts, of the Canticle's palpably erotic material is founded on a well established allegorical interpretation, traceable back to Origen (*c.* 185–*c.* 254), whereby the male and female spouses (Sponsus and Sponsa) are taken to symbolize, respectively, Christ and the individual Christian soul (or, in some cases, the whole Christian Church). Thus the Sponsa with her 'passionate desires and longings' represents the soul [anima] in its urgent yearning for Christ, and the many expressions of mutual love, 'that soul's total fulfilment in Him'.[6] In the first section of No. 11 the words are those of the Sponsa; but by omitting the phrase 'it is the voice of my beloved that knocketh', Schütz, perhaps

[5] See Gottfried Grote (ed.), *Heinrich Schütz: Cantiones sacrae*, NSA, 8, Preface, ix.

[6] See Robert L. Kendrick, ' "Sonet vox tua in auribus meis": Song of Songs Exegesis and the Seventeenth-Century Motet', *SJb*, 16 (1994), 103. This article (pp. 99–118) also provides information of much interest about works by Italian and German composers, based on the Canticle.

shunning too symbolic an interpretation, leaves the character's gender unclear. The elegantly pictorial opening provides a slow-moving theme in the tenor line, for the words 'Ego dormio' (I sleep), which is answered by its inversion, half a bar later, in the bass; then immediately, at bar 3, this tranquil pairing, transferred to the upper voices, is combined with a flowing pattern in quavers, again shared imitatively between tenor and bass, for the words 'et cor meum vigilat' (but my heart waketh). In the process, by a musical representation of perfect clarity, the heart is shown to be, even in sleep, constantly vigilant for the moment of intimate communion with Christ. Designedly more fragmented is the setting of the eager demand 'Aperi mihi' (open to me) in bars 14–16, where the texture is permeated by a falling three-note pattern, rising in stepwise sequences in all parts, and its subsequent combination, in finely shaped counterpoint, with a parallel phrase for 'soror mea, columba mea, immaculata mea' (my sister, my dove, my undefiled) (see Ex. 13).

Ex. 13

In outline the structure of the motet, with its varied repeat for added coherence in the final section, is as follows:

Fig. 1

Section	Bars	Text opening	Key sequence
I	1–13	'Ego dormio'	d–F
II	14–26	'Aperi'	F–D
III(a)	26–34	'Quia caput'	d–G
III(b)	34–40	'et cincinni mei'	C–A
IV	40–53	'quia caput meum' (a varied repeat of III (a) & (b), plus a 4-bar codetta)	D–F

It will be seen that, in conformity with normal practice of the time, No. 11, as the first of a linked pair of motets, cadences finally in F major, and by thus side-stepping the basic D minor Dorian mode, greatly enhances the feeling of continuity with No. 12, its ensuing partner.

In 'Vulnerasti cor meum', the text of which is largely unrelated to that of the first motet, it is the thoughts of the Sponsus (Christ) which are expressed: 'Thou hast wounded my heart my sister [altered by Schütz to 'dearest daughter'], my spouse with one of thine eyes, with one chain of thy neck'. As in the preceding work there are four clearly defined sections, the last of which, again a variant of its predecessor, reaffirms the basic 'tonality'. The emphasis placed at the opening of each section on the word 'Vulnerasti' and its associated theme—marked by a prominent falling tritone, d'' to $g\sharp'$, in the soprano line—leads one to suspect a further hidden meaning, whereby the 'wounds' relate symbolically to those of Christ's Passion and the charming physical attributes, to the earthly vanities of the self-seeking Christian soul. The substitution of 'filia carissima' (dearest daughter) for 'soror mea' (my sister) in the opening phrase of the text is one of a number of minor alterations which Schütz made to the passages he took from Musculus. It may be seen as a loving reference to his younger daughter, Euphrosina, born in November 1623, or more prosaically, as the choice of a word of three syllables (filia) for one of only two (soror) in order to provide, in the context, for smoother musical declamation.

An alteration of more substance occurs in Nos. 24–5, the paired Christmas motets, 'Supereminet omnem scientiam' and 'Pro hoc magno mysterio', SWV 76–7, where added intensity is achieved by changing the text's original focus from God the Father to God the Son, and the wording from the third to the second person singular. In translation the long text of No. 24 reads: 'Thy great love, O Lord Jesus, surpasses all knowledge. Thou hast shown it to us, unworthy people, out of thy goodness and mercy. By taking on human, rather than angelic nature, thou hast glorified it with the garment of immortality and carried it above the heavens, above all choirs of angels, above Cherubim and Seraphim, to the right hand of the Father. The angels praise thee, the principalities adore thee, and all the powers of

heaven tremble at God having become Man.' Very bold in conception, the
first motet opens fugally, with subject/answer entries—in the order
TBAS—successively on dominant and tonic, delivering a single-note theme
in repeated crotchets, plus a vigorous countersubject in quavers which
descends scalewise over a minor seventh (or octave). At bar 20, with fine
effect, a slow-moving chordal pattern in D minor, throws special emphasis
on the single phrase, 'humanam et enim' (with reference to Christ's taking
on of human nature), and this, from bar 22, in combination with a swift
pattern for 'rather than angelic nature', tapers off magically to a delicate
two-voice texture (see Ex. 14). Finally, in bars 43–51, recurrent references to
'tremunt' (tremble) invoke a leaping melisma and a vocal *trillo* in all
voices—a device which is rather more striking to the eye than to the ear.

In the second motet, the final part of the same text is set: 'For this great
mystery of love, I bless and glorify thy holy name, O Christ my king, son
of Mary, son of the living God'—with a final paean to the Holy Trinity. At
the opening a combined sense of awe and adoration is created by means of
an augmented triad or dissonant suspension in each voice-part as it reaches

Ex. 14

the second syllable of the word 'mysterio', and, in immediate contrast, by a plainly chordal setting of an entirely consonant nature for the ensuing words 'I bless and glorify thy name'. Remarkably symmetrical in structure, the motet has three broad sections: two outer ones in 4/2 time and of twelve bars each, and a central one in 6/4 time and of nine bars duration, which, by the use of 3 + 3 crotchets per bar and a hemiola pattern for the words 'et sancto spiritu' provides apt musical symbolism for the pervading references to the Holy Trinity.

Equally advanced in style is No. 31, the fine single motet, 'Veni, rogo, in cor meum', SWV 83, set for high voices (SSAT) and based on a pseudo-Augustinian text of a deeply introspective character: 'Come, I beseech thee, into my heart, and intoxicate my soul with the abundance of thy joy, that I may forget temporal things. Support me, Lord, my God, and put joy in my heart; come to me, that I may see thee'. Amongst its more advanced elements are the use of wider voice-ranges and unusual (even unvocal) intervals, such as the tritones which feature prominently in the jagged figure set to 'ista temporalia' (temporal things), in bars 25–7. As in No. 9 the opening is set in two halves, but in response to the text's meaning, to music of such vividly contrasted character—a slow descending theme for the first phrase, and high-pitched, melismatic 6/3 chordal patterns in quavers to represent the 'soul's intoxication'—as to make virtually impossible any subsequent theme-combination (see Ex. 15). Variety is achieved at bar 33, where (for the penultimate section of the work) the words 'et da laetitiam in corde meo' (and put joy in my heart) are given a forthright fugal setting

Ex. 15

(a)

(b)

in triple (3/2) time; and unity in the final section, from bar 44, where recurrences of the word 'veni', in the phrase 'veni ad me' (come unto me), elicit a four-note pattern, exactly similar in pitch and rhythm, but in reduced note-values, to that used (by S.1 and A) for 'Veni, rogo' at the opening of the whole work.

Still closer to the monodic style is No. 30, the Passiontide motet 'Inter brachia salvatoris mei', SWV 82, based on an excerpt from the *Manuale* of St Bernard. Set in four clearly defined sections, the text reads in translation: 'Within the arms of my Saviour I wish to live and desire to die'; 'Safe will I sing'; 'I shall exalt thee, O Lord, for thou hast sustained me'; and 'Let not mine enemies triumph over me'. Despite its brevity, the text is composed on a grand scale, with phrase repetitions, scoring contrasts, and brilliant vocal *passaggi* providing scope for a continual variety of musical expression. Divergent theme-fragments represent 'life' and 'death' throughout the opening section, the former involving a rapid six-note pattern (for 'et vivere volo'), and the latter a slower cadential figure, by means of which, in bars 5/6, F Ionian transposed is confirmed as the basic modal centre. At bar 16, a new triple-time, largely homophonic, setting is provided for 'et vivere volo', on a thematic pattern adapted from that used for the same words in the opening paragraph; and from bar 28 there follows an extended working of the 'death' motif, in which suspended dissonances, with echappée-note decoration, in all voices transform the mood, creating a sudden grimness of effect (see Ex. 16). Giant melismas on the word 'decantabo' (I will sing), set in dotted rhythms in the three highest voice-parts, create an enlarged paragraph for the brief text of the second section; while, to achieve formal par-

Ex. 16

ity, the words of the final paragraph, set to a single theme, are given largely syllabic treatment, with much closely wrought imitation. Nearly a century later, parts of the colourful text of this motet served an even deeper purpose as a basis for the aria 'Sehet, Jesu hat die Hand uns zu fassen ausgespannt' (See the Saviour's outstretched hands!), which follows the crucifixion scene at Golgotha in J. S. Bach's St Matthew Passion.

As noted earlier, the normal practice with motets in two or more inter-linked *partes* is for the first and each subsequent part except the last to cadence finally in a 'key' other than the home 'tonic'. This process is found in its most elaborate form in Nos. IV–VIII, a Passiontide series on texts from St Anselm's *Meditations*, in which the pattern of 'keys', at their beginnings and endings is: 'Quid commisisti, o dulcissime puer' E–A; 'Ego sum tui plaga doloris' E–C; 'Ego enim, inique egi' e–B; 'Quo, nate dei, quo tua descendit humilitas' b–G; and 'Calicem salutaris accipiam' e–E. And since, in view of their 'key' schemes, none of these motets can with reason be performed separately, this series provides, with a total of 205 bars in 4/2 time, easily the longest work in the collection. In texts and music of calculated austerity, the Passion theme is explored in five stages, in which the worshipper expresses his indignation at Christ's unjust condemnation; admits his contribution to the Saviour's suffering; contrasts his egotism with the Lord's humility; seeks ways to repay him for his compassion; and vows to renew his commitment to his faith in the presence of the congregation. Particularly striking amongst the many ways in which the composer illuminates the texts is his treatment of the concept of egotism. Both the second and third *partes* begin with a sliding four-note semiquaver pattern, descending and ascending, set to the word 'ego' (see Ex. 17a and b) and in *Pars* 2, at bar 17, a fourfold repetition of the same word, with imitative patterns in minims between the soprano and tenor, and between the alto and bass a crotchet beat later, a remarkable impression is created of the sinner beating his breast in anguished remorse. As a means of symbolizing the first person singular (and its possessive pronoun), the running figure in semiquavers, referred to above, is found in a number of contexts throughout the collection, set mainly to such 'ego-linked' phrases as 'in vita mea' (No. 3, bar 22), 'super me' (No. 30, bar 49), and 'orationem meam' (No. 35, bar 28). However, in one unique case—in No. 20, 'Quid detur tibi?, at bars 21–2—the figure also appears, in all four voice-parts, set to the word 'sagittae', apparently in an unambiguous reference to the composer's name in its Latin form (see Ex. 17c). While it is perfectly possible (perhaps even likely) that the parallelism provided by this single reference occurred simply by chance, it is tempting to surmise that the composer may have intended through it to create for his work an even more personal slant than usual.[7]

In the three-part sequence of Atonement motets—'Domine, ne in furore tuo', 'Quoniam non est in morte', and 'Discedite a me', Nos. 33–35, based

[7] For further information on these and other possible interconnections, see Roger Bray, 'The Cantiones sacrae of Heinrich Schütz re-examined', *Music & Letters*, 52 (1971), 299.

Ex. 17

on the whole of Psalm 6 in the Vulgate—Schütz makes his most adventurous use, in this collection, of the monodic concerto style with obbligato
continuo. Notable features in No. 33 include, at the opening, a chromatic
ascent from B flat to E flat in the soprano line, supported by root-position
chords of E flat, C, F, D, G, and C minor, with their intervening dominants,
in the continuo part; a sheer downward leap of a diminished octave (*f″* to
f#′ in bars 10/11, to colour the word 'miserere' (have mercy); and a simultaneous false relation—an alto F natural against a bass F sharp—in bars
18–19, to delineate 'infirmus sum' (for I am weak) (see Ex. 18). In the

Ex. 18

central motet the texture is reduced to the three lowest voices only, thus providing an increased darkness of vocal colouring for the sombre text, 'For in death there is no remembrance of thee: in the grave who shall give thee thanks?', and an even more declamatory style is adopted, in which single voices with continuo accompaniment operate within very narrow pitch ranges, with largely syllabic word-setting. Madrigalian features are found in bars 8–11 where a 'sospirando' (sighing) minim rest is inserted between the second and third syllables of 'Laboravi' (I have toiled), and collisions between the adjacent notes $e\flat'$, d', and c' give vividly realistic expression to the words 'in gemitu meo' (in my groaning), and, in bar 21, where a descent of an octave, from g to G scalewise in the bass, colours the words '[lacrimae] meis' (my [tears])—possibly as a further manifestation of 'sagittarian' symbolism. The third part—with the opening text 'Depart from me, all ye workers of iniquity'—has an angular first theme, with an internal tritone step, the shape of which returns from bar 21 for the words 'orationem meam' (my prayer); and on two separate occasions, in bars 20 and 25, sections of unmeasured *falsobordone* are introduced, in four-part harmony, for the words 'suscepit Domine' (the Lord will receive). With their emotionally charged forms of expression, these works represent the farthest point to which Schütz was prepared to travel within the boundaries, however widely stretched, of the traditional motet concept. In his only later collection of a comparable nature, the *Geistliche Chor-Music* of 1648, he turned to the mainstream of Protestant motet writing, and with works by Hassler, Lechner, Praetorius, Schein, and others as models, provided grandly structured settings of a cooler, somewhat more picturesque, but (as we shall see later) none the less deeply expressive character.

Much simpler music is contained in the so-called *Becker Psalter*, a collection of versified psalms, set for four (SATB) voices, the first version of which Schütz published in 1628, with a dedication to the Dowager Electress Hedwig, the widow of Johann Georg's brother, Christian II.[8] Cornelius Becker, the author of the texts, was a professor at Leipzig university, whose complete German psalter 'to which the melodies commonly used in Lutheran churches are adapted' first appeared in 1602, with the prefatory observation that it was intended mainly for devotional use in the home. Behind Becker's work—as a model, but also as a rival for possible supersession—lay the German psalter of Ambrosius Lobwasser (a translation of the Calvinist psalter of Clément Marot and Théodore de Bèze, with Huguenot melodies set by Goudimel) which was completed as early as 1565, but not published until 1573, and which rapidly won widespread popularity in Lutheran Germany. In 1602, in an extension of Lobwasser, Schütz's first patron, the Landgrave Moritz of Hesse, also produced a

---

[8] The original title reads: 'Psalmen Davids / Hiebevor in Teutsche Reimen / gebracht durch D. Cornelium Beckern / Und an jetzo / Mit Einhundert und / Drey eigenen Melodeyen, darunter / Zwey und Neuntzig newe, und / Eylff Alte, / Nach gemeiner Contrapunctus art in / 4. Stimmen gestellet, / Durch Heinrich Schützen / Churf. Sächs. Capellmeister.

German psalter. This originally had melodies only, some of them of Moritz's own composition; but ten years later, after turning towards Calvinism, he published a second edition with four-part harmony, which is almost certain to have come to Schütz's attention and may well have spurred him to attempt a version of his own. Whether or not the composer was entirely happy with Becker's rather commonplace verse is unclear; but he may well have been encouraged by his knowledge of some four-voice settings of them by the Leipzig composer, Seth Calvisius, which had already been published, in 1605, and enjoyed considerable success.[9]

Begun in the early 1620s, as appropriate devotional material for the choirboys in his charge at Dresden, the psalter was rapidly expanded by Schütz from 1625, following the death of his wife Magdalena in September of that year. Its first edition of 1628 comprised settings of 103 melodies of which, according to the title-page, ninety-two were new and eleven old, some of the latter being drawn from sacred lieder of the earliest Lutheran times, such as 'Ach Gott vom Himmel sieh darein', 'Ess spricht der Unweisen Mund wohl', 'Ein feste Burg ist unser Gott', 'Es wollt uns Gott genädig sein', and 'Aus tiefer Not schrei ich zu dir'. Subsequently, with a second edition of the volume in 1640, and a substantial enlargement and revision of it in 1661, the total number of settings was brought to 159.[10]

By his use on the title-page of the expression 'in the ordinary contrapuntal style' (nach gemeiner contrapunctus Art) Schütz indicates a straightforward type of setting, involving either four-square chordal harmony or some slightly more elaborate type of part-writing. His intention was clearly to gain for his work the widest church, school, and domestic usage, even in places where the choral resources were meagre or relatively untrained. An indication of the scope he is prepared to envisage is given in the preface, where he writes 'should anyone wish to put some of these melodies to secular use, or should a composer or organist wish to set hymn texts to them, they should arrange the discant part (that which leads either the choir or the principal voices) in slow notes with interposed pauses and thus it is hoped find satisfaction'.[11] The plainest type of chordal writing he uses can be seen, with Becker's somewhat crabbed text underlaid, in Ex. 19, which shows the opening line of the setting of Psalm 84. The upward chromatic progression in the soprano part, and its supporting harmony, it will be noticed, parallels almost exactly the graceful chordal sequence at the start

[9] One lasting result of Becker's work was his version of Psalm 23, 'Der Herr ist mein getreuer Hirt', which J. S. Bach used, in April 1731, for his church cantata, BWV 112, of the same name.

[10] Amongst his settings in the 1661 edition, that of Psalm 47, 'Frohlocket mit Freud' (Exult with joy), SWV 144, is modelled on the treble part of a gagliarda, 'All' Lust und Freud' by H. L. Hassler, from his *Lustgarten neuer teutscher Gesäng* of 1601.

[11] Wolten aber jemand etliche dieser Melodeyen zu weltlich fürkommen / oder aber wann einen Componisten oder Organisten einen Choral darüber zuführen belieben möchte / der setze ihm den Discant (welcher die Chor oder Hauptstimme führet) mit langsamen Noten und interponirten Pausen abe / wird verhoffentlich sich begnüget finden.

Ex. 19

Wie sehr lieb-lich und schö-ne   sind doch die Woh - nung dein!

of the composer's double-choir setting of the same psalm, with its biblical text, 'Wie lieblich sind deine Wohnungen', SWV 29, in the *Psalmen Davids* of 1619 (see Ex. 8).

Although officially adopted in 1661 as the standard psalter in Saxony, the collection failed, unhappily, to achieve the wider dissemination and lasting recognition for which the composer had clearly hoped. Schütz was, in a sense, too cerebral a composer to have been able to succeed readily in this type of work. The various tiny settings display all the technical perfection that one would expect; but the composer's own melodies tend to lack the obvious attractions most likely to win favour in congregational worship; and his arrangements of the traditional chorale melodies reveal too often a degree of subtlety inappropriate for their purpose. During his lifetime, the *Becker Psalter* suffered inevitable competition from a host of similar anthologies; and of these it was the renowned *Cantional* (1627) of J. H. Schein and the *Praxis pietatis melica* (1648) of Johannes Crüger, which were eventually to gain with congregations the most widespread popularity.

6

The return to Venice in 1628: the *Symphoniae sacrae* I

By early in 1628 the finances of the Dresden court were becoming seriously eroded by the exigencies of the Thirty Years War, even though Saxony was managing still to avoid direct involvement in the conflict; and as a result many of the Kapelle musicians were being forced to endure severe economic hardship. In a petition submitted by Schütz on Passion Sunday 1628 to the elector's advisors, those most acutely affected were identified as the singers and instrumentalists whose services had not been required for the performance of *Dafne* at Hartenfels castle in April, 1627, or for the music at the electoral assembly held at Mühlhausen, later in the same year. In a heartfelt plea, it was stated that many of these 'had received hardly more than a month's pay during a whole year';[1] but nothing, it appears, was done to ease their plight. In reaction to these immediate problems, and to the strict limitations on musical activity to which the court was committed, Schütz decided that this would be an appropriate time for him to revisit Venice and examine, at first hand, the latest developments there; and on 22 April 1628 he wrote to the elector, seeking his permission and financial support. It is impressive evidence of the composer's longing to make ever greater progress in his art that, at the age of 42, and as head of one of the most important musical establishments in northern Europe, he should have been prepared to set aside all his immediate concerns, undertake a long and difficult journey, and engage in an extended period of further study.

It is likely that, in addition to his problems at Dresden Schütz's desire to revisit Italy was spurred by some novel ideas which were being advanced at court by one of his former pupils, Johann Nauwach. A one-time choirboy in the Dresden *Hofkapelle*, Nauwach had been sent by the elector, in 1612, to be educated at Turin and Florence; and on his return to Dresden in 1618, had served for seven years as court lutanist before being elevated in 1625 to the rank of chamber musician. In 1623 he published, at Dresden, the work by which he is particularly remembered, his *Libro primo di arie passeggiate a una voice per cantar e sonar nel chitarrone* (First book of ornamented arias for solo voice with theorbo accompaniment), settings of Italian texts in which, apparently for the first time, and if so somewhat belatedly, the

---

[1] *GBS* No. 27, 93.

monodic style of Caccini was brought to northern Germany. In addition to some modest compositions of his own, Nauwach's volume included a number of arrangements of works by other composers, including Caccini's 'Amarilli', with many inserted *passaggi* (florid decorations), and a setting of Guarini's 'Cruda Amarilli' based on a madrigal by Sigismondo d'India. Subsequently, in 1627, he published, again at Dresden, and in collaboration with the poet Opitz, his *Teutsche Villanellen* which contained some of the earliest examples of the German continuo song.

For Schütz the urge to explore these techniques at their source must have seemed irresistible; and in August 1628, after much (not unusual) difficulty in securing the elector's agreement, he left for Venice and, following many 'costly delays' en route, arrived there early in November. It is not easy nowadays to grasp fully the fearsome problems which must regularly have confronted coach-travellers during the early-seventeenth century. A journey from Dresden to Venice—assuming a route via Munich, Innsbruck, Bolzano, and Verona—would have involved a distance of well over 450 miles, a not inconsiderable part of it over mountainous terrain. The 'costly delays' to which Schütz refers would no doubt have resulted from inclement weather, inferior roads, broken wheels, lame horses, and many other inevitable tests of a traveller's resolution. It is hardly surprising, therefore, that on his arrival the composer wrote to Johann Georg asking for extra money to help defray the additional expense he had incurred, and to cover the cost of the 'many delightful new musical works [and the instruments]' which he had been commissioned to acquire.[2] On a happier note he referred in the same letter to various developments in the city's music he had found since his previous visit, alluding particularly to compositions written for 'princely banquets, comedies, ballets and other such productions'.

His first concern, however, was to make contact, either personally or through a close study of their work, with as many as possible of the principal Italian musicians and composers of the time, living in or near Venice. Not only Monteverdi who, as he was later to remark, had 'guided him with joy and showed him happily the path he had long sought',[3] but also Ignazio Donati and Alessandro Grandi, both of whom were pioneers of important new forms of the period—Donati, with his small-scale concertato works on sacred texts (four volumes, 1612, 1616, 1618, and 1619), and Grandi with his three sets of *Motetti con sinfonie* (of 1621, 1622, and 1629), the

[2] *GBS* No. 28, 95: 'Auch sonst zu erkeuffung vieler newer schöner musikalische sachen, ein mehrers vonnöthen sein will. Immassen ich dan vorspüren thue, das von der zeit an, da ich hiebevorn das erste mahl dieser örter gewesen binn. Sich dieses gantze werk sehr geendert, undt die Jenige Music welche zu fürstlichen Taffeln, Comedien, Balleten undt derogleichen represntationen di[e]nlichen ist.' (Letter of 3.11.1628 from Schütz to the Elector Johann Georg).

[3] Probably through personal advice from Monteverdi, and certainly from the example of his concertato-style settings, such as the canzonetta for two sopranos 'Chiome d'oro, bel thesoro',—marked 'concertata da duoi violini, chitarone o spinetta'—from his seventh book of madrigals, a work which Schütz was later to adapt for his own canzonetta 'Güldne Haare, gleich Aurore', SWV 440.

subtle sonorities of which appear to have provided Schütz with the most immediate models for his chamber-style monodic works for voices and obbligato instruments.[4]

The fruits of his study and intensive creative endeavour appeared eventually, on 19 August 1629, with the publication, by Gardano of Venice, of his first collection of *Symphoniae sacrae*, a volume containing twenty concertato works (five of them the second *partes* of paired settings) in the *stylus mixtus*, for solo voices and obbligato instruments. His texts are all drawn from Latin sources, like those of the *Cantiones sacrae* but, in this later set, solely biblical ones from the Vulgate versions of the Psalms (see chapter 5, footnote 2, concerning the numbering of Latin psalms), the Song of Solomon, the second Book of Samuel, and St Matthew's gospel. His choice of Latin was no doubt dictated partly by the proposed publication of his work in Italy, and partly by the ready availability in Venice of suitable Latin biblical texts, many of which had previously (and in several instances repeatedly) been set by Italian composers. This, however, was the last occasion on which he was to adopt Latin consistently for a complete set of compositions.[5] It is noteworthy that in the 1629 print the emphasis on Latin extends not only to the title-page and the dedicatory epistle, but also to the composer's name (Henricus Sagittarius) and to the special designation 'Opus ecclesiasticum secundum', the latter possibly intended to sanction a distinctive breadth of denominational usage. Curiously, no earlier collection of his is marked 'Opus ecclesiasticum primum'; but there can scarcely be a better claimant to the title than his only other exclusively Latin work, the *Cantiones sacrae* of 1625.

Some idea of the impact which the latest Venetian music had made on him in 1629 is given by the collection's lengthy dedicatory preface, addressed by Schütz to the Lord Johann Georg, the Crown Prince of Saxony, a future employer whom he knew to be not only deeply interested in music,[6] but also well enough versed in Latin to appreciate his elegant literary style. Amidst a wealth of adulatory prose, he describes some of the changes in music he has encountered during his visit, referring particularly to the various new devices with which the latest Italians composers 'seek to entice modern ears'; it is 'to the [cultivation] of these', he declares, that 'I have directed my mind and energies'.[7] From the evidence provided eventually by his own work, it may be deduced that the novel features to

---

[4] See Jerome Roche, 'What Schütz learnt from Grandi in 1629', *The Musical Times*, 113 (1972), 1074.

[5] In such later collections as his two sets of *Kleine geistliche Konzerte* (1636/9) where, out of a total of 55 works, only 11 (all in the second set) have Latin texts, plus a further five with Latin ones added as alternatives to the German.

[6] The compositions of Johann Georg II include a psalm: *Laudate Dominum omnes gentes* a 4, with instruments including six trumpets and timpani. Listed in a *Dresden Instrumental Chamber Catalogue* of 1681: see Spagn., Doc. 18, 224 and 232.

[7] *GBS* No. 31, 103. The relevant passage reads, in the original: 'Venetis apud veteres amicos commoratus, cognovi modulanti rationem non nihil immutatam antiquos numeros ex parte deposuisse, hodiernis auribus recenti allusuram titillatione; ad cujus ego normam ut aliqua tibi de me[a]e industriae penu pro instituto depromerem, hu[n]c animum et vires adieci'.

65

which he refers include melodic patterns with a high degree of structural symmetry and scope for graceful ornamentation; delicately varied harmonic and instrumental colour; the articulation of form by the juxtaposition of declamatory and aria styles and by contrasts of scoring and metre; and the use of immediate and long-range repetition, of both vocal and instrumental passages, to enhance formal coherence.

It is, however, by the choice and deployment of his obbligato instruments that Schütz moves most strikingly beyond the range of his Italian models. The customary accompanying ensemble of two violins and continuo, much favoured by the Italians, is found in only six pieces in the collection (SWV 257, 258, 260, 261, 265, 266). All but one of the remaining fourteen works feature a typically German variety of wind instruments, with strings (violins or viole) indicated, in only few cases, as optional alternatives. The single exception is No. 3, 'In te, Domine, speravi', SWV 259, in which, uniquely, an alto soloist is supported by a violin, a trombone (or bassoon), and organ continuo. The wind instruments detailed throughout the collection comprise three types of flute—designated 'fiffaro' (a transverse flute or Querpfeiffe, on the evidence of Praetorius's *Syntagma musicum*),[8] 'flautino' (a descant recorder), and 'flöte' (a treble recorder)—together with bassoon or dulcian (the English 'curtal' in varying sizes), trombetta (trumpet), cornett, cornettino (a small cornett, pitched a fourth or fifth higher), and trombone (in alto, tenor, and bass sizes). In one decidedly unusual instance, involving the paired Song of Songs settings, 'Anima mea liquefacta est' and 'Adjuro vos, filiae Hierusalem', SWV 263–4, the scoring indicated—two fiffaros, with a pair of cornettinos as alternatives—is strangely ill-suited to the tessitura (a to eb'') prescribed in the written parts. In a recent study it has been suggested, as a possible solution to the problem that, in order to match the compass specified (and in particular to provide for the four lowest notes), Schütz may have intended by the term 'fiffaro' to indicate the bass flauto traverso, which has g as its lowest note; and by the term 'cornettino' (listed by Praetorius, under the heading 'kleiner Zink', as having a compass of e' to e'''), the cornetto muto, a 'pastoral' instrument, with a range of g to a'', of simpler construction than the standard cornett but greater sweetness of tone.[9] Although undoubtedly ingenious, this interpretation is weakened by its suggested involvement of two instruments (as principal and its alternative) which appear not to have been employed in any other of Schütz's works. Elsewhere, throughout the collection, the use of the alternative instruments indicated would be likely so to undermine the richness of effect that they can hardly have been included other than as makeshifts. However, in the manner of the times, it

---

[8] M. Praetorius, *Syntagma musicum II, De Organographia* (Wolfenbüttel, 1619); repr. in *Documenta musicologica* I, 15 (Kassel, 1958), 35.

[9] See Robert L. Kendrick, op. cit. (in Ch. 5, n. 5), 107. As a solution to the problem he suggests that, if 'cornettino' was in fact substituted for 'cornetto muto', it may have been as a result of a misreading of Schütz's handwritten instructions by his Venetian printer.

is not unlikely that more freedom than is immediately apparent in the composer's instructions, may have been envisaged in the way the instruments might be deployed. In some contexts, for example, flutes or cornetts might temporarily replace the violins, or vice versa, so as to emphasize important changes in text expression, or a harpsichord or lute might substitute for the organ in order to achieve, where suitable, a more delicate sonority in the continuo accompaniment.

Delicacy is well exemplified at the start of No. 4 'Cantabo Domino in vita mea', (I will sing unto the Lord as long as I live), SWV 260, a setting of Psalm 103: 33 for solo tenor with two violins and continuo, where the soloist's opening cry of 'Cantabo' is supported, somewhat in the manner of a minstrel declaring the burden of the story he is about to unfold, by a chordal flourish best suited to a harpsichord or other plucked-strings instrument. As the setting develops it shows a remarkable combination of textural simplicity and structural intricacy. Individual lines of the psalm-text are set to alternating melodic patterns of contrasted character; fluctuations between duple and triple time reflect changes in style and text-expression; the largely syllabic treatment is varied by some brilliant vocal melismas (on 'cantabo' from bar 35, and 'psallite' from bar 118); and subtle changes in melody and harmony, at bars 80 and 100, for example, enrich the effect of long-range repetitions. In broad outline the structure of the Symphonia is as follows:

Fig. 2

Section	Bar	Time	Commentary
A	1	C & 3/2	Tenor solo: opening 'flourish' and contrasted settings of themes (i) (bar 1) and (ii) (bar 3) of first line of text (see Ex. 20a).
B	22	C	Sinfonia for strings (or flutes as substitutes), expanding the preceding vocal patterns in cross rhythms (see Ex. 20b).
C	33	3/2	Tenor solo; a new theme for next phrase of the text, with a 'giant' melisma on 'cantabo'.
D	61	3/2	Tenor and strings; 'Alleluia' on a variant of the opening flourish: spaced entries by soloist, bound by scalic patterns on violins.
E	80	C & 3/2	Tenor solo: original motifs from A, reshaped for a repeat of the opening phrase of text (see Ex. 20c).
F	100	C	Tenor and strings (or flutes); further varied forms of the opening themes (expanded to 18 bars): followed (at bar 120) by 'psallite' melismas in semiquavers, set antiphonally between voice and violins.
G	135	3/2	Tenor and strings; an inverted version of 'Alleluia' motif (from section D, bar 61), with a new string scalic pattern. The last 4 bars have 'Alleluia' repeat set again to a variant of the opening flourish, with *passaggio* ornamentation.

Schütz

Ex. 20

Even more elaborate is the structural use made of thematic recall in Nos. 9 and 10, the paired settings, 'O quam tu pulchra es' (O how beautiful thou art), SWV 265, and 'Veni de Libano' (Come with me from Lebanon, my spouse), SWV 266, for tenor and baritone soloists accompanied by two violins, with harpsichord and cello continuo. The text, drawn freely from the Song of Solomon 4: 1–5 and 7, is divided between the two settings, with the line 'O quam tu pulchra es' functioning in each as a recurrent refrain. At the start of No. 9, the bass soloist presents two short motifs in triple time (marked x and y in Ex. 21a) and these, from bar 33, provide the material for a brief orchestral sinfonia, and thereafter play an increasingly important role as the work evolves. At bar 112, a new idea, z, in arpeggio form, is introduced by the strings which, at a final return of the opening text-phrase, combines with the two original motifs (x and y) to form a tightly-woven contrapuntal texture (see Ex. 21b). The *Secunda Pars*, based on a still freer version of the biblical text, is concerned with different, and consistently less fragmentary, thematic material; but from bar 80, in order to provide an exceptional type of coda, motif z from *Pars 1*, is combined with overlapping entries of motif y in shortened note-values on the strings, to create an even more elaborate contrapuntal complex and in this way rounds off the paired settings with effective symmetry and an increased intensity of expression (see Ex. 21c).

In many of the settings, the composer's choice of his principal obbligato instruments (and his decisions about the way they are deployed in the introductory and interposed sinfonias) seems to have been determined very largely by their descriptive capabilities. Examples are to be found in the second of another pair of Song of Songs settings, No. 17 'Invenerunt me custodes', (the watchmen that go about the city found me), SWV 273, where an ensemble of four bassoons suggests, with stepwise patterns, the heavy pacing of the watchmen on their rounds; and still more obviously in Nos. 19 and 20 (from Psalm 80: 1–3), 'Buccinate in neomenia tuba' (Blow up the trumpet in the new moon) and 'Jubilate Deo', SWV 275–6, where an ensemble of cornett, trumpet, and bassoon adds great brilliance to the joyous, festive texts with their many allusions to musical instruments. Although in some cases conceived as independent movements, the sinfonias more usually anticipate or recall—in various ways, both subtle and obvious—the melodic substance of adjacent vocal sections and thus contribute to the overall sense of formal integration. In addition to the examples mentioned earlier, attention may be drawn to two places in No. 2 'Exultavit cor meum', SWV 258, the first at bar 39, where the solo soprano starts a new section, for 'Et exaltatum est cornu meum' (and my horn is exalted) with a melodic pattern, in 3/2 time, drawn in double augmentation from the last four bars of the preceding sinfonia; and the second at bar 63 where, reversing this procedure, the violins take up and expand a phrase first heard—to the words 'super inimicos meos' (against my enemies)—at the end of the preceding vocal section.

Ex. 21

(a)

O quam tu pul - chra, tu pul - chra es   a - mi - ca me - a

Elsewhere, there are to be found instances where the sinfonias are used simply to enlarge settings with unusually short texts. A fine example is No. 15 'Domine, labia mea aperies' (Ps. 50: 15), the entire text of which translates as 'Lord, open thou my lips: and my mouth shall show forth thy praise'. Scored for soprano and tenor, with cornett (or violin), tenor trombone, and bassoon as supporting instruments, the work comprises four closely integrated sections: a lengthy fugal sinfonia (bars 1–31); a vocal duet, with continuo support, for the first text phrase (bars 32–58); a further vocal duet for the second text phrase, with lively, imitative instrumental interventions (bars 59–92); and a repeat of the opening sinfonia, slightly modified so as to accommodate added voice-parts which present, repeatedly, the final words only of the text, 'laudem tuam' (bars 93–124). In each section the thematic material is derived, as a variation, from a tiny 'head-motif', $c''d''b'$, first heard on the cornett at the start of the opening sinfonia; and in order to provide full integration, the vocal countertheme, set against the repeat of the sinfonia in the final section, is drawn from figuration in semiquavers (again outlining the 'head-motif') which features prominently in the penultimate section. Although there are altogether 41 bars of purely instrumental writing as against 83 in which the voices are involved, the overriding significance of the sinfonia material creates most powerfully the impression of a work dominated by instruments.

In No. 13, 'Fili mi, Absalon', SWV 269, for solo bass and four trombones, the famous version (from II Samuel 18: 33) of David's lament over the death of his son, the trombone chorus (fulfilling by its instrumental colouring an association traditional at least since early Renaissance times with ceremony, mystery, and the afterlife) provides an opening sinfonia of 42 bars, which foreshadows, in an extended imitative complex, the thematic material of the ensuing vocal section. A second sinfonia, from bar 81, is unrelated thematically to its surroundings, *except* in the final three bars, which outline, an octave higher, the start of the ensuing bass solo, almost as if supplying an unusual type of theatrical 'prompt'. In a wholly symmetrical pattern, each instrumental sinfonia leads to a solo vocal section with continuo accompaniment only, and immediately afterwards to a further one in which the sombre sonority of the full trombone ensemble gives added depth of feeling to the king's despairing words. Most searingly emotional, in the last of these more richly scored sections, are the repeated broken cries of 'Absalon, Absalon', descending over ever-widening intervals—a major third, a fifth and an octave—to provide increasingly mournful colouring to the work's final plagal cadence (see Ex. 22). Entirely similar in structure and scoring, with equally majestic sinfonias for the trombones, is No. 14 'Attendite, popule meus', SWV 270, a 'companion' to SWV 269 rather than a 'paired' setting, since it is markedly different in mode (F Ionian as against G Dorian in No. 13) and expression. A surprising feature of the work is the sparse content of its text, 'Give ear, O my people, to my law: incline your ears to the words of my mouth. I will open my mouth in a parable: I will utter dark sayings of old: which we have heard and known, and our fathers have told us' (from Psalm 77: 1–3). After so portentous an opening it seems strange that there is no continuation, nothing in fact to indicate the grand purport of the ensuing psalm text (no less than sixty-nine further verses) which refers, in vivid summary, to God's providence to his people and anger

Ex. 22

at their sinfulness, and to such historical events as the release of the Israelites from captivity in Egypt. The effect is musically impressive, but theologically somewhat barren. It is perhaps the case, however, that, in the context of a religious service, the work would have achieved greater justification by being 'paired' with a sermon of ample content on the same biblical theme.[10]

At the opposite extreme in the scoring spectrum are the relatively few setting which have no independent instrumental sections. One such is No. 18, 'Veni dilecte me', an exquisitely beautiful setting of passages from the Song of Songs (4: 16 and 5: 1), in which the solo voices and instruments are allocated to two judiciously contrasted ensembles—one comprising a soprano, three trombones (with a tenor singer as a possible substitute for the second trombone), and organ continuo; and the other, a soprano and tenor with

---

[10] Other instances of the use of similarly 'incomplete' texts include: 'Meister, wir haben die ganze Nacht gearbeitet', SWV 317, in *Kleine geistlich Konzerte* II (the miracle of the multitude of fishes, from Luke 5: 5), which ends with the words of Simon, 'I will let down the net', and thus fails to describe the actual miracle.

theorbo accompaniment. In a precisely balanced scheme, a motet-style texture by the four-part ensemble (delivering the Sponsa's words, 'Come my chosen one into my garden') alternates with a type of chamber duet for the soprano and tenor soloists (giving the reply of the Sponsus 'I am come, my sister, my spouse, into my garden'), with the music of each section, after the first, providing a simple variation of that in its similarly-scored predecessor. A climax is established finally with the words 'Eat, O my friends: drink, yea drink abundantly, O beloved' where all the forces are combined in an apt expression of communal delight. Necessarily very different is the scheme adopted in the paired settings, 'Benedicam Dominum in omni tempore' and 'Exquisivi Dominum', SWV 267–8, where the vocal (STB) soloists are accompanied only by a cornett (or violin) and organ continuo, and independent sinfonias, though not impossible, are in fact precluded. Of particular interest in these works is the manner in which the treble instrument contributes what amounts almost to an extra 'voice' to the imitative textures, though one whose upper range often exceeds vocal capability. The passage in Ex. 23 shows the finely interlocked type of imitative writing which results, and the manner in which, unusually (though in conformity with the cornett's line above), the voices adopt a quasi-instrumental style,

Ex. 23

and in the process suggest momentarily what a purely instrumental sonata or concerto by Schütz might have been like.

In order to gauge the effectiveness of his groupings of instruments and voices, Schütz, during his limited time in Venice, had probably to rely more upon his aural imagination than upon any opportunities to hear his work in live performance. In only one case—the Song of Songs pairing 'Anima mea liquefacta est' and 'Adjuro vos, filiae Jerusalem', SWV 263–4—do the problems appear not to have been fully overcome. Apart from an apparent misnaming of the obbligato instruments (a possible solution to which was considered above, and in footnote 9), the textures, produced, with their sustained and close-knit imitative writing for combined instruments and voices and, at times, unusually high level of dissonance, are of a density, which can hardly fail to jeopardize the clarity of the text. The balance might, of course, be considerably improved by the use of flutes or recorders, as the mildest-toned of supporting instruments, but the basic problem would remain still not entirely resolved.

Schütz's commitment to the Italian style makes it highly probable that he would have expected, within the limitations imposed on sacred as opposed to secular (theatrical) music, various forms of improvised ornamentation to be applied to his settings, in particular to sections of a declamatory nature. For voices, and in some cases for instruments also these would be likely to have ranged from the various forms of trill (including the *trillo*, the vocal tremolo first employed by Caccini in *Le nuove musiche* of 1602), to the appoggiatura, the acciaccatura, and the fleshing out of bare intervals with interpolated notes, especially at the approach to cadences. An indication of the underlying Italian practice is contained in the preface to a volume of madrigals by Bartolomeo Barbarino (*Il Pesarino*), published in Venice in 1614, in which he draws a distinction between 'simple' and 'ornamented' vocal parts. The former, he declares, are designed 'either for those who lack the ability [and thus do not wish] to ornament, or for those who, having sufficient knowledge of counterpoint, are able to invent ornamental passages [for themselves]'; and the latter 'for those who, while wishing to ornament, lack the knowledge . . . to be able to invent [suitable] variations'. Schütz leans unequivocally towards the first of these alternatives, the so-called 'simple' option. The predominance of syllabic writing in short note-values found in many of his settings tends to limit the scope for frequent ornamentation, but there are numerous cadences approached by long-held notes, and passages involving wide-ranging intervals, which seem to invite more or less elaborate forms of treatment. It is perhaps in the single-voice items, with the largest amount of declamatory writing (Nos. 1–6 in the collection) that the most scope is afforded for elaboration; and it is very possibly significant that in No. 4, 'Cantabo Domino in vita mea' a cadential *passaggio* is actually written into the final bars, as if to demonstrate how effectively a restrained type of improvised decoration may be introduced.

It is not surprising, when one considers the limited time-scale under which he was working, that the composer appears to have left, for his 1629 collection, no preliminary versions of works, ready for improvement before publication. Only nine months elapsed between his arrival in Venice in November 1628 and the issue of his collection in the following August; and if one allows a sufficient period for his initial studies and for the eventual engraving and printing processes, there can hardly have been more than six months left for completing the actual task of composition. Furthermore, during this period he was committed, on behalf of the electoral Kapelle (as he revealed later in a letter of 30 April 1630), to securing the services of the Mantuan violinist, Francesco Castelli, and to the purchase of music and instruments, including 'three new cornetts and six cornettini', which he was no doubt able to secure in Venice, and 'five violins', in search of which he may well have had to journey as far afield as Cremona. It remains remarkable testimony to his powers of concentration that, despite the pressures to which he was subjected, and the short time available to him, he was able to produce a group of works of such outstanding originality and finesse.

7

Dresden and Copenhagen, 1630–6: the *Musikalische Exequien*

In September 1629 Schütz began his journey home, together with his newly enrolled violinist, Francesco Castelli, and his colleague and former pupil, Caspar Kittel who, with the elector's support, had spent the previous five years studying in Venice. After staying for some days at the home of Philipp Hainhofer in Augsburg, the party finally reached Dresden on 20 November. Amongst important events during the following year were the marriage of the elector's daughter Maria Elisabeth to Duke Friedrich III of Holstein-Gottorf in February, and services to mark the centenary of the Augsburg Confession, early in June, for both of which Schütz was required to provide music. Towards the end of the year he was greatly saddened by the death, on 19 November, of his friend, Hermann Schein, the renowned Cantor of St Thomas's Leipzig. In his memory (and very probably by his death-bed request) Schütz composed the beautiful six-voice motet *Das ist je gewisslich wahr*, SWV 277, based on a text from I Timothy 1: 15–17, 'This is a true saying, and worthy of all acceptation, that Christ Jesus came into the world to save sinners; of whom I am chief'. A later version, which was included in the *Geistliche Chor-Music* of 1648, reveals subtle changes in the composer's thinking in a number of minor revisions; these include some re-ordering of the voice-parts, various small, but effective, expansions of the original (at bars 74–5, 91–2), and a simplification of the final 'Amen' (bars 132–6), whereby the florid semiquaver passages of the original soprano and tenor lines are reduced to crotchet scalic movement without undue sacrifice of the underlying melodic outline.

In the autumn of 1631 further distress was caused, on a personal level, by the deaths of the composer's father and father-in-law, and in the public domain by the decision of the elector to ally the forces of Saxony with those of the Swedish king, Gustavus Adolphus II, in the struggle against the Catholic League, despite an agreement reached earlier in the year by the German electors to avoid direct involvement in the war. The immediate outcome was the defeat of the Catholic forces under Field Marshal Tilly, at the Battle of Breitenfeld in November 1631, a success achieved more by Swedish musketry than effective participation by the Saxons, who were driven ignominiously from the field.[1] However a typical reversal of fortune

---

[1] See C. V. Wedgwood, *The Thirty Years War* (London 1938), 391.

at Nordlingen in 1634 brought victory for the imperial army, and led eventually to the signing of a peace treaty at Prague in May 1635, by which a united German front was created against the Swedes, and a temporary cessation of hostilities agreed.[2] Inevitably, the burden on Saxony's finances, resulting from her military involvement, created even greater hardship than before for the Dresden Kapelle, and from 1632 musical activity at court dwindled virtually to nothing.

In February 1633 a welcome opportunity to escape from the dispiriting situation at Dresden presented itself with an invitation to Schütz from the Crown Prince Christian of Denmark to visit Copenhagen and supervise the music for his marriage to Johann Georg's daughter Magdalena Sibylla. Despite the elector's personal interest in the event, he appears to have shown his customary reluctance to grant Schütz the necessary leave of absence, and it was not until the middle of September that, in the company of Matthias Weckmann and Daniel Hämmerlein, he was able to leave for Denmark, via Hamburg. Weckmann, it appears, went no further than Hamburg (probably remaining there for study with Jacob Praetorius, the organist of St Petri), while Hämmerlein, a gifted instrumentalist whose contribution to the anticipated musical events was likely to be of much value, continued the journey with Schütz, and the pair reached Copenhagen early in December. Soon after his arrival Schütz was accorded the title of visiting Kapellmeister by the Danish king, Christian IV, together with a generous annual stipend.

After long and painstaking preparations the actual wedding took place on 5 October 1634 and was followed by a fortnight of associated celebrations. Four elaborate theatrical works are known to have been performed, each of which must certainly have involved music by Schütz; but while the librettos have survived largely intact, there remains now only one tiny, and very incomplete, portion of the music, the canzonetta 'O der grossen Wundertaten', SWV 278, for four sopranos (the music for the third of whom is lost), 2 violins (whose parts are also missing) and continuo. The dramatic presentations appear from the main librettos all to have been given in German; however, copies of the texts in German were provided only for privileged, high-born audiences within the palace, while for those attending performances in the courtyard in front of the palace, the less well educated, a Danish text was supplied.[3]

Some idea of the magnificence of the festivities may be gained from a brief survey of the theatrical works which were performed.[4] The first was a so-called 'Sing-Ballet', in which the leading personages present at the wedding were represented, symbolically, by mythological characters: King Christian by Neptune, who is portrayed clearing the land of monsters and

[2] Loc. cit.

[3] See Mara R. Wade, 'Heinrich Schütz and "det Store Bilager" [the Great Wedding] in Copenhagen (1634)', *SJb*, 11 (1989), 32–52.

[4] See ibid., 34–44, where the information is set out in greater detail.

war; the bridegroom by the 'Young' Neptune; the bride by Pallas Athene; and the noble guests by several assorted gods and goddesses. The libretto provides for three curiously unrelated theatrical interludes, in which: (i) Pan attempts to seduce Deianira and is driven off by Heracles; (ii) Orpheus mourns the loss of Euridice, while Mercury, distilling the essence of these events, foresees, for the young couple, a new reign of peace and amity throughout the realm and (iii) the prince-elect (as the 'Young' Neptune) is saved from the clutches of a fearsome dragon by Pallas Athene, Fame (Fama), and the Virtues, and the couple's love is finally sealed by the attentions of Amor. Each scene, in succession, involves either a chorus, an aria, or an instrumental interlude, and the whole work culminates in *ballet-de-cour* style with a grand final dance. The textual evidence suggests that the arias may well have involved recitative-style monody on the latest Italian pattern; and in setting them Schütz is likely to have gained his first opportunity to exploit the new theatrical techniques he had studied in Italy— those referred to in a letter of 6 February 1633, to Friedrich Lebzelter, the Saxon agent in Hamburg, in which he reveals how he had learnt (very probably from Monteverdi) the ways in which 'a comedy of diverse voices can be translated into declamatory style and brought to the stage and enacted in song'.[5] In the absence of a surviving score or part-books there is, unhappily, nothing to offer in support of this conjecture.

The second and third theatrical works were a *Comoedia de Raptu Orithyjae* and a *Comoedia de Harpyjarum Profligatione*, both written by the poet, Johann Lauremberg, and both based, again, on the type of mythological scenes which provided the widest scope for allegorical interpretations, flattering to the royal family and their guests. In the first of these Jupiter details the favours he has bestowed on the frozen kingdom of Aquilo (representing the crown prince), and describes how, with help of various of the gods, he has assisted Aquilo to win Orithyja (Magdalena Sybilla) as his bride. The other play, loosely following parts of the Argonauts' story, tells of the actions of Calais and Zetes (representing the future heroic sons of the royal couple) in rescuing Phineus from the clutches of the Harpies, and in the process bringing peace and prosperity to the world. In both cases it appears from the texts that numerous opportunities were provided for songs and choruses appropriate to nymphs, satyrs, sailors, and other secondary characters.

Since the two 'Comedies' were linked by their common mythological source, they were intended, naturally, to be performed in immediate succession. Unhappily, however, a fearsome storm on the night of 9 October caused the second work to be postponed for three days and in the interim the originally-planned final presentation, a 'morality play with fireworks' entitled *Tragoedia von den Tugenden und Lastern* (virtues and vices), was

[5] *GBS*, No. 41, 126. The passage reads in the original: '. . . wie eine Comedi von allerhandt Stimmen in redenden Stylo übersetzet undt auf den Schaw undt singende agiret werden könne . . .'

1. Schütz: portrait in oils by Christoph Spetner

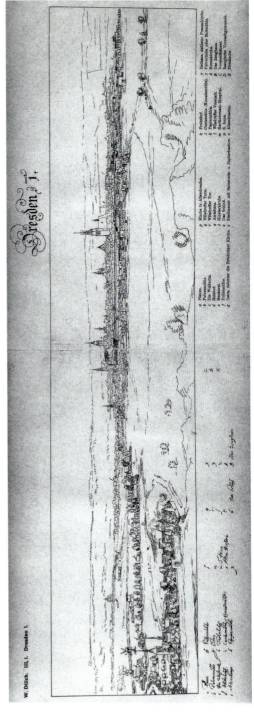

2. Weissenfels and Dresden: two pen-and-ink sketches by Wilhelm Dilich (1571/2–1650), dated 1626–9

L'Altra Parte della PIAZZA DI S. MARCO di Venetia.

I.S. Marco

3. St Marks, Venice: seventeenth-century engraving (Victoria and Albert Museum)

ENSIFER Imperio, Cum bis Vicarius essem
Imperio turbas, fulmina sustinui;
Totius ut fermè factæ Germanidos oræ
Consilium in medium, ME posuig, meum,
Cunctando ut Veniat quondam medicina, laboro,
Ut populus CÆSAR, principe, salvus eat,

Lucas Kilian.
Sculpsit:

E. R

4. Johann Georg I: engraving from 1630 by Lucas Kilian

DAFNE.

Auff deſz Durchlauchtigen/
Hochgebornen Fürſten vnd Herrn/
Herrn Georgen/ Landtgrafen zu Heſſen/
Grafen zu Catzenelnbogen/ Dietz/
Ziegenhain vnd Nidda;
Vnd
Der Durchlauchtigen / Hochgebor-
nen Fürſtinn vnd Fräwlein/ Fräwlein Sophien
Eleonoren/ Hertzogin zu Sachſen/Gülich/Cleve
vnd Bergen / Landtgräfinn in Thüringen/
Marggräfinn zu Meiſſen/ Gräfinn zu
der Marck vnnd Ravenſpurg/
Fräwlein zu Ravenſtein
Beylager:
Durch Heinrich Schützen/ Churfürſtl.
Sächſ. Capellnmeiſtern Muſicaliſch in den
Schawplatz zu bringen/
Auß mehrentheils eigener erfindung
geſchrieben von
Martin Opitzen.

In Vorlegung David Müllers/
Buchführers in Breßlaw.

5. Title-page of *Dafne*, Torgau, 1627

6. Portrait of Johann Georg I by an unknown artist, from the first half of the
seventeenth century

7. Schütz's house in Dresden, at the corner of Neumarkt and Frauenstrasse

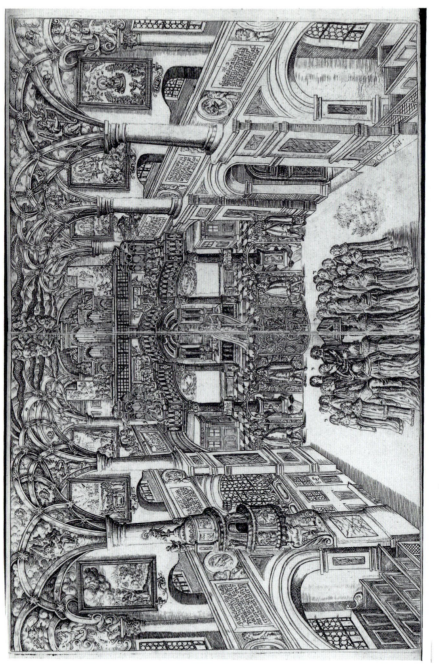

8. The Dresden Court Chapel, with Schütz in the circle of his choristers: engraving by Conrad David (1604–81) as a title-page illustration for a *Geistreichen Gesangbuch* of 1676

given. This, cast in a somewhat more pensive vein, provided telling contrasts between good and bad rulers; and to judge from the various 'musicieren' cues given, offered scope mainly for instrumental music.[6] It is likely, however, that the greatest excitement during the evening was generated by the grand firework display, an event originally intended (but slightly misfiring in the unfortunate circumstances) as a grand culmination to the whole series of celebrations.

In May 1635, after learning of his mother's death early in February, and aware no doubt that Johann Georg was pressing for his return to Dresden, Schütz left Denmark. At his leave-taking he was asked by King Christian to deliver a letter to Johann Georg containing a request that he might be permitted to return soon to Denmark to 'complete the work that he has begun with our *Kapel*'; and on that occasion he was presented with a gold chain, bearing a portrait (probably of the king or the crown prince), and a sum of 200 thalers. Following his arrival back in Dresden in June 1635, a service was held in celebration of the Peace of Prague, the music for which, one may readily assume, was given under his direction.

Later in the year the deaths occurred of two of Schütz's close personal friends. The first, early in August, as a result of the plague, was that of Christoph Cornet, a minor composer with whom Schütz had maintained frequent contacts since their student days together as Kassel, and who had succeeded Georg Otto as Kapellmeister there in 1618. At his funeral there was performed a newly-composed, and doubtless specially commissioned, German *Nunc dimittis* by Schütz (SWV 352a). Scored for a solo bass, accompanied by two violins and continuo, the work is remarkable for the two-octave tessitura, *D* to *d'*, and unusually virtuosic style, of its voice part. A later version, containing some detailed, and enlightening, revisions was included in Schütz's second set of *Symphoniae sacrae* of 1647 (see p. 117). The other death, on 3 December, was that of Count Heinrich the Younger of Reuss, known as 'the Posthumus' because he was born some weeks after the death of his father in 1572. Ruler of the principality of Reuss in which Schütz was born, Posthumus was as well known for his musical accomplishments as for his political vision and deeply religious character.

For the Count's obsequies, Schütz composed the largest and most important of his many funeral works, the *Musikalische Exequien* SWV 79–81.[7] The setting (the text details of which will be given later) is in three movements, comprising: (i) a 'Concerto in the Form of a German Burial Mass' for six solo voices, SSATTB,[8] with a matching six-part Capella for voices

---

[6] Mara R. Wade, op. cit., 43.

[7] Günter Graulich (ed.), Heinrich Schütz, *Musikalische Exequien* [Op. 7] *SSA*, 8. This edition has exceptionally full editorial information.

[8] These are supplemented by two short solo sections for an additional bass, included somewhat stangely in the alto partbook: see Graulich op. cit., Preface, xxxix, under *Ordinance* for the concerted motet or German Burial Mass, fol. 1. In his edition of the work (see n. 7 above) Graulich suggests (Preface, xxviii, under 'Notes on Performance') that 'this can probably be explained by the constitution of the Chapel Royal in Gera, where there appears to have been

and/or instruments and continuo; (ii) a valedictory motet for two SATB choruses with optional continuo; and (iii) a setting of contrasted texts for two unequal choruses, SATTB and SSB, with optional instrumental support and obbligato continuo.[9] Some as yet unresolved mystery surrounds the circumstances of the work's creation. It is known that, well in advance of his demise, the Count chose a number of biblical and chorale verses which he wished to have inscribed on his coffin, and that these texts were the ones adopted by Schütz (at the Count's request) for the first part of his work. What remains unclear is whether Posthumus had discussed with the composer how he wished his chosen texts to be set—and, indeed, how the whole wider plan for his funeral music might be fulfilled—or whether he had kept his intentions secret until very shortly before his death. The difficulty arises from a statement in the title of the printed work that 'it had been sung for His Late Grace . . . during his lifetime to a discreetly registered organ', which cannot readily be reconciled with an apparently equally authoratative statement, on the title-page of the Order of Service for the funeral, that the texts had been 'set to music at the behest of Her Most Gracious Ladyship, the widow of His Late Grace, and of his Sons'. Since the interment did not take place until 4 February 1636, two months after the Count's death, it is perfectly possible that Schütz could have composed his settings during this intervening period. But the apparent contradiction between the two statements remains. A possible explanation, offered by Günter Graulich, is that there may have been two commissions, one by the Count for the first part of the work, which was completed and performed for him during his lifetime, and the other by his family, immediately after his death, for the remaining two parts.[10] This theory gains substance when, in terms of the time-scales available, one compares the complexity of Schütz's task in assembling the grand mosaic of texts of the first part into a coherent pattern, and devising for their setting a wholly original musical structure, with the relatively less demanding creative burden presented by the other two parts.[11]

Although it is no longer accessible, because of building alterations, the copper coffin containing Posthumus's body has survived in the vault of the Salvatorkirche at Gera. In 1922 a photograph was taken of it by the city archivist of the time, which shows that, though the outlines of the original inscriptions are still visible, they are no longer legible. However, in an appendix added to the Count's funeral sermon, and published at Gera in

a male alto able to sing bass'. This theory serves well enough for the duet for two basses from bar 458, but leaves unexplained the S.1/B duet from bar 210, where there seems to be no need for a bass/alto substitution.

[9] An extended survey of the *Musikalische Exequien* is provided by Werner Breig in *SJb*, 11 (1989), 53–68, under the successive headings: hypotheses; prehistory; the composer's instructions; composition and first performance; publication; and the outcome.

[10] Graulich, op. cit., Preface, xxvii.

[11] See Gregory S. Johnston, 'Textual symmetries and the origins of Heinrich Schütz's *Musikalische Exequien*', *Early Music* 19, No. 2 (May 1991), 213–25.

1636, the officiating pastor Christoph Richter, provided details of 'all the sayings from Holy Scripture and Christian Hymns / which . . . Lord Heinrich the Younger and Eldest of the Reuss family . . . had marked on the coffin he had had made in readiness' (Derer Sprüche Göttlicher Schrifft und Christlicher Kirchen Gesänge / Welche . . . H. Heinrich der Jüngere und Eltiste Reuss . . . auff Dero in Bereitschafft gehabten verzeichnen lassen). And these texts correspond precisely with those set by Schütz.[12]

The first part of the funeral composition is based on the form of a Lutheran Missa Brevis, with German-texted settings which provide a three-fold Kyrie and a Gloria. As a special elaboration, the three invocations of the Kyrie section are preceded by four biblical passages: (i) as an Introit, 'Naked I came forth from my mother's body' (Job 1:21), a text not actually inscribed on the coffin; (ii) the linked texts 'For to me to live is Christ, and to die is gain' (Philippians 1: 21), and 'Behold the Lamb of God' (John 1: 29), from the head of the coffin, where they are separated by a crucifix; and (iii) 'For whether we live, we live unto the Lord' (Romans 14: 8), from the lid at the head of the coffin. The first two passages are set for three solo voices (TTB and SST, respectively) and the third for two (AB); and all three lead in turn to a German paraphrase, in full Capella scoring, of the standard liturgical clauses—'Herr Gott, Vater im Himmel', 'Jesu Christe, Gottes Sohn', and 'Herr Gott, Heiliger Geist', each ending with the customary phrase 'erbarm dich über uns' (have mercy upon us). In the much longer second part, representing a Lutheran Gloria, ten coffin texts (three from St John's Gospel, two each from the Psalms and Isaiah, and one each from Genesis, Philippians and the Wisdom of Solomon), set for from one to six solo voices, alternate with eight chorale stanzas (also inscribed on the coffin) which are scored, with elaborated versions of their traditional melodies, for the full Capella ensemble. The overall Gloria pattern, with the items numbered in sequence, may be shown as follows:

Fig. 3

Bible texts	Chorales
(1) Also hat Gott die Welt geliebt (John 3: 16) (SSATTB)	(2) 'Er sprach zu seinen lieben Sohn' (verse 5 of 'Nun freut euch lieben Christen g'mein')
(3) Das Blut Christi, des Sohnes Gottes (I John 1: 7) (S.2, T.2)	(4) 'Durch ihn ist uns' (v. 6 of 'Nun lasst uns Gott dem Herren')
(5) Unser Wandel ist im Himmel (Phillip. 3: 20) (S.1, B.1)	(6) 'Es ist allhier ein Jammerthal' (v. 3 of 'Ich hab mein Sach' auf Gott gestellt')
(7) Wenn eure Sünde gleich Blutrot wäre (Isaiah 1: 18) (T.1 & T.2)	(8) 'Sein Wort, sein Tauf, sein Nachtmal' (v. 5 of 'Nun lasst uns Gott')

[12] Graulich, op. cit., Preface, xxvi, n. 24; and see picture of the coffin on xlv.

Bible texts	Chorales
(9) Gehe hin mein Volk, in einer Kammer (Isaiah 26: 20) (A solo)	—
(10) Der gerechten Seelen sind in Gottes Hand (Wisdom 3: 1–3) (SSB)	—
(11) Herr, wenn ich nur dich habe (Psalm 73: 25–6) (T.1 & AATB)	(12) 'Es is das Heil und selig Licht' (v. 4 of 'Mit Fried und Freud ich fahr dahin').
(13) Unser Leben währet siebenzig Jahre (Psalm 90: 10) (B.1/A & B.2)	(14) 'Ach, wie elend ist unser Zeit' (v. 1)
(15) Ich weiss, dass mein Erlöser lebt (Job 19: 25–6) (T solo)	(16) 'Weil du vom Tod erstanden bist' (v. 4 of 'Wenn mein Stundlein vorhanden ist')
(17) Herr, ich lasse dich nicht (Genesis 32: 27) (S.1 & S.2/ Tutti)	(18) 'Er sprach zu mir: Halt dich an mich' (v. 7 of 'Nun freut euch, lieben Christen g'mein')

To provide an ordered pattern, four chorales are placed on either side of a central section of three consecutive bible texts (9, 10, and 11), and, for extra symmetry, two pairs of chorale stanzas are derived from identical sources: Nos. 2 and 18 above, from 'Nun freut euch lieben Christen'; and nos. 4 and 8 from 'Nun lasst uns Gott dem Herren'. Included within the central core of coffin texts is an outstandingly beautiful setting of the verses from The Wisdom of Solomon, 'The souls of the righteous are in the hand of God, where no torment can trouble them' (Der Gerechten Seelen sind in Gottes Hand, und keine Qual rühret sie an), which Brahms was later to choose for massive fugal treatment in the third part of his *German Requiem* of 1868. Set for SSB, Schütz's section begins with a chordal trio of memorable grace and purity (see Ex. 24); after which, in a solemn imitative passage, the bass muses gently on the folly of those who lack faith in an afterlife, while the sopranos, with a tiny seven-note pattern for the phrase 'but they are at peace' (aber sie sind in Frieden), repeatedly offer words of hope and re-assurance.

Amongst various prefatory 'ordinances', supplied for the guidance of performers, the composer refers to an essential transposition which applies to the first part of the work. 'For the benefit of the singers', he writes, 'I have written out the basso continuo part, with the chords I have in mind to be played on the organ, a fourth lower, even though I am well aware that a fifth lower would be more natural for the organ, and would probably have made

Ex. 24

things easier for an inexperienced organist'.[13] His problem arose from a natural desire to retain the notation appropriate to the Aeolian mode (the one chosen for the first part), and at the same time arrive at a pitch which would 'benefit the singers'. Simple notation would have been possible if the normal transposition of down a fifth, with a B flat in the signature, had been employed; but this would have resulted in an uneasily low pitch for at least some of the singers. He therefore preserved the plain Aeolian notation for the singers, and at the same time lowered the pitch of the organ part by a fourth; and thus was able to achieve, at the expense only of the organist's peace of mind, an acceptable pitch, centred on E (although one which, with changed standards of pitch, is still on the low side for present-day performers). In another observation from the same ordinance (see footnote 12), concerning the adaptation of the chorale melodies, whether major or minor, to the overall modal scheme, he asks to be forgiven by 'understanding musicians' for having had occasionally 'to transgress the *Ninth Mode* [Aeolian] in order to accommodate the chorale tunes'. In practice,

[13] Graulich, op. cit., Preface, xxxix, under '*Ordinance* for the concerted motet or German Burial Mass, fol. 1'.

the most significant result is the addition of a short phrase leading to a cadence in the minor at the end of each major-mode chorale melody, in order to conform to the minor-mode setting of the ensuing solo (or ensemble) entry.

The second part of the work is a deeply expressive setting for two SATB choruses, with optional continuo and unspecified supporting instruments, of 'Herr, wenn ich nur dich habe' (Lord, when I have only thee, I long for no other, either on earth or in heaven), a 'coffin' text (from Psalm 73, 25–6) used previously in the 'Gloria' section of Part 1, between bars 391 and 427, and the one chosen by Posthumus for the sermon at his funeral. The setting comprises four sections (ending at bars 23, 41, 61, and 98), each of which provides for increasingly close-knit antiphony between the two choruses and culminates in a sonorous tutti climax. Although set in the Aeolian (A minor) mode (with a visual consistency, only, to Part 1, in view of the latter's transposed form), the motet shows throughout a striking predominance of major chords—including from the outset, A, D, G, and C,—which contributes, no doubt by design, to a mood of exceptional lightness and exaltation. For the final part the composer provided, once again at Posthumus's request, a setting of the German Nunc dimittis, in which he shows the most inventive, and indeed most theatrical, side of his genius. Somewhat in the manner of his ceremonial motet for the Electoral Diet in Mühlhausen in 1627, 'Da Pacem, Domine, in diebus nostris', SWV 465 (see pp. 33–4 above), he employs two choruses of unequal constitution, each with its own separate text, and ensures balance between them by their positioning in the performance area and by appropriately placed *submisse* (soft) and *fortiter* (loud) markings for the larger ensemble.[14] After an initial intonation, to impart a solemn liturgical character, the first 'chorus concertatus', a five-part SATTB ensemble, situated 'next to the organ', begins a complete version of the Song of Simeon (Luke 2: 29–32), 'Lord now lettest thou thy servant depart in peace'; and from bar 9 the second chorus, an SSB trio 'placed at a distance' (in ferne geordnet), enters with an imitative setting of the beautiful text, from Revelation 14: 13, 'Blessed are the dead who die in the Lord, they shall rest from their labours, and their deeds shall follow after them' (see Ex. 25). In the process two separate, but closely intertwined, scenes are strikingly portrayed—on the one hand, of the faithful congregation in solemn liturgical worship, and on the other, of the disembodied soul of the departed, 'in the distance', in peaceful communion with heavenly spirits.[15] In an ordinance relating to this final section

---

[14] The dynamic contrasts indicated by these terms could be dramatically enhanced by a withdrawal of the instruments, or by the use of solo voices, for the *submisse* passages.

[15] A 'scenic' arrangement which compares interestingly with that of Schütz occurs in an *Actus musicus*, entitled *Lazarus*, and dated 1649, by Andreas Fromm (1621–83). In the preface he writes: 'The profane chorus [should be placed] down in the church near the congregation, to be more audible, and because Hell is down below . . . the heavenly chorus, on the other hand, should be up on high . . . before he comes up to Heaven, Lazarus should sing in the church below. The Prologue should stand in one place, away from the organ.'

Ex. 25

Schütz suggests that 'by making one or two copies of their second choir [music], and by setting it up at different places around the church, according to the possibilities that present themselves . . . the effect of the work might be greatly enhanced'.[16] Clearly his intention was to create, in miniature, a spaced choral effect; but whether this is to be achieved by placing one or two extra second choruses in separate locations, or by allowing a single chorus to move from place to place during the performance is not made plain. The first alternative would appear to assume the presence of a larger number of performers than for any other part of the work, while the second might well jeopardize the solemnity of the occasion by introducing an excessive amount of perambulation.

[16] Graulich, op. cit., Preface, xl, under '*Ordinance* for the Song of Simeon, fol. 16'.

With the *Musikalische Exequien* Schütz created a major landmark in the history, still far from fully explored, of Protestant funeral music. With some of its selected texts it points forward to the *German Requiem* of Brahms— not only with 'But the souls of the righteous are in the hand of God', already mentioned, but also with 'Blessed are the dead which die in the Lord from henceforth'. It is, however, linked more strongly to the liturgy and is thus more positively Christian in character than its nobly spiritual, but more 'humanity-orientated', successor. Brahms's work continues to live inspiringly in the concert-hall; but for a great many funeral works, created in tribute for a single occasion, there remains often, and somewhat paradoxically, little likelihood of an 'afterlife', once each has served its initial purpose. No doubt it was with this in mind that, with reference to the opening part of the work, Schütz remarked in the first of his prefatory Ordinances: 'Anyone who likes this work of mine may find that it can be used to good effect . . . as a substitute for a German *Missa*, perhaps for the Feast of the Purification or on the 16th Sunday after Trinity'.[17]

---

[17] Graulich, op. cit., Preface, xxxix (see n. 13).

8

War and desolation, 1636–45. The *Kleine geistliche Konzerte*

Despite hopes that a sustained period of peace would follow the Treaty of Prague in 1635, the war continued almost uninterruptedly as France entered the struggle with the aim of shattering, finally, the remaining power of the Habsburgs and Spain. For the next thirteen years central Germany became the main theatre of conflict between the warring armies; and since the soldiers involved frequently lacked pay and provisions, they tended to support themselves by acting virtually as brigands, looting and murdering as they passed through the land, and bringing ruin and desolation in their wake. In the words of the poet Andreas Gryphius (from his sonnet 'Tränen des Vaterlandes', 1636), 'The steeples lie in embers, the church is razed to the ground, / The town hall crouches in terror, the strong are cut down, / The maidens are despoiled and all we now can see there / Is fire, plague and death, the heart and soul pierced through.'[1] Yet further reference to the misery created by the war is found in the dedicatory preface to the first of Schütz's two collections of small sacred concertos (*Kleine geistliche Konzerte*),[2] Part 1 of which was issued in Leipzig late in 1636, as his first published work since the *Symphoniae sacrae* of 1629, and Part 2 in Dresden, three years later. 'Praiseworthy music', he wrote, 'has not only fallen into great decline through the constant perils of war . . . but in many places has ceased altogether, suffering the general ruin and disorder which invariably results from unholy strife'. He has created, he says, 'sundry little concertos, so that the talents given me by God in such a noble art do not remain quite unused'.[3] Although individually quite modest in scale, and as a whole invariably reported on disparagingly by the composer, these exquisitely fashioned miniatures were to become eventually some of the most widely admired and frequently performed of Schütz's works. Their

[1] 'Die Türme stehn in Glut, die Kirch ist umgekehret,/Das Rathaus liegt im Graus, die Starken sind zerhaun,/Die Jungfern sind geschändt, und wo wir hin nur schaun,/Ist Feuer, Pest und Tod, der Herz und Geist durchfähret.'
[2] *GBS*, No. 45, 135–6.
[3] 'Welcher gestalt unter andern freyen Künsten / auch die löbliche Music / von den noch anhaltenden gefährlichen Krieg-Läufften . . . nicht allein in grosses Abnehmen gerathen / sondern an manchen Ort gantz niedergeleget worden / stehet neben andern allgemeinen Ruinen und eingerissenen Unordnungen / so der unselige Krieg mit sich zu bringen pfleget / vor männigliches Augen . . .

special characteristics will be considered in more detail, later in the present chapter.

During the following months the composer was increasingly preoccupied with family matters. In April 1637, in an attempt to set up a financial trust in favour of the Schütz family's daughters, not only his own but those also of his brothers Johann and Benjamin, he encountered difficulties through the negligence of the assigned administrators, the city fathers of Chemnitz, with resultant problems which appear never to have been fully resolved. Soon afterwards, in relentless succession, two family deaths brought further deep distress to the composer. Firstly, that of his brother Georg, in the late spring of 1637; and secondly that of his elder daughter, Anna Justina, aged seventeen, early in 1638.

The death of Georg imposed an added burden upon the composer since he felt obliged, in the circumstances, to assume responsibility for the education of his brother's children. It gave him particular pleasure, however, that for one of his sons he was able to find a place as a choirboy in the Dresden Kapelle. Very possibly it was Georg's death, and its ramifications, which presented the principal obstacle to a return visit to Denmark that Schütz appears to have envisaged at this time. As early as February 1637 he had petitioned the elector for leave of absence, partly to retrieve some of 'his best pieces of music' which he had left behind on his previous visit, but mainly to accept the generous offer of employment which he had received from Crown Prince Christian. There is however no evidence that this journey to Denmark took place, and the likelihood is that Matthias Weckmann went there in his place.

In November 1638, despite the financial constraints imposed by twenty years of war, elaborate festivities, lasting a week, were mounted in Dresden to celebrate the marriage of the Crown Prince Johann Georg to Princess Magdalena Sybilla of Brandenburg. The climax of the proceedings was reached with the performance of an 'Opera-Ballet' entitled *Orpheus und Euridice*, with a libretto by August Buchner and music by Schütz. The libretto only has survived, and there is nothing to indicate the precise character of the music involved. Since, however, under the supervision of the dancing master, Gabriel Mölich, particular emphasis was placed upon a series of ballet scenes—featuring nymphs and naiads, the death of Euridice from snake-bite, the crossing of the Styx with Charon, and an underworld peopled by Ixion, Tantalus, Tityus, and the daughters of Danae—it is very likely that Schütz took the opportunity to delight the Dresden court with dance music composed in the latest Italian styles.[4] During the winter months of 1638/39 his main concern was family business in Weissenfels; and following his return to Dresden in the spring he supervised the publication of the second part of his *Kleine geistliche Konzerte*, which he dedi-

---

[4] See Walter Salmen, 'Der Tanz im Denken und Werken von Heinrich Schütz', *SJb*, 15 (1993), 25–31.

cated, with apologies for its 'simplicity', to Prince Frederik, the youngest son of the Danish King.[5]

By 1639 the number of musicians in the electoral ensemble at Dresden, formerly thirty-nine in 1632, had been reduced to only ten, and it had become increasingly difficult to maintain performances of any real substance in the palace church. However, during the succeeding years up to 1647, a gradual recovery to twenty-one members took place, largely as a result of a proposal by Schütz (submitted to the elector in September 1645) that the three basic groups of musicians—choirboys, adult singers, and instrumentalists—should be increased in turn, with the adult vocalists being drawn mainly from foreign sources 'even partially from among the Italians'.[6] In the meantime, from September 1641, a separate ensemble was founded by the crown prince, Johann Georg. Originally it comprised only four members—a singer who also played the theorbo (Philipp Stolle), another unspecified instrumentalist (Friedrich Werner), an organist (Matthias Weckmann), and a director of the instrumental music (Augustus Tax); but by the beginning of the following decade it already numbered, under the direction of G. A. Bontempi, some twenty-two musicians and was thus at least the equal in size of the elector's ensemble.

Notwithstanding his difficulties at Dresden, the exalted position which Schütz continued to hold amongst German musicians of the period is clearly evidenced by the many invitations he received, and accepted, over the ensuing decade, to act as an honorary Kapellmeister, or in some cases simply as an advisor *in absentia*, to various prominent courts, German and Danish. The first of these, from October 1639 for a period of fourteen months, took him to the court of Duke Georg of Calenberg at Hildesheim where, in the absence of detailed records, he may be assumed to have contributed to the raising of standards at the court Kapelle. Then, in 1642, he was invited to pay a further visit to Copenhagen and attend the court as their principal Kapellmeister. Payment of his salary there began early in May; but since he is believed to have been in Dresden at the end of September to direct the music at the baptism of Prince Johann Georg's first daughter, it is very likely that he did not travel to Denmark until October. On his journey he was accompanied by two of his Dresden colleagues, Andreas Gleich and Clemens Thieme, the latter a noted bassoonist who, in 1663, became Konzertmeister at Zeitz. During his stay, which lasted until April 1644, Schütz's duties included the direction of the music, now lost, but presumably of some elaboration, for the double wedding of King Christian's twin daughters, held in November 1642.

Of greatest interest are the contacts he enjoyed, at various periods from 1644, as Kapellmeister-*in-absentia* to the court, at Wolfenbüttel, of Duke August the younger of Brunswick-Lüneburg. The Duke's wife, Sophie

[5] See facsimile of the dedicatory letter in W. Ehmann and H. Hoffmann (eds.), *Heinrich Schütz, Kleine geistliche Konzerte* Vol. 10 part 1 (Bärenreiter, Kassel, 1963), in Preface, xxvii.
[6] *GBS*, No. 57, 158.

Elisabeth, a member of the renowned *Fruchtbringende Gesellschaft*, enjoyed a considerable reputation for her achievements both as an author and as a composer. From surviving correspondence it can be seen that she formed a close association with Schütz, during which, from time to time, she sought his advice about her compositions. In a letter from Brunswick, dated 22 October 1644 (in which he first seeks her approval for the purchase of a *positif* organ from Hamburg for the court chapel) Schütz refers to the notable improvement 'from my modest instruction' which he has observed in some arias by her that he has received, and states his readiness to discuss with her 'immediately and most diligently the completion of our musical work which we have at hand'.[7] This last reference is very probably to a court spectacle entitled *Theatralische neue Vorstellung von der Maria Magdalena* (New theatrical presentation [of the story] of Mary Magdalene), destined for performance in Wolfenbüttel at the end of 1644 or early in the following year.[8] The text is now generally believed to have been contributed by the court poet, Justus Georg Schottelius, while the music, which is no longer extant, was probably the combined work of the Duchess Sophie Elisabeth and Schütz, with the larger portion contributed, no doubt, by the latter. There have survived, in a collection entitled *Fruchtbringender Lustgarten*, which Schottelius edited and published in Lüneburg in 1647, the texts of two song-poems believed to have come from the work: 'Frölich auf, ihr Himmels Volk' and 'Nun hat recht die Sünderin', the settings of which, attributed to Schütz, are now lost. A number of letters, exchanged between Schütz and Sophie Elisabeth between 22 June 1655 and 2 January 1656, reveal how long continuing an association the composer maintained with the Wolfenbüttel court.[9] Amongst the musicians who, on his recommendation, were accepted for service there, were Johann Jacob Löwe von Eisenach (one of Schütz's former pupils at Dresden) as Kapellmeister, together with a male soprano, a bass, and two choirboys from Kassel. Later, in 1663, Löwe became Kapellmeister at Zeitz (again on Schütz's recommendation) and was replaced at Wolfenbüttel by Martin Coler.

Various events of a primarily social nature occupied Schütz during the first half of 1645. In February he travelled to Brunswick to attend, as godfather, the baptism of the third child of Delphin Strungk, the organist of St Mary's church in the city; and on 10 April, it is highly likely, though not certain, that he visited Wolfenbüttel for the birthday celebrations of Duke August. Subsequently he moved to Leipzig and from there wrote on 21 May to Johann Georg to announce his intention of returning as soon as possible, after his long absence, to Dresden.

[7] Spagn., Doc. 19, 239 and 241.
[8] See Judith P. Atkin, 'Heinrich Schütz's *Die Bußfertige Magdalena* (1636)', *SJb*, 14 (1992), 9–24, a detailed account of the text and its probable authorship, including an appendix providing, in facsimile, the anonymous text from 1636, identified as the original source.
[9] Spagn., Docs 23, 25, 27, 28, and 29.

One can hardly suppose that Schütz was not fully conscious of the outstanding merits of his two sets of *Kleine geistliche Konzerte*. His reference to the collection, in the preface to the second part, as 'a small and unworthy work', limited by the 'wickedness of the times',[10] surely owes more to the courteous humility of phrase he so often displayed in dedicatory epistles than to any lack of confidence in his work. No doubt as a result of the war the scope for the printing and publication of music had been greatly reduced, and the likelihood of performances of elaborately scored works at the many impoverished court Kapelle of the time virtually eliminated; but as the consistently varied nature of his earlier major collections indicates, it was more his constant urge to explore new genres which determined his continuing publication policy than the pressure of external events, however formidable.

The small sacred concerto, involving the setting of a religious text for one or more solo voices in monodic style with continuo accompaniment, was established early in the seventeenth century by Ludovico Grossi da Viadana with his *Cento concerti ecclesiastici. A una, a due, a tre e a quattro voci. Con il basso continuo per sonar nell' organo*, published in Venice in 1602, with two additional volumes following in 1607 and 1622. Although modest in their artistic aims, these works soon gained widespread renown, partly because of the novelty of the techniques they employed, and partly because of the enlarged repertory they provided, with their limited scoring and undemanding style, for court chapels and country churches with slender performance resources. Subsequently, with the new genre firmly established, the sacred monodic style was vividly exploited by Monteverdi and several of his associates and followers, including Grandi, Rovetta, Donati, and Giulio Belli, many of whose settings appeared in large collections, such as those assembled by Nikolaus Stein (Frankfurt, 1621) and Lorenzo Calvi (*Symbola diversorum musicorum*, 1620 and 1624). In Germany the earliest important works to follow Viadana's example were, in the Catholic south, the *Cantiones Ecclesiasticae . . . cum Basso generale* (Dillingen, 1607) by Gregor Aichinger, organist to the Fugger family in Augsburg; and, in the north, the *Opella nova* Part 1 (Leipzig, 1618) by Hermann Schein, in which the emphasis is on chorale texts and melodies, set for one or two voices and continuo, in some cases with additional obbligato instruments.

The fifty-five concertos in Schütz's collection are ordered, in each volume, according to the nature and number (from one to five) of the voices involved, with the higher voices and smaller ensembles taking priority. Instruments other than the continuo are used in only two concertos, the German and Latin versions of the Annunciation story 'Sei gegrüsset Maria', SWV 333 and 'Ave Maria, gratia plena', SWV 334, to be discussed later. Three principal sources are drawn upon for the texts: the Bible (psalms, gospels, and epistles), the liturgy (introits, graduals, and

---

[10] See *GBS*, No. 47, 139 for the dedicatory letter in *Kleine geistliche Konzerte* II.

responsories), chorale stanzas, and in a few cases German versions of patristic writings, similar to those attributed to St Augustine and St Bernard of Clairvaux which are found in the *Cantiones sacrae* of 1625. Latin texts are present in only eleven items, all of them in Part 2; but there are also a few cases where subsidiary Latin versions have been inserted by the composer into the German-texted liturgical settings, presumably with a view to widening their denominational appeal. Although Schütz may well have intended his concertos as much for domestic or school use (in the traditional Lutheran manner) as for church worship, it is noteworthy that the texts chosen are appropriate to a wide liturgical range, one which embraces Advent, Christmas, New Year, Epiphany, and Passiontide, and such special functions as funerals, confirmations, and ordinations. Although three years separate the publication of the two sets of concertos, the collection as a whole shows a broad consistency of style. The main distinguishing feature of the second set is the use, in some works, of what may be termed 'ensemble declamation', in which several singers contribute separate monodic passages, in recitative style, bound together by continuo harmony. The technique is evident particularly in the 'Epistle' settings, on verses from Romans, 'Ist Gott für uns' (If God be for us, who can be against us?), SWV 329, and 'Wer will uns scheiden' (Who shall separate us from the love of God?), SWV 330; and in the tormentedly penitential five-voice (SATTB) setting, 'Aufer immensam' (Restrain, Lord, your terrible anger, withhold the bloodstained scourge), SWV 337, on a hymn text by Georg Klee, with which the entire collection ends.

Most advanced in style are the solo-voice settings found early in each part of the collection: 'Eile, mich, Gott, zu erretten' (Make haste, O God, to deliver me: let them be ashamed and confounded that seek after my soul), SWV 282; and 'Was hast du verwirket' (What crime have you committed, O Jesus Christ, dearest child), SWV 307. The first of these—for soprano, and marked 'In Stylo Oratorio'—is set in a wholly declamatory style in which, following Italian models, the musical content is determined by the rhythm and expressive content of the words. Very fine is the use, in the last two bars, of an augmentation, at low pitch, of the preceding phrase (in bars 30–1), to give extra weight to the words 'Mein Gott, mein Gott, verzeuch nicht' (My God, make no tarrying). Similar in style, the other monody is set for a (male) alto voice, with a dark emotional colouring that well matches its pseudo-Augustinian penitential text, a German version of the Latin ones used previously by Schütz for the motets 'Quid commisisti, o dulce puer' and 'Ego sum tui plaga doloris', SWV 56–7 in his *Cantiones sacrae*. The remorseful repetitions of 'Ich' (Oh, I am the cause of your sorrow, I am guilty of your death) in the concerto provide a notable parallel to those of 'Ego' in Latin settings, remarked upon in chapter 5 (see p. 58).

Madrigalian devices of particular vividness are found in several of the solo concertos for male voices. In the tenor setting, 'O süsser, o freundlicher' (O sweet, O amiable, O gracious Lord Jesus Christ'), SWV 285, the mood of yearning and delight is captured by the characteristic device of a chromatic ascent over a perfect fourth. In this case the composer's debt to Italian practice of the time, and the barely concealed eroticism of his approach, becomes clear when one compares his opening phrase with that of the madrigal (complete with oxymoron), 'O dolcezze amarissime d'Amore' (O most bitter sweetness of love)[11] by Sigismondo d'India (see Ex. 26). Later in the concerto (from bar 28) repeated cries of 'O' are set in ascending melismas to provide telling contrast with the otherwise consistently syllabic treatment. At the other extreme the bass solo concerto 'Ich liege und schlafe', SWV 310 (on a text from Psalm 3: 5–8), contains a remarkable example, one among many in the collection, of virtuoso vocal writing—a melisma of twenty-four notes, thrice repeated with minor variations, to colour the word 'Selah', a Hebrew expression of uncertain (possibly musical) meaning, found frequently in the psalms at verse-endings. Although in most cases lengthy melismas are used to illustrate words such as 'singing', 'joy', 'praise', or 'splendour', the intention here seems to have been mainly to provide the singer with an opportunity for personal display.[12] Even more extreme is the effect sought in the final bars of the tenor concerto 'O Jesu, nomen dulce', SWV 308, where a 'giant' melisma of sixty-six notes is set to the word 'portabo' (I shall carry) in the context 'and so I shall carry your name, sweetest Jesu, in my mouth for ever'. Possibly the aim in this case was to symbolize through the immense *passaggio* not only the act of 'carrying' but also its 'endlessness'.

In the two- and three-voice concertos the composer turns, apparently instinctively, to an imitative contrapuntal style, with resultant settings that parallel (though with greater finesse, and an added continuo line) those of

Ex. 26

[11] From Sigismondo d'India, *Le Musiche* (Milan 1609), on a text from *Il pastor fido*, Act III.

[12] Another example is provided by the Christmas concerto 'Hodie Christus natus est', SWV 315, in which both 'canunt' and 'gloria' are coloured by elaborate melismas, of varying length. Interestingly, this setting is now known to have been modelled on an Ave Maria by Viadana.

the traditional *bicinia* and *tricinia*, the simple two- and three-voice forms much favoured in Lutheran choir schools for teaching purposes. One elegant procedure, found chiefly in the duet settings, is to present the initial theme (which may contain several short ideas) in one voice-part alone, with continuo support, and then repeat it in the other part, with the original voice supplying imitation or a new countertheme. A fine example is provided by 'O lieber Herre Gott', SWV 287, for two sopranos, based on an ancient Advent Collect in a translation by Luther. In this case, the first soprano's opening theme, twelve bars in length, comprises three distinct fragments (starting at bars 1, 6, and 10), each of which is subsequently linked with the second voice in two-part imitative writing. Then, after a middle section in triple time—for the words 'ihn mit Freuden empfahlen' (receive him with joy)—which provides the emotional climax of the work, the final thirty bars present a contrapuntal complex of great refinement. By

Ex. 27

again separating the text section into three segments—'durch denselbigen deinen lieben Sohn/Jesum Christum/Amen' (through thy selfsame beloved son/Jesus Christ/Amen)—and setting each to a distinctive melodic fragment, the composer introduces a series of simple interwoven patterns which are preserved, with delicate variations, until the final bar (see Ex. 27).

·A related scheme of at least equal ingenuity is found in 'Herr, ich hoffe darauf', (Lord, I have trusted in thy mercy, my heart shall rejoice in thy salvation), SWV 312, for two sopranos, a setting of Psalm 13: 5–6. In this case the opening theme, for soprano 1, has no less than four contrasted elements, set to 'Ich hoffe darauf / dass du so gnädig bist / mein Herz freuet sich / das du so gerne hilfst' (But I have trusted / since thou art so gracious / my heart rejoices/ that thou hast so gladly helped me), starting at bars 1, 3, 5, and 8, respectively. Segment 3 stands out by virtue of its melismatic treatment, in dactylic rhythms, of the word 'freuet' (rejoice), and both it and segment 4 are given extra force by being immediately repeated. Then from bar 16 the second soprano enters to provide imitative treatment of each thematic idea in succession, including an ingenious combination of segment 3 with a diminution of segment 4. In the central section the two voices in turn provide rapid declamatory patterns for the phrase 'Ich will dem Herren singen, dass er so wohl an mir' (I will sing unto the Lord, for he hath dealt bountifully with me), before interlinking them in close imitation. And finally, in a highly effective repetition scheme, the third and fourth theme-fragments from the opening paragraph return, with the vigorous melisma (set originally to 'freuet') providing equally apt colouring for the word 'Alleluja'. Notable especially for its assured use of invertible counterpoint to underline text expression, is the duet setting for soprano and bass, 'Wann unsre Augen schlafen ein' (When our eyes droop in sleep, then let the heart be a weapon: hold over us thy right hand, that we fall not into sin and shame), SWV 316, based on the third stanza of the ancient chorale 'Christe, der du bist der helle Tag'. At the opening the soprano provides two contrasted ideas, a slow descending chromatic passage to represent 'sleep' and a rising melisma in quavers to symbolize the protective shield of the 'valiant heart'. At bar 4, the bass enters, and using the same thematic fragments provides a finely shaped imitative pairing which, after some expansion, returns from bar 38 with the parts inverted at the twelfth. Then at bar 49 two further themes are introduced in combination, one comprising a descending minor scale, initially g to G, in minims (a smoother version of the chromatic opening theme) to signify the 'right hand's' guardianship, and the other a short bass figure in crotchets for the phrase 'that we fall not'; these also appear inverted, from bar 57, this time in double counterpoint at the tenth. And during the final bars, with a delightful touch of madrigalian 'negative' word-painting, limping syncopations are introduced for the words 'sin and shame', despite the overall message that these can be *avoided* in the ways advocated (see Ex. 28).

Ex. 28

Certain structural principles of unity and variety are common to virtually all the concertos. Unity results most frequently from the use of short-range repetitions, melodic sequences, and a balanced scheme of 'keys' and cadences; and variety, from changes of metre (between 4/4, 3/2, and 6/4), contrasts between syllabic and melismatic writing, and the temporary adoption within settings of new 'key' (or modal) areas. Long-range repetition, in the sense of a true recapitulation, is found only rarely; but an instance of some note occurs from bar 42 of the three-voice (SSB) concerto, 'Rorate coeli desuper', SWV 322, where there is an unusually full reprise of the opening text, with each of its associated themes in various modified shapes. As a further means of securing cohesion, several of the concertos contain interpolated 'Alleluja' sections which repeatedly interrupt the basic text as a form of refrain. One notably elaborate example occurs in the duet (SS) concerto, 'Habe deine Lust an dem Herren' (Delight thyself also in the Lord), SWV 311, a setting of Psalm 37: 1–5. At bar 91, over ten repetitions of a four-bar ostinato bass (drawn, mysteriously, from the continuo line between bars 65 and 69) there are placed nine markedly different 'Alleluja' patterns—the inexact match resulting from the inclusion of both solo and duet versions of the single idea of pattern six, set over two statements of the ostinato figure. Variety is achieved partly by a change of metre from $\mathbf{c}$ to 3/2 (and with it an increase from four to six bars) for the sixth, seventh, and eighth ostinato patterns; partly by the use of melodic shapes in which the accentuation falls on each syllable of 'Alleluja' in turn; and partly by a reversion to $\mathbf{c}$ time for the final, majestic pattern, marked, with one of Schütz's rare tempo indications, *Tarde*. Noteworthy in this work is the manner in which Schütz rearranges his material so as to intensify both its textual and musical impact. In order to give prominence to Psalm 37's 'hopeful' message, he sets verses 4 and 5 ('Delight thyself also in the Lord' and 'Commit thy way unto the Lord') as an outer framework, and encloses within it verses 1–3 ('Fret not thyself because of evil-doers', 'for they shall soon be cut down like the grass', and 'trust in the Lord and do good') as a darker centre-piece. It is precisely because of the type of care in the disposition of his texts shown here that Schütz is able, in these concertos, to achieve so richly varied a range of musical structures.[13]

Amongst the concertos in the first set there are three which are duplicated elsewhere in Schütz's output. One of these, the three-voice (SST) setting, 'O Herr hilf', SWV 297, was included later, in an amplified version, as SWV 402, in *Symphonia sacrae* III of 1650 (see pp. 133–4); while the other two, 'Ich hab mein Sach Gott heimgestellt' (I have commended myself to God's care), SWV 305, and 'Siehe, mein Fürsprecher ist im Himmel' (Behold, my advocate is in heaven), SWV 304, are revised versions of earlier works, the former of the five-voice aria, SWV 94, which Schütz composed on the death of his sister-in-law in 1625, (mentioned earlier on page 32), and the latter of the motet 'Ecce advocatus meus apud te', SWV 84, No. 32 in the *Cantiones sacrae* of 1625. In the last of these the revision involves mainly an enlargement (from 16 to 20 bars) of the central tenor solo—'En qui peccatum non fecit, peccata nostra pertulit', in the Latin version—apparently as a means of 'easing' the extreme intensity of the earlier setting's complex vocal line. Yet another extensive link, of great interest, occurs between 'Herr, wenn ich nur dich habe', SWV 321, for two sopranos and tenor, and the setting of the same text, at bar 391, in the first part of the *Musikalische Exequien*. The sixteen-bar tenor solo of the funeral work (which may be assumed to have preceded the concerto) is wonderfully expanded to seventy-eight bars in the three-voice setting, partly by a much varied treatment of the basic theme during the first forty bars and partly by the introduction of entirely new material, in a rapid syllabic style, for the words 'Wenn mir gleich Leib und Seele verschmacht, so bist du doch, Gott, allzeit meines Herzens Trost und mein Teil' (My flesh and my heart faileth: but God is the strength of my heart, and my portion for ever) with which the text-section ends.

In addition to 'Wann unsre Augen schlafen ein' and 'Ich hab mein Sach Gott heimgestellt' mentioned above, there are in the collection five other settings of chorale texts with adaptations of their associated melodies: 'O hilf, Christe, Gottes Sohn', SWV 295, 'Nun komm, der Heiden Heiland' SWV 301, 'Wir glauben all an einen Gott', SWV 303, 'Ich ruf zu dir', SWV 326, and 'Allein Gott in der Höh', SWV 327. Two of them, SWV 327 and SWV 303, are settings of *Altargesänge* (altar hymns)—Lutheran versions, respectively, of the Gloria and Credo; while the other three (which are

---

[13] For a fuller analysis of this concerto see Anne Kirwan-Mott, *The Small-scale Sacred Concertato in the Early Seventeenth Century* (UMI Research Press, Ann Arbor, Michigan, 1981), 139.

amongst those noted earlier as having alternative Latin texts) are hymns appropriate to various seasons of the Church's year. As with his other, comparatively rare, elaborate settings of chorale texts, Schütz, in these concerto versions, avoids plain statements of their associated melodies. Occasionally he places the first phrase in some clearly recognizable form at the opening, as if to 'announce' the hymn's title, but thereafter introduces only fragments of the original theme, often disguised by repetition and ornamentation or buried deeply inside his textures. In the process the settings become suffused with the essential character of their all-important basic melodies, but without recourse to a literal presentation. At the same time, as if to emphasize their grand traditional status, the composer brings to bear upon them a striking range of technical skills, including canon, invertible counterpoint, ostinato patterns, and cantus firmus treatment. In his setting (SSTT) of the Gloria substitute by Nikolaus Decius, 'Allein Gott in der Höh sei Ehr', the principal unifying factor is an ostinato pattern in the continuo bass which, in two segments at different pitches, underpins each verse. In a varied scheme the four stanzas are scored in turn for the two sopranos, the two tenors, the first soprano, and a four-voice tutti, in each case with continuo support. Only in the first and last stanzas is the basic chorale melody at all clearly outlined; and by means of repetition and melodic decoration the hymn's original slender material is expanded to form a work of substantial proportions. Even more complex treatment is accorded to the Advent chorale 'Nun komm, der Heiden Heiland', a reworking by Luther of both the text and melody of 'Veni Redemptor Gentium', an Ambrosian hymn of eight four-line stanzas, with seven syllables to each line. Schütz sets the first stanza only (for SSBB) and, in the course of four clearly defined sections, expands each line musically by means of imitation, antiphony, sequential repetition, and melismatic ornamentation. During the first two sections a principal role is played by canon. In section 1 an outline of the first phrase of the melody is combined with a countersubject in shorter note-values to provide a canon 4 in 2 distributed between the pairs of upper and lower voices. In section 2, successive duet and trio textures (S. 2/B.2, S.1/B.1, and S/S/B.2), based freely on the second line of the melody, are set in canon 2 in 1. The second of these, between bars 22 and 28, conveys, by means of Lombardic rhythms and delicate melismas, a charming aura of childlike innocence for the words 'der Jungfrauen Kind erkannt' (The Virgin's child revealed) (see Ex. 29). In the third and fourth sections, the opening line of the chorale (text and melody) reappears with vivid effect as a cantus firmus in the bass (B.2 and continuo), which at different pitches persistently supports rapid versions of the third-line theme and text in the upper voices. Finally, reductions in the note-values (from semibreves to minims and then to crotchets) in the cantus firmus lead gradually to a climactic version of the last line of the chorale (identical in Luther's version of the melody to the first) in which a return of canonic and stretto-like patterns for the full ensemble provide a final texture of outstanding richness.

Ex. 29

Found amongst the final settings in Part 2, the Annunciation dialogue, differs from the other concertos as the only one to incorporate obbligato instruments (in addition to the continuo), and the only one to exist in separate, German- and Latin-texted, versions: 'Sei gegrüsset, Maria, du Holdselige', SWV 333 and 'Ave, Maria, gratia plena', SWV 334. The dialogue between Mary (a soprano) and Gabriel (a male alto or high tenor) is enclosed between two identical symphonias of an appropriately simple character for an ensemble of five obbligato instruments—unspecified, but probably of a uniform tonal character, either strings or wind, with SSATB ranges—which in these two contexts, and in a final Capella chorus, make their only contribution. The text, from Luke 1: 28–38, is reduced in both versions by the omission of verse 32 (second half) and verse 33, and the problem of creating a dialogue in which one character (Gabriel) has much the largest amount of text is charmingly resolved by providing Mary with the (non-biblical) response, 'What greeting is that?', to Gabriel's opening salutation, and thus giving verbal expression to the description (in verse 29) of her 'troubled thoughts'. The two concertos are of equal length (103 bars) and involve essentially the same music with identical figured-bass lines. However the Latin version, which must surely have been the later of the two to be written, tends to involve more syllables and thus, at times, more unwieldy vocal patterns—in Mary's first utterance, for example, where 'Qualis, qualis est ista salutatio?', with twelve syllables, replaces 'Welch ein Grüss is das?', with only five. In his setting of this passage, and parallel ones which occur later, Schütz contrives, by means of differences in pitch and

99

verbal accentuation, to achieve a strong contrast between Gabriel's grave, low-pitched, greeting in measured rhythm, and Mary's thoughtful reaction, in which a high vocal range is used to suggest her nobility of character, and off-beat patterns her natural bewilderment. These clear contrasts of pitch—low/humble and high/exalted—accord well with numerous traditional portrayals of the Annunciation scene, such as the stone relief at Santa Croce by Donatello, in which the archangel, on bended knee, looks up with profound reverence to the aristocratic figure of the standing Virgin.

It is interesting to compare Schütz's German setting of the scene with the very fine one which Schein published in Leipzig in 1626 in the second part of his famous *Opella nova*. Though not dissimilar in scoring and structure, with soprano and tenor roles allotted to Mary and the Angel, and an instrumental introduction (scored impressively for four trombones and continuo), Schein's work is longer and considerably more complex than that of Schütz. The opening instrumental music, for example, leads directly into the first vocal entry, and thereafter intervenes twice in the central dialogue, with impressive effect; and the vocal writing, particularly for the role of Gabriel, is decidedly more elaborate than that in the later work, involving several ornamental passages of a melismatic character. Arguments may be given in favour of both types of setting; but it is difficult not to conclude that by its very simplicity Schütz's version comes the closer of the two to the heart of its subject. His vocal writing, plain and largely syllabic, provides an immediacy of expression which Schein's, for all its surface beauty and rich artifice, never fully attains; his continuo bass, with its close imitative links with the voice-parts, has greater vitality than Schein's more static pro-

Ex. 30

100

vision; and his portrayal of Mary, with four spaced utterances of her bewildered cry 'Welch ein Grüss ist das?' as compared to only one, delayed until bar 24, in Schein's work, gives her a fuller, altogether more substantial, 'presence'. Mary's final words, 'Behold the handmaid of the Lord; be it unto me as thou hast said', evoke from the two composers markedly different interpretations. In Schein's version the Virgin's graceful humility is emphasized with almost theatrical vividness by a sudden drop of an octave (from $c\sharp''$ to $c\sharp'$) for the murmured words 'I am the handmaid of the Lord'; and her submission to the divine will finds expression in decorative passage-work as the final cadence is reached (see Ex. 30a). Schütz, on the other hand, sets the passage high in the voice range, and by means of two repeated-note phrases in a strong, rising sequence, focuses particularly on Mary's resolution and firmness of faith (see Ex. 30b). And by setting the word 'du' ('thou', in the context 'as thou hast said') on a long note and at the highest point of each phrase, he appears to suggest that the Virgin's thoughts have turned finally from the messenger at her feet, and are focused instead, in her moment of extreme rapture, on the hallowed source of the message.

9

Change and controversy, 1645–56; the death of the Elector Johann Georg I

Dismayed by the desperate straits to which the Dresden Kapelle had been reduced, and aware that, with increasing age, he was less able than formerly to fulfil the demands of his work at court, Schütz decided, in 1645, that the time had come for him to seek honourable retirement. On 21 May he wrote to the elector asking that he should be released from his full-time duties with an annual pension of 200 thalers, and given permission to move to Weissenfels, where he hoped to make a permanent home with his sister, Justina.[1] In his reply, Johann Georg denied him the chance of a full retirement but, as a compromise, consented to his staying in Weissenfels, during either the autumn or winter months of the ensuing years. However, partly because of the demands made from many quarters on his expertise, and partly because of his natural urge to travel, he appears to have been unwilling or unable to keep strictly by the terms of this requirement; and as is suggested by his frequent movements during the succeeding years—to and from Weissenfels, Dresden, Calbe an der Saale, Weimar, and Leipzig—there was some inevitable neglect of his duties at Dresden. A long-term result of this was a complaint, made in a letter to the elector, dated 16 May 1649, by Johann Georg Hofkontz, a tenor singer in the electoral Kapelle who, not for the first time, was seeking appointment as vice-Kapellmeister. 'It is known to Your Serene Highness and to practically everyone else', he wrote, 'that he [Schütz], although entrusted as a shepherd, has for many years paid little attention to his flock, but has abandoned it, moving from one province to the next, taking little care about the proper provision for Your Serene Highness's ensemble'.[2] The fact that Hofkontz was inclined to blame Schütz for the repeated denials of the position he sought was no doubt a principal cause of his disgruntlement; but it is probably indicative of the weight of his complaint that, by the early summer of 1649, Schütz returned to Dresden and remained there for at least the next two years.

[1] *GBS*, No. 56, 157.
[2] Staatsarchiv Dresden Loc. 8687 Kantoreiordnung fol. 271 v. 'So ist doch E. Churf, Durchl., und fast jedermännlichen bekannt, das Er, wie sonstem einen Hirten gebühret, viel jahr hero seiner Schaffe wenig geachtet, sondern sie verlaßen, von Ein provinz in die andern geröyset, E. Churf. Durchl Capelle hat mögen versorget werden'.

In the late summer of 1646 Schütz was asked by a certain Christian Schirmer (of whom nothing further is known) for his opinion about a dispute which had arisen between Paul Siefert, first organist at the Marienkirche, Danzig, and Marco Scacchi, choirmaster to the Polish court in Warsaw.[3] The conflict had originated in the early 1640s at Danzig in a prolonged feud between Siefert and the elder Kaspar Förster, the Kapellmeister at the Marienkirche; and, as a result of this, Scacchi, incensed by Siefert's claim that the Italians had lost the ability to write good counterpoint, had published, in the summer of 1643, a Latin treatise, *Cribrum musicum ad triticum Siferticum* (Musical sieve for the Syfert wheat), in which he criticized in acrimonious detail Siefert's competence as a contrapuntist, basing his arguments on a collection of chorale motets by the Danziger, entitled *Psalmen Davids, nach französischer Melodey* (1640). Subsequently, early in 1645, Siefert had issued an equally strongly worded reply, entitled *Anticribatio musica ad avenam Scacchianam* (Musical counter-sieve for the Scacchi oats) as a 'visible demonstration of the most stupid errors' (ocularis demonstratio crassissimorum errorum) in his opponent's challenge. And so, uneasily, and largely unnecessarily, since the opponents were arguing from quite different—German and Italian—stylistic viewpoints, the sad confrontation had persisted. In his reply to Schirmer, in 1646, Schütz tried diplomatically to express some sympathy for Siefert's opinion, while at the same time praising Scacchi fulsomely as 'an extremely well-grounded musician'.[4] Subsequently, in a further letter, of 1648, in which he related some of Scacchi's precepts to those he had learnt from Gabrieli in his youth,[5] and more particularly in the preface to his *Geistliche Chor-Music* of 1648, to be considered in chapter 11, Schütz gave further reasons why his sympathies lay principally with the Warsaw Kapellmeister's views.

During the winter of 1646 Schüzt was present in Weimar for celebrations to mark the birthday of Eleonora Dorothea, the wife of Duke Wilhelm of Saxe-Weimar, providing for the occasion a 'Song of Thanks', SWV 368, 'Fürstliche Gnade zu Wasser und Lande' for tenor, two instruments and continuo, on a text by Christian Timotheus Dufft. And in the following year on 1 May, shortly after returning to Dresden from Weissenfels, he published his second collection of *Symphoniae sacrae*, SWV 341–67, containing twenty-seven concertato settings of German sacred texts, which he dedicated to Prince Christian of Denmark. Amongst other works which probably originated around the mid-century, but remained unpublished, are the dialogues 'Vater Abraham' (the parable of the rich man and

[3] See Walter Werbeck, 'Heinrich Schütz und der Streit zwischen Marco Scacchi und Paul Siefert', *SJb*, 17 (1995), 63.
[4] *GBS*, No. 59, 163.
[5] Ibid., No. 60, 189: 'Attamen unicum hoc confiteor, et protector, quod hoc simili modo (quo Dnus Marcus Scacchius in Cribo suo Dnum Syfertum) ego in juventute mea bone memoria Johanne Gabriele Preceptore meo quoque fuerim instructus ac institutus.'

Lazarus, from Luke 16: 24–9), SWV 477, and 'Es gingen zweene Menschen' (the parable of the Pharisee and the publican, from Luke 18: 24–31), SWV 444, which, according to the watermarks on manuscripts preserved at Kassel, can be dated *c*.1642 and *c*.1647, respectively.[6] Unusual in the 'Vater Abraham' dialogue is the use of different modes to contrast the principal characters—Phrygian for the 'Rich Man' and G Dorian for 'Abraham'—and the overall 'key'-scheme, which moves from A Aeolian in the opening sinfonia to G Dorian for the final vocal ensemble. Very striking also are various chillingly intense melismas for a pair of violins which depict the torments in Hell of the Rich Man (and those of his brothers who fail to repent). From the same period there date also some of the composer's surviving group of secular songs to German texts. Typical of the genre is 'Tugend ist der beste Freund' (on the rewards of Virtue), SWV 442, to a poem by Martin Opitz, from his *Deutscher Poëmatum Erster Theil* (Breslau, 1629). Set for a pair of sopranos, with an accompaniment for two violins and continuo, the work is organized in the manner of a miniature cantata, with a series of recurring sections, which involve separately the voices and instruments. The poem has four stanzas, each of seven lines, with matching rhyme and syllable patterns; and these are set to two contrasted sections of music, for stanzas 1 and 3, and 2 and 4, respectively. The instrumental component comprises an opening symphonia (of thirteen bars) and two ritornello sections, which preface in turn each of the two different vocal passages. An overall structure is thus evolved as follows: symph./ritorn. 1; stanza 1/music A; ritorn. 2; stanza 2/music B; ritorn. 1; stanza 3/music A; ritorn/ 2; stanza 4/music B; coda (6 bars).

In August 1647, the composer was afforded much joy by the engagement of his twenty-three-year-old daughter, Euphrosina, to a Leipzig lawyer, Christoph Pincker. The wedding followed at Dresden on 28 February 1648; but sadly the young bride died in childbirth only seven years later on 11 January 1655. Amongst the numerous expressions of sympathy received by the composer were letters of condolence from Bernhard, Bontempi, Buchner, Dedekind, and Ziegler. The year 1648 also saw the publication of the *Geistliche Chor-Music*, SWV 369–97, with a dedication, dated 21 April, to the mayor and councillors of Leipzig; and on 24 October the signing, by the exhausted combatants, of the Peace of Westphalia which at last brought an end to the Thirty Years War. It was not, however, until July 1650, following the removal of the Swedish occupying forces from the town, that services were held at Dresden to celebrate the peace. Amongst the music performed for the occasion was Schütz's majestic setting with 'trumpet and timpani chorus' of Psalm 136, SWV 45 (No. 24 in the *Psalmen Davids*). Some four months later, in celebration of the double marriage of the elector's youngest sons, Christian and Moritz, to the princesses Christiana and Sophia Hedwig of Holstein-Glücksburg, more than three

---

[6] See Clytius Gottwald, 'Neu Forschungen zu den Kasseler Schütz-Handschriften', *SJb*, 12 (1990), 31.

weeks of festivities were held at Dresden. A high point of the event appears to have been the performance of a ballet-opera *Paris und Helena*, the cast of which included Johann Hofkontz, Philipp Stolle, Christoph Bernhard, Christoph Kittel, and Prince Johann Georg; the music, which has not survived, has been supposed by some, not unreasonably, but without firm evidence, to have been provided by Schütz.

Towards the end of 1650, Schütz published, and dedicated to Johann Georg, the last, and grandest, of his three sets of *Symphoniae sacrae*, comprising twenty-one sacred concertos scored for five to eight obbligato parts (vocal and instrumental) with, in some cases, one or more additional, 'complementum', choruses. When presenting this collection—'my little work', as he described it—to the elector, he included with it, on 14 January 1651, his famous 'Memorial' (noticed earlier as a main source of information about his early years up to 1615) in which he again sought permission to retire on a suitable pension and to be granted the right to retain 'to [his] grave' the title of Kapellmeister. 'With the imminent waning of my strength', he wrote, 'it is perhaps possible that I shall experience . . . what has happened to one not poorly qualified old cantor . . . whom I know well, who . . . has written to me and complained bitterly that his young town councillors are quite dissatisfied with his old-fashioned music and therefore would like very much to be rid of him, saying . . . to his face that neither a tailor nor a cantor of thirty years are of use to anyone'; and while he would 'anticipate none of this from my lords the sons of your Electoral Highness' he is concerned that he might 'encounter it from some other newly arrived young musicians who, with the rejection of the old, usually give preference to all of their new ways, although for poor reasons'.[7] None of this appears, however, to have made the slightest impression on Johann Georg; the memorial was returned, apparently unread, and several subsequent attempts to broach the matter proved equally fruitless during the elector's lifetime.

On 11 October 1652 the wedding took place in Dresden of the elector's daughter Magdalena Sybilla, by then the widow of the Danish crown prince. Included amongst the planned celebrations was *Der triumphierende Amor*, a 'grand ballet of gods and goddesses, together with dances of nymphs, shepherds, and shepherdesses', the music of which (now lost) was very probably by Schütz. However, because of a death in the elector's family, the performance had to be cancelled. More pleasurable, no doubt, was an invitation which the composer received in August of the following year to write the preface to Caspar Ziegler's treatise, *Von den Madrigalen*, in which an attempt is made to show German writers how to shed their rigid poetic forms in favour of a more flexible madrigal style, one which Ziegler eulogized as 'a beautiful kind of verse, most suitable for music'.[8] An important effect of this enterprise was an increased cultivation

[7] Spagn., Doc. 2, 123 and 130.   [8] *GBS*, No. 85, 236.

of the continuo lied at the hands of such notable composers as Constantin Dedekind, Heinrich Albert (a cousin of Schütz), and Adam Krieger.

The ensuing years were troublous ones for Schütz. One particular cause of his distress was the lack of salary payments to the court musicians, by reason of which most of them had been reduced to penury. Appeals on their behalf in letters from the composer to Christian Reichbrodt, the elector's secretary, seem to have elicited little if any response. Writing in May 1652, Schütz referred particularly to the misery endured by a much admired bass singer—unnamed but almost certainly Georg Kaiser who had given long service—who, so he said 'has, from poverty, recently pawned his clothes, and now paces about his house like a beast in the forest'.[9] In two further letters he raised matters through which he felt his reputation had been seriously impugned. In the first of these, addressed to various of his patrons at court, including Reichbrodt and Jacob Weller, and dated 21 August 1653, he expressed his consternation at having been commanded by the elector apparent not only to take over from the vice-Kapellmeister (Hofkontz, who had succeeded to the post in 1651) the relatively humble function of providing the music for the regular Sunday services, but also to alternate in these, Sunday by Sunday, with the crown prince's director, G. A. Bontempi, 'a man three times younger than me, and castrated as well, and [thus to] compete with him for favour, pro loco, before biased and largely ill-qualified audiences and judges'.[10] In the second letter,[11] dated 23 August 1653, and addressed directly to the elector apparent, the composer rejects most bitterly the unwarranted censure he has had heaped upon him from many quarters regarding the large number of Italian musicians employed at court, most of whom had in fact been engaged over many years by the prince himself. Later, the rapid promotion and inflated salaries of the Italians, together with the fact that most were practising Catholics serving in a Lutheran court, became the source of much resentment amongst the German musicians.

Further evidence of the distressed state of the electoral Kapelle is given in a letter, of 3 December 1654, from Hofkontz and the organist, Christoph Kittel, to Jacob Weller, the senior court preacher, begging that 'a single quarter of their salary only, to preserve their miserable lives', should be granted to 'those four or five persons through whom the most necessary forms of worship are still maintained . . . with singing and playing'.[12] Three

[9] *GBS*, No. 83, 230: '. . . aus Armuht seine Kleider vor etliche Zeit wieder verpfändet, und seithero in seinen Haus, nicht anders als eine Bestie in Walde verwildet.'
[10] Spagn., Doc. 3, 133 and 135: 'an solchen Sonntagen . . . ich mit des Herrn Churprintzens Director als einen 3 mahl jüngern als ich, undt hirüber Castrirten menschen, ordentlich und stetig umbwexeln [*soll* crossed out] und unter, ungleichen undt zum gueten theil unverstandigen zuhörer und Richter urtheil mit ihm gleichsamb pro loco disputieren soll.'
[11] Spagn., Doc. 4, 137 and 142.
[12] Spagn., Doc. 7, 149 and 152: 'Sie doch nur denen 4, oder 5, Personen, durch welche der höchstnothwendige Gottesdienst mit gesang u, klang noch erhalten Und Verrichtet wird, ein eintziges Quartal besoldung zu erhaltung ihres elenden Lebens nur mochte angeordnet Und gegeben werden.'

days later Weller passed on to the elector the five musicians' plea, pointing out 'that, if they were to leave, there would remain almost no one who could simply sing hymns and a German 'Our Father' in church'.[13] However, nothing appears to have been done to remedy the situation, and the decline in the elector's musical resources continued during the remaining eleven months of his reign.

Throughout much of 1656 Schütz remained actively engaged at Dresden. Entries in the court diaries of the time show that he directed a performance there of his *Resurrection History* early in April, and during the following three months led the Kapelle in services on the principal feast days of the Church. However, during the latter part of this period life at court was overshadowed by the serious illness of the elector, who became confined to his private quarters, unable even to attend church. By early autumn the deterioration in his health became the cause of mounting anxiety; and finally on 8 October he died, aged seventy-one. The obsequies which followed showed a degree of solemnity and elaboration fully in keeping with the exalted rank of the deceased.[14] The funeral, which took place between 2 and 4 February 1657, began with a service in the palace church at 7 a.m., after which a vast procession was formed which comprised the deceased elector's family, court members of all ranks, grandees from surrounding German cities, and distinguished representatives from Bohemia, Hungary, Denmark, Sweden, and Austria. Once assembled, this concourse moved with great solemnity to the Kreuzkirche for another service at 4 p.m. On the second day a further, somewhat smaller procession was mustered which marched, bearing the coffin, some twenty miles to Freiberg for the burial of the deceased in the royal tomb in the cathedral; and on the next day, before the mourners returned to Dresden, yet another service, again preceded by a procession, was held at 11 a.m. in Freiberg, with a sermon delivered by Jacob Weller. Under the leadership of Schütz and Bontempi, there were involved no less than forty-five musicians (singers and instrumentalists), whose role consisted mainly in leading the singing of numerous hymns, both in church and in procession. A minor mystery surrounds the two matching settings of the German Nunc dimittis (Herr, nun lässest du deinen Diener im Friede fahren'), SWV 432–33, which Schütz is known have composed as a memorial to his deceased friend and employer. There would seem to have been a natural context for them, before and after the sermon on the *Canticum Simeonis* which the court preacher Christoph Laurentius is known to have delivered at the early service on the first day; but since the programme, so detailed in every other respect, makes no mention of them, one must assume that they were intended by the composer simply as

---

[13] Spagn., Doc. 7, 151 and 154: '. . . diese Fünffe, so bis anhero fast einig und allein den Gottes dienst bestellet, weichet und also fast niemand sein würde der nur den Corall und ein deütsches Vater Unser in der Kirchen würde sing konnen . . .'

[14] See Spagn., pp. 7–16 for an extended account of the Elector's funeral.

a separate tribute of a purely personal nature.[15] Both works are for six voices (SSATTB—with lost first soprano lines in each case, now supplied editorially) and optional continuo, and both begin similarly with chordal passages in expressive harmony. But thereafter they unfold in strikingly different ways: in SWV 432 with wide-ranging melismas for all voices in ¢ time on the word 'fahren' (depart), and in SWV 433 with lengthy tripla sections, flowing and dignified, for both 'fahren' and 'ein Licht zu erleuchten die Heiden' (a light to lighten the Gentiles). Together the settings represent a deeply sincere tribute from the composer to the royal master from whom he had gained so much; and also, perhaps, a final absolution for the minor wrongs which he and his fellow musicians in the elector's employ had on so many occasions been compelled to endure.

[15] Werner Breig, *NSA* 31, xii–xiii.

10

The Music of 1645–7: the *Seven Words of Christ* and the *Symphoniae sacrae* II

The exact origins of the short Passiontide setting, *Die Sieben Worte Christi am Kreuz* (The Seven Words of Christ from the Cross), SWV 478, are uncertain.[1] The work was not published during Schütz's lifetime, and the only record of it from that period occurs in a Naumburg catalogue of 1657, where its final chorus is listed. After the composer's death the composition remained lost until 1855, when its original partbooks were discovered at Kassel by Otto Kade and transcribed into score, a year later, by Friedrich Chrysander. The highly charged emotional style of the work, together with the technical mastery it displays, suggests a likely date of origin in the mid-1640s, probably around the time of the 'Vater Abraham' and 'Es gingen zweene Menschen' dialogues, with which it appears to have most in common—though its unique character makes it difficult to relate very closely to other works by the composer—but before the last two volumes of his *Symphoniae sacrae*. Because of the skilful course around the twin hazards of sentimentality and banality which a sensitive treatment of its subject necessarily demands, it is not surprising that, apart from the expressive choral work derived, *c.* 1795, either by Haydn, or his brother Michael, from the former's fine sequence of orchestral movements based on *The Seven Last Words*, Schütz's setting has had few successors of distinction.

The texts adopted by Schütz are derived from two different sources: a condensed account of the Crucifixion of Christ and his final words from the Cross, from the renowned gospel harmony published in 1526 by Johann Bugenhagen;[2] and the first and last verses of the ancient Passion chorale 'Da Jesus an dem Kreuze stund' by Johann Böschenstein (1472–1539). Bugenhagen's biblical text, amalgamated from all four gospels, is one which was used for the concluding part of their Passion settings by a number of sixteenth- and seventeenth-century composers, mainly but not exclusively, for works in a through-composed, motet style. In addition to the Seven Last Words, the text contains abbreviated linking passages of narrative, also drawn from several gospels, which are designed to provide only

---

[1] *Die sieben Worte unsers lieben Erlösers und Seeligmachers Jesu Christi*, NSA, 2.
[2] *Die Historia des Leidens und der Auferstehung unsers Herrn Jesu Christi aus den vier Evangelisten* (Wittenberg, 1526).

the gist of the biblical account.[3] Schütz bases the central part of his work on this condensed text, and for his outer framework (within which there is an inner one for instruments alone), adopts the first and last verses of Böschenstein's hymn, starting respectively, 'Da Jesus an dem Kreuze stund' and 'Wer Gottes Marter in Ehren hat'. The other seven stanzas (2 to 8), which are not used by Schütz, contain in turn poetic versions of each of Christ's seven last sayings.

The provenance of the Seven Words and their positioning in Schütz's work is as follows:

Fig. 4

(1) Vater, vergieb ihnen, denn sie wissen nicht was sie tun.

Father, forgive them, for they know not what they do. (Luke 23: 34)

(2) Weib, siehe, das ist dein Sohn, [Johannes], siehe das ist dein Mutter.

Woman, behold thy son [John], behold thy mother. (John 19: 26–7)

(3) Wahrlich, ich sage dir, heute wirst du mit mir im Paradies sein.

Verily, I say unto thee, today shalt thou be with me in paradise. (Luke 23: 43)

(4) Eli, Eli lama asabthani?

My God, my God, why hast thou forsaken me? (Matthew 27: 46) and (Mark 15: 34)

(5) Mich dürstet.

I thirst. (John 19: 28)

(6) Es ist vollbracht.

It is finished. (John 19: 30)

(7) Vater, ich befehle meinen Geist in deine Hände.

Father, into thy hands I commend my spirit. (Luke 23: 46)

Since the sayings are located in different gospels no definitive order can be established for them. It seems likely, therefore, that the sequence adopted in particular areas may have depended simply upon local custom. The order used by Schütz corresponds to that found in Böschenstein's hymn, and is retained in a later setting of the Seven Words by Augustin Pfleger (Gottorf, 1670). It differs, however, from the sequence used in the Latin-texted motet Passion by the Frenchman Antoine de Longueval (*c.*1510, probably the oldest extant setting in a through-composed style), where the sayings 2 and 3, and 6 and 7 (as shown in Fig. 4) appear in reversed order. Changes found in other similarly constructed Lutheran Passions, include the reversal of sayings 2 and 3 in a Latin-texted work by Balthazar Resinarius (Wittemberg,

---

[3] In one instance compression has led to a curious error. Following Jesus's fifth Word 'I thirst', the narrative section, which reads in the original (John 19:29) 'and they filled a sponge with vinegar, and put it upon hyssop' (sie fülleten einen Schwamm mit dem Essige und legten ihm um einen Ysopen), is condensed to become 'they took a sponge and filled it with vinegar and hyssop' (sie nahm einen Schwamm und füllet ihn mit Essig und Ysopen'), thus distorting the meaning of hyssop as a plant whose twigs were used in Jewish rites for sprinkling. This compression is not peculiar to Schütz's work; it is found as early as 1568 in a St John Passion by Joachim a Burck, and in settings by Demantius (1631) and Selle (1643).

1543), and of sayings 4 and 5 in a German St John Passion by Leonhard Lechner (Nuremberg, 1594).

Schütz's setting is scored for five solo voices (SATTB), and a group of five unspecified instruments (also designated SATTB with the appropriate clefs), together with a single continuo part, which is no doubt intended to serve both ensembles. The mode, corresponding to that of the ancient melody associated with Böschenstein's hymn, is Phrygian, but rendered by means of D sharps and F sharps, particularly at cadence points, close to a modern E minor. The part of Christ is taken throughout by the second tenor—rather surprisingly since the traditional practice in Passion settings was to represent the Saviour by a bass soloist—and the words of the thieves crucified to the left and right of Jesus (the only other characters) by the alto and bass soloists, respectively. For the narrative sections, in an entirely surprising manner, three of the soloists—soprano, alto and tenor 1—are employed, both individually and on three occasions, with the bass added, as a four-part ensemble, possibly as a way of distributing the musical interest as widely as possible amongst the participating singers. In order to highlight the intensely emotional settings of Jesus's words, a plain musical style is employed for both the solo singers' narration and the sayings of the thieves, with narrow melodic ranges and a sparing use of repetition or rhetorical figuration. Schütz, however, does not fail to exploit his differing voice-types for dramatic and pictorial ends. A fine example is provided by the dialogue between Jesus and the two thieves. By scoring the words of the thief on the left-hand side for an alto (the voice-type commonly used to portray Judas in Passion settings) he creates a vivid contrast not only with the robust bass-voice colouring of the words of the faithful robber—'Lord, remember me when thou comest into thy kingdom' (Herr, gedenke an mich, wenn du in dein Reich kommet)—but also with the expressive tenor-voice character of Jesus's reassuring response—'Verily I say unto thee, today shalt thou be with me in paradise (Wahrlich, ich sage dir, heute wirst du mit mir im Paradeis sein), the third of the Last Words. Furthermore, by using a soprano narrator to introduce this interchange, he carefully enhances its wholly male-voice character. By his adoption of a four-voice (SATB) ensemble for the narrative section which precedes the fourth Word—the climactic cry of 'Eli, Eli, lama asabthani'—the composer appears to invite the listener to witness in imagination a small group standing at the foot of the Cross, who, with their sombre rising sequences on the phrase 'schrei Jesus laut und sprach' (Jesus cried with a loud voice and said), give apt expression to their mingled astonishment and despair.

The five-voice settings of the two Böschenstein stanzas (designated *Introitus* and *Conclusio*), were clearly intended by the composer to be supported by the instrumental ensemble, and the instruments involved (on the evidence of those used similarly in Intermedium 2 of the *Christmas History* (see p. 151) to be viols, in treble tenor and bass sizes. Very unusual, however, is the way he requires his players to perform the independent, thirty-bar symphonia, mentioned earlier, immediately after the *Introitus* and (exactly repeated) before the *Conclusio*, as an inner framework to the central gospel account. As a rare example of purely instrumental writing by the composer[4] this short section is greatly to be treasured; but its style, appropriately enough in the context, is very subdued and in practically every respect decidedly more vocal than instrumental in character. Throughout the central part of the work the two topmost instruments of the ensemble (marked 'Vox suprema instrumentalis' and 'Altus instrumentalis'), supported by the continuo, provide tiny sections of imitative writing to accompany the sung Words of Jesus, and thus provide the 'halo' of instrumental sound which was to become increasingly common in Passions of the period, and which reached its most compelling form in the setting of Christ's words throughout J. S. Bach's St Matthew Passion.

With the aim of achieving the maximum realism of effect, Schütz allows himself some liberty in his treatment of the biblical text. Two devices, found particularly in the fourth, sixth, and seventh of Jesus's utterances, are rhetorical repetition and the splitting of melodic phrases by means of rests. In the fourth of these, for example, the opening word 'Eli' occurs three times in a descending pattern, with intervening rests, before the last two words 'lama asabathani', again separated by rests, are reached; and then the whole passage recurs, this time with a single 'Eli' and a repetition of the final words.[5] And in the setting of the seventh utterance, the opening word, 'Vater', is repeated no less than three times against fragmentary imitations on the viols; the climax of this passage is reached with top e' at its second repetition in bar 4, after which the melodic line descends a full octave with a single repeat of the final phrase, 'in deine Hände' (see Ex. 31). In each case, by inserting rests, the composer succeeds in conveying most vividly the Saviour's gasping utterances under the torture of crucifixion. Particularly striking is the use he makes of the device in the setting of the sixth Word, 'Es ist vollbracht' (It is finished) where, after an initial rapid statement, the words move gradually upwards (to top e') in minims, with a minim rest interposed between each, and with a descending imitative pattern in long notes for the upper instrument (x in Ex. 32). Strangely moving at this point is the way Schütz, no doubt unconsciously, has transferred the madrigalian *sospiro* (sigh) from its common association with profane love, to love in its most sacred form.

It remains to consider whether or not Schütz makes any use of the anonymous melody associated with Böschenstein's hymn. Amongst German authorities, Moser[6] says emphatically not, and suggests that a lost sacred

---

[4] The nearest parallel is provided by the simple instrumental prelude and postlude attached to the Annunciation settings, SWV 333 and 334, in the second set of *Kleiner geistliche Konzerte*.

[5] In a strange departure from tradition, the German *translation* of this 'Word' is allotted also to Jesus rather than to the Evangelist.

[6] Mos/Pf, 494.

Ex. 31

melody of folk origin may have served Schütz as the basis of his chorus settings; and Kretschmar,[7] who also proposes a link with an ancient folk
melody, provides little evidence in support of his view. As we have seen earlier, particularly in connection with the *Kleine geistliche Konzerte*, Schütz,
in his elaborate polyphonic settings of chorale texts, tends to avoid a strict
cantus firmus form of treatment, preferring to infuse his textures with tiny
motifs drawn from the hymn's melody; and it is possible that some similar
process may have been employed, however covertly, in the oratorio's opening chorus. The connection is most evident in the initial phrases of the two

Ex. 32

[7] H. Kretschmar, *Führer durch den Konzertsaal*, Part 2, Vol. 1, *Kirchliche Werke* (Leipzig,
1921), 43. 'Für die [Introitus]', Schütz hat 'durch ihre dorische Färbung interessante, aus dem
alten Volkslied: "Wer das Elend bauen will" herstammende eine Vorliebe'.

melodic lines (chorale and introit), which share a descent of a major second and upward leap of a minor third, in each case from b' and returning to b' (marked x and y in Ex. 33), and a semitone rise and fall, from bar 14, again from b', on 'und ihm sein Leichnam [war verwundt]' (marked z in Ex. 33). At later stages in Schütz's polyphonic texture an upward leap of a minor third continues to fulfil an important role, and it may well be significant that the interval of a third, both rising and falling, features prominently in the voice-part of both the first and second (final section) of Jesus's utterances.

Ex. 33

If our conjectural dating of the work is reasonably accurate, it must have appeared at a time when composers were beginning, in defiance of the traditional ban on the use of instruments and non-liturgical texts during Holy Week, to compose Passion settings of increasing elaboration. One of the earliest examples, the second St John Passion of Thomas Selle (Hamburg, 1643), involves motet settings (so-called 'intermedia') of biblical and hymn texts, together with a large body of instruments, including flutes, bassoons, cornetts, a trombone, strings (violins and viols), and organ, which functions both as an accompaniment and as a means of characterization. In a lengthy preface Selle makes it clear that he is prepared 'in accordance with local custom' to allow the work to be performed in a number of different ways, most radically without either the Intermedia or the instruments,[8]

[8] Selle states that, to conform to local custom, the work may be performed: (i) without Intermedia or orchestra; (ii) without Intermedia but *with* orchestra; (iii) with Intermedia but

thus showing a degree of caution which was only gradually shed by his successors. It is hard to imagine, in view of its essential scoring characteristics, that any similar type of simplification could have been envisaged by Schütz for the *Seven Words*. If his miniature oratorio was in fact ever accepted within the severely orthodox religious ambience of Dresden, it is most likely to have been performed, somewhat in the manner of the more elaborate forms of Passion music in J. S. Bach's time, as an entirely separate devotional act, beyond the framework of accepted liturgical practice.

In May 1647 Schütz published at Dresden, with a dedication to the Crown Prince Christian of Denmark, his second set of *Symphoniae sacrae*, a collection of twenty-seven concertos to German texts, for from one to three solo voices, two obbligato instruments, and continuo. As customarily with Schütz, the works are set in order according to the size of the ensemble involved—from three to five parts—and with the high-voice settings preceding those for low voices. The precise scoring in individual works is left deliberately unclear by the composer. On the title-page the obbligato instruments are described as 'two violins or other similar instruments' (Zwei Violinen oder dergleichen Instrumenten), and in several of the settings a tenor soloist is proposed as a possible substitute for a soprano. It seems, therefore, that rather than presenting a definitive setting in each case, Schütz has preferred to provide a type of 'blueprint', which, if so desired, may be 'realized' in performance in a variety of ways. For his texts he draws, apart from a few chorale stanzas, entirely from the Lutheran bible; some are passages from the New Testament and the Apocrypha, but predominantly it is psalm verses, either from single psalms or combined sources, which are chosen.

Valuable insights are provided by a 'dedicatory epistle' addressed to the Danish Crown Prince and a 'discourse to the reader', attached to the collection. In the former, Schütz recalls how, during his visit to Denmark in 1642–4, many of the settings in his 'modest little work', then still in manuscript, had been performed at the Danish court 'by the King's special request', and received there with acclaim. The subsequent delay in publishing the works, he declares, was caused partly by wartime difficulties, and partly by his desire to enlarge and revise the collection. Since several of the works have survived in both their original and revised forms, it is possible (as we shall see later, pp. 118–20) to gain useful glimpses of the composer's methods of work. In the 'discourse' he describes how his earlier collection with Latin tests—the *Symphoniae sacrae* I of 1629—had been well received in Germany and performed there in many places, with the original texts replaced by German ones; and this, he declares, had proved 'a particular incentive to him to attempt a similar type of work in our German mother tongue'.[9] But at the same time he expresses concern that many of his fellow

without orchestra; (iv) with both Intermedia and orchestra. For details see the edition of the Passion (ed. R. Gerber) in *Das Chorwerk*, 26.

[9] *GBS*, No. 64, 178: '. . . eine besondere Anreitung seyn dergleichen Wercklein auch in unsere Deutschen Muttersprachen zu versuchen.'

German musicians lack the expertise to deal correctly with the latest Italian styles, particularly in the performance of 'black notes' ('schwartzen Noten', by which he means ones of short value) in passages of rapid figuration; these, he says, are too often scampered through without proper regard to the music's steady pulse. Also he stresses, for string players, the importance of cultivating a long-drawn style of bowing, if they are to achieve the proper results and 'avoid offending the judicious ear'.

In a further paragraph references are made to Monteverdi, whom Schütz had certainly met, and may to some extent have studied with, during his visit to Venice in 1629. In one, of a somewhat puzzling nature, he alludes to an opinion which he says the 'astute' Italian composer expressed, in the preface to his eighth book of madrigals (the *Madrigali guerrieri et amorosi* of 1638), that 'music [in the current Italian style] had reached its final perfection'.[10] The surviving preface, however, includes no such assertion by Monteverdi, and one can only suppose that Schütz may have been privy to some earlier version of it which, perhaps out of modesty, his Italian mentor decided eventually not to publish. In a further reference he acknowledges that, in his Symphonia No. 16, 'Es steh Gott auf', SWV 356—a setting of Psalm 68: 1–3 for two tenors, two violins, and continuo—he has 'followed to some degree' two works by Monteverdi: 'Armato il cor d'adamantina fede' and 'Zefiro torna', each of them duets for two tenors and continuo from his *Scherzi musicali* of 1632. He hastens to add, however, that he hopes 'nobody will entertain suspicions about his other settings', since he is 'not accustomed to adorn [his] work with foreign plumage'.[11] In addition to their vocal scoring and general style, Schütz draws from the first of Monteverdi's *Scherzi* its triple-time rising arpeggio figuration for his opening vocal section (from bar 14), and from the second, its two-bar ostinato (*ciaconna*) pattern which, with one shift of pitch, he maintains in the bass from bars 108 to 175. The German work lacks none of the vigour and brilliance of vocal writing of its models but, possibly in view of its sacred text, avoids the starker forms of emotional contrast which so markedly characterize the Italian composer's works.

Clues about the variety of instrumentation Schütz is prepared to contemplate are found in the fourth item in the collection, a setting of the German Magnificat. After an opening section with two violins, the scoring specified involves, in succession, several pairs of instruments which help in some degree to characterize the changing ideas and emotions of the text: two violas or trombones at bar 40 for 'and his mercy is upon them that fear him'; two cornetts or trumpets at bar 64, for 'He hath shewed strength with his arm': two 'flautini' (descant recorders) at bar 88, for 'He hath put down the mighty from their seats'; two violins again, at bar 122, for 'He hath holpen his servant Israel'; and 'two cornettini or violins' at bar 141, for 'As he promised to our fathers, Abraham and his seed for ever'. In this way he

[10] '. . . nach der scharfsinnigen Claudio Monteverdens Meynung die Music nunmehr zu ihrer entlichen Vollkommenheit gelanget seyn soll.'
[11] '. . . als der nicht gefliessen bin mit frembden Federn meine Arbeit zu schmücken.'

seems to indicate not only how a range of 'similar instruments' may, at least in this specific case, be accepted as substitutes for the basic violins, but also how appropriate changes of instrumentation can be made during the course of a work. It must remain an open question whether, with his original discretionary advice, he was referring only to this setting or whether he intended that the substitution principle might be applied more generally. But the increased variety of expression and the structural articulation attainable in a setting such as 'Zweierlei bitte ich, Herr, von dir' (Two things have I required of thee, Lord), SWV 360 on verses from Proverbs 30, in which the varying moods can be effectively captured by using flutes for the opening symphonia, trumpets (or cornetts) from bar 36, cornetts again from bar 61, violins from bar 73, descant recorders from bar 120, and violins finally from 148, argue powerfully the desirability of such a course. Certainly in present-day performances, whenever suitable players are available, this practice is frequently encouraged.

In a number of the settings the instruments contribute to a special vividness of effect by linking with the voices in spirited imitative exchanges. One example occurs in bars 94 to 114 of No. 3, 'Herr, unser Herrscher' from Psalm 8, 'O Lord, how excellent is thy name in all the world', SWV 343, where animals under the 'Lord's dominion'—sheep, oxen, wild beasts, birds, and fishes—are depicted in sharply-etched vocal patterns, each of which is immediately taken up by the accompanying instruments (see Ex. 34). In such closely woven textures as this, an important reciprocal influence between instruments and voices can be observed, whereby elaboration in the instrumental parts (not least in the passages involving 'black' notes) begins increasingly to pervade the solo vocal writing. As a result the singers are frequently confronted by new technical challenges, often involving rapid figuration, extended melismas, and jagged rhythmic patterns. However, the fully integrated style of the writing means that truly idiomatic forms of instrumental music are hardly ever to be found—not even in the separate sinfonias, which still customarily draw their thematic material from adjacent vocal sections.

Some of the most extreme vocal demands are presented, as is the case generally at this period, to the bass soloists. In Symphonia No. 12, 'Herr, nun lässest du deinen Diener im Friede fahren', SWV 352, a setting of the German Nunc dimittis (the revised version of the work written for Christoph Cornet's funeral in 1635) the bass singer's opening section, of seventeen bars, has a two-octave compass (*D* to *d'*) and embraces long and complex melismas on the word 'fahren' (depart) in rapid scales and arpeggios. In making such demands on his singer, Schütz very probably had in mind the outstanding abilities of his Dresden bass, George Kaiser ('who is not to be let go, for ... another like him cannot be had'),[12] very much in the

[12] Spagn., Doc. 5, 143 and 145: Letter, of 30 September 1653, from the Crown Prince Johann Georg to the Elector: 'die 2 Bassisten der Keÿser worbey Ich zuerinneren, das Ja E. GN. selbigen nicht weck lassen wollen . . .'.

Ex. 34

way that Purcell, later in the century, provided similarly testing passages—such as bars 245–8, 'For though the Lord be high, yet hath he respect unto the lowly', in his anthem 'I will give thanks unto thee, O Lord'—for his renowned Chapel Royal bass, John Gostling. In an altogether different vein, but hardly less demanding technically, are the curious double echoes required of the soloist, in bars 116–21 of the German Magnificat setting, which vividly convey the 'emptiness' with which the rich are sent away.

The German Nunc dimittis, mentioned above, is one of several settings in the collection which have survived in both early and revised versions, and thus provide concrete examples of Schütz's methods of working. In some cases the revisions are concerned mainly with the refinement of details, and do little to affect the overall character of the work; in the Nunc dimittis, for example, during a long melisma on 'allen' (all), between bars 60 and 64, lively dotted-rhythm patterns replace the plainer dactylic ones in the earlier version, and minor but effective reshapings are made, in bars 21, 45, 64, and 79, to one or other of the original violin parts. In other settings, however, the composer's more radical concern is to tighten his structures by pruning away excess material. A striking example is provided by No. 8, for solo alto, 'Herzlich lieb hab ich dich, o Herr' (Heartfelt love have I for thee, O lord), SWV 348, in which, from bar 60, the original twenty-two bar vocal line is shortened in the re-working to 18 bars. In Ex. 35, sections of the voice-part from each of the versions are set one below the other to show how, in the later one, an immediate elimination of two bars has been achieved.

Ex. 35

An even more substantial revision is to be found in No. 6, 'Ich werde nicht sterben' (I shall not die, but live, and declare the works of the Lord), SWV 346a/346, for solo soprano or tenor, in the final version of which bars 109 to 124 are almost entirely recomposed. In place of the anapaestic arpeggio patterns set, with somewhat inapt accentuation, to 'Ich rief an dem Namen des Herren' (I called upon the name of the Lord) in the original setting, a more precisely pointed, melodic pattern is introduced, which allows space for the supporting violins to provide, with fine effect, echoing interventions (see Ex. 36). Less significant modifications include the replacement, at bars 111–2, of the original tonic cadence at the end of the preceding symphonia with one on the dominant, so as to highlight the ensuing vocal entry in the tonic; and a more logical allocation of 'Presto' and 'Tarde' markings, during bars 114–22, to add contrast to the settings of the two halves of the sentence 'I called upon/the name of the Lord'.

The first version of 'Ich werde nicht sterben', the text of which, a compilation from psalms 118, 116, and 34, expresses a determination to continuing living in the face of great suffering, probably dates from 1641, when, in

Ex. 36

a letter to the elector of 7 March, Schütz revealed that he had only recently recovered from a serious illness.[13] When the revised setting was published in the 1647 collection a further work was added to it—No. 7, 'Ich danke dir, Herr' (I thank thee, Lord . . . for thou hast delivered my soul from death), SWV 347—and the connection between the two, already evident in their texts, was affirmed by making them as linked *partes* and by recalling the opening section of No. 6 as a conclusion to the second work. No early version of SWV 347 has survived, and it is very unlikely that the works were designed as a pair in 1641, particularly since No. 6 ends in its original 'key', rather than cadencing on a different degree of the scale as was normal with linked settings. Only two other works in the collection are marked similarly as a pair, No. 14 'Verleih uns Frieden' (Grant us peace in our time, O Lord), SWV 354, and No. 15 'Gib unsern Fürsten' (Give our Prince and all in authority peace and good government), SWV 355, each based on a chorale stanza (the former a translation by Luther of the Latin antiphon 'Da pacem, Domine') of obvious relevance to the still current war situation. Although identical in mode (G Dorian) and scoring (S/T and 2 'violini') the two works differ considerably in tone. While the first setting is passionate in expression, with numerous short-scale contrasts of tempo and dynamics, and a powerfully scored final section, with vocal and instrumental 'fanfares' for the words 'there is none other that fighteth for us than thou, our God', the second, in which the secular authority appears to be identified as the surest foundation of peace and prosperity, is more restrained, with calm

[13] *GBS*, No. 48, 141.

120

imitative writing in 3/2 time, for the phrase 'that we may lead a serene and quiet life', providing its chief element of contrast. Of the plainchant melody on which the original chorale of No. 14 is based, only the first line is traceable, set in a disguised form in the upper voice part in bars 20 to 24.

The 'fanfare' motifs found in 'Verleih uns Frieden' provide one example amongst several in Schütz's settings of the so-called *stile concitato*, which Monteverdi introduced with striking effect in *Il combattimento di Tancredi e Clorinda* in 1624, and again used in his eighth book of madrigals, the *Madrigali guerrieri et amorosi* of 1638. In his preface to the madrigal collection the Italian composer contrasts the new 'agitated' style with the 'soft' (*molle*) and 'moderate' (*temperato*) styles and, citing Book 3 of Plato's *Republic* (which, incidentally, he misnames *Rhetoric*), claims for it the ability to express 'the accents of a brave man who is engaged in warfare'. In order to enhance his settings of texts which, as he puts it, 'express anger or disdain', Monteverdi employs rapidly repeated notes, pounding rhythms, and fanfare-like arpeggios. Although the results are vividly stirring they are hardly new; as Denis Arnold pointed out, effects of a similar nature had been current in battle pieces, by Jannequin and others, since at least the middle of the sixteenth century.[14] In Schütz's case the technique is applied to two different types of text: those involving military metaphors or actual references to warfare, as in the case of 'Verleih uns Frieden'; and those in which words of praise or jubilant acclaim are found in purely religious, though not necessarily more restrained, contexts. The typical arpeggio figuration features prominently in No. 19 'Der Herr ist mein Licht und mein Heil' (The Lord is my light and my salvation), SWV 359, a setting of Psalm 27 for two tenors and continuo, in matching sections between bars 52 and 57, and bars 73 and 76, where rapid syllabic writing for the singers, to express the text-phrases 'though an host should encamp against me' and 'though war should rise against me' (v. 3), is accompanied by fanfares on the supporting instruments—most aptly, in the context, cornetts or trumpets, though they are not actually specified. However, in the case of No. 5 'Der Herr ist meine Stärke' (The Lord is my strength, my song of praise, and my salvation), SWV 345 (S or T soloist), based on a composite text comprising two separate verses from Exodus and a single verse from Psalm 104, it is worship and adoration, rather than warlike action, that are treated in *concitato* style. Between bars 31 and 37, the words 'so mighty, so sacred, so awesome, so wondrous' (Exodus 15: 11), are characterized by ascending scale passages in rapid dactylic rhythm, shared, in yet another example of close-set imitation, between the voice and each of the accompanying instruments (see Ex. 37 for a short excerpt from the passage). In both these cases, it may be added, the effect of the 'agitated' section is greatly enhanced by the suddenness with which it emerges from a relatively placid background.

[14] Denis Arnold, *Monteverdi*, Master Musicians Series (London, 1963), 96; 3rd edn., 1990, 88.

Ex. 37

Amongst other settings of composite texts the most ingenious is No. 25, 'Drei schöne Dinge seind', SWV 365, in which the 'three beauteous things most pleasing to God and Man'—the unity of brothers, friendship between neighbours, and marital harmony—are set out and commented upon in passages drawn from six sources: the apocryphal Ecclesiasticus, Psalm 133, Proverbs, and the Epistles to the Galatians, Hebrews, and Ephesians. The basic passage from the Apocrypha was one which attracted many composers of the period; and for our present purposes it will be of interest to compare Schütz's elaborate working with one by Schein, in a similar but simpler vein, published in his *Israelsbrünnlein* (Little Streams of Israel) of 1623.[15] Both composers employ textures of much the same size and richness—Schein, SSATB and continuo, and Schütz, TTB, two violins, and continuo—and both, not surprisingly, make considerable play with the number 'three', with its express Trinitarian associations. Schein provides three sections, each of which includes a statement of all three 'beauteous things', preceded (as a type of 'refrain') by the opening phrase of the text. Thus, in total, he presents nine (3 × 3) settings which embrace both the

[15] J. H. Schein, *Neue Ausgabe sämtlicher Werke*, ed. A. Adrio (Kassel, 1963–), Vol. 1, 130.

'refrains' and the 'beauteous things'. Also he sets many of his textures for three voices (SSA or ATB), in most cases reserving tutti scoring for the section endings. Schütz also provides three main sections, but allots only one 'refrain' (the basic phrase) and one 'beauteous thing' to each. His whole pattern, however, takes on far greater proportions by the inclusion within each section of two further parts: an immediate 'interpretation' of each 'beauteous thing' (an example of which is given below), and a moralistic concluding passage, both of which are drawn from his wider biblical sources. In the process the fifty-two bars of Schein's setting are increased in Schütz's version to no less than 247. Nevertheless, within their very different frameworks the two works display equally great musical beauty. In the course of his continuous polyphonic texture Schein provides a different, or in some cases slightly varied, setting for each 'beauteous thing' as it returns, and introduces such delicate madrigalisms as a snatch of canon to symbolize the first 'unity of brethren' and a long melisma on 'Wohl begehren' for the final 'agreement between a man and his wife'. Schütz's more varied scheme includes instrumental symphonias and lengthy solo vocal passages, in addition to trio sections for the three male voices. Amongst the solo sections, none are more lively, nor more entertaining, than those in the first of the 'interpretations' (from bar 35), in which the 'unity of brethren' is related, somewhat obscurely, to 'the precious ointment upon the head that ran down upon the beard, even Aaron's beard: that went down to the skirts of his garments', from Psalm 133: 2. In the first of these, for tenor 1, the last phrase of the psalm text above is set to music of altogether remarkable jollity (see Ex. 38a); and in the second, for the bass (from bar 51), the concluding phrase—'as the dew of Hermon descended on the mountains of Zion'—is furnished with one of the composer's most vividly extravagant pieces of vocal mountaineering (see Ex. 38b).

Finally, special consideration may be given to No. 10, the splendid setting of Psalm 150, 'Lobet den Herrn in seinem Heiligtum' (Praise the Lord in his sanctuary). The work is scored for solo tenor with a prescribed accompaniment for two violins and continuo. However, the text, by its nature, provides a strong incentive to vary the instrumentation, in the manner apparently sanctioned by Schütz. Violins are certainly appropriate for the lively opening symphonia, and as accompanists for the first vocal entry, the melodic shape of which is derived from the initial instrumental pattern. But thereafter it seems entirely logical to adopt, as far as the pitch and other details of the scoring permit, a range of instruments which to some extent (but by no means always literally) correspond with those suggested by the text. Thus trombones provide a clear choice, in bars 35–8, for 'Lobet den Herrn mit Posaunen' (praise the Lord with the sound of trombones [the trumpet in AV]), while descant recorders (Blockflöten) might serve, in bars 42–61, for 'Lobet ihn mit Psalter und Harfe' (praise him with the psaltery and harp), and possibly an organ improvisation for the untexted passage, marked 'Symphonia', in bars 62–5. Then, in a series of contrasted

Ex. 38

(a)

(b)

instrumental colours, clarini could provide, in bars 70–83, for 'Lobet den Herren mit Pauken und Reigen' (praise the Lord with the timbrel and [round]-dance'), recorders again, in bars 84–92, for 'lobt ihn mit Saiten und Pfeifen' (praise him with stringed instruments and pipes [organs in AV]), and violins again, with undulating figuration, in bars 94–104, for 'lobt ihn mit wohlklingenden Cymbalen (praise him with well-tuned ["high-sounding" in AV] cymbals')—where the use of the word 'Cymbalen' rather than 'Becken' probably denotes the small, cup-shaped, 'biblical' cymbals, played rather like castanets, which Praetorius lists as 'Schellen'. And to achieve a last, resplendent effect, rich instrumental support could well be provided for the second utterance, marked 'Tarde' (slowly), of 'Alles was Odem hat lobe den Herren' (let everything that hath breath praise the Lord), a phrase already stamped (as also in SWV 38 from the *Psalmen Davids* of 1619, see p. 43) by the special emphasis which the composer constantly reserved for ideas that best expressed his deepest convictions.

In the ensuing final paragraph, by setting the word 'Amen' to a tiny melodic pattern, first heard in quick-fire imitation between the violins in the fifth bar of the opening symphonia, Schütz indulges, with obvious relish, in a remarkable piece of long-range thematic recall. As so often in his work, it is careful attention to symmetry and structural coherence which remains pre-eminent amongst his compositional concerns.

11

The music of 1648–50: the *Geistliche Chor-Music* and the *Symphoniae sacrae* III

In 1648, the year of the Peace of Westphalia, which at last brought an end to the Thirty Years War, Schütz published his Op. 11, entitled *Musicalia ad Chorum Sacrum* or *Geistliche Chor-Music*,[1] a set of twenty-nine motets, in a classic polyphonic style, on German biblical and chorale texts, for five, six, and seven voices, set out, in the composer's customary manner, with those for the smaller vocal groups given priority. In his dedicatory epistle, addressed to the Burgomaster and Councillors of Leipzig, the composer refers to the widely acknowledged eminence of the choir at St Thomas's church in their city, into whose care he wishes his new works to be entrusted. Its director, until his death in 1630, was Schütz's greatly admired friend, Johann Hermann Schein; and he had been succeeded by Tobias Michael (the son of Rogier Michael, the former Kapellmeister at Dresden), a gifted church composer in whose career Schütz had long taken a close interest. Over the years the choir (later to come under the charge of J. S. Bach) had gained a reputation not only for the artistry of its performances but also for the excellence of the training it was able to offer apprentice church musicians; and no doubt it was partly with this in mind that the composer designed his latest motet collection to serve a didactic as well as an artistic and religious purpose.

In the preface, one of the most important of his printed statements, Schütz is at pains to outline a general musical philosophy which he believes could profitably guide aspiring German composers of the period. After acknowledging the success which the Italian manner of composition with basso continuo had enjoyed in Germany, he advises his younger contemporaries against adopting this style too heedlessly, without having first mastered such primary compositional skills as 'the orderly management of the modes, the handling of various types of fugue and double counterpoint, the differentiation of styles, and [most particularly] the mastery of self-sufficient polyphonic writing for voices'.[2] It was on these foundations, he observes, that 'in Italy, the true university of music, where it was customary

---

[1] *NSA*, 5.
[2] *GBS*, No. 7, 193: 'die Dispositiones Modorum: Fugae Simplices, mixtae, inversae; Contrapunctum duplex; Differentia Styli in arte Musicâ diversi; Modulatio Vocum; Connexio subjectorum', etc.

for beginners first to compose a short sacred or secular work diligently without basso continuo', he himself had 'first learnt the basic skills of his profession'.[3] It is likely that such a forthright statement of his views marked him out as a reactionary in the eyes of some of his colleagues; but it is noteworthy that, until quite recently, equally strict regimes of study have continued to be seen, in numerous academies, as essential to the basic study of composition. Furthermore, he was by no means alone in holding to such opinions. In a letter to Heinrich Baryphonus, of 16 January 1651, his friend and former colleague, Samuel Scheidt, expressed similar, though less temperate, views: 'Much of our music today', he wrote, 'is so clearly false and worthless that I am astonished that everyone neglects the manner in which the old and loved composers used to write.' Later in his preface, Schütz remarks also upon 'the eagerness with which I await news of a treatise by a musician well known to me, who is renowned for his skill, both in theory and practice', a work likely to be 'of particular use to us Germans'.[4] Although its author is not named, it can hardly be doubted that he is referring to the Warsaw Kapellmeister, Marco Scacchi, in connection with whose dispute with Paul Siefert he had been called upon to act as an arbiter in 1646 (see p. 103). The treatise in question, entitled *Breve discorso sopra la musica moderna*, was published in Warsaw in 1649, and appears to have fulfilled many of the hopes which Schütz had entertained for it.

Some apparently contradictory remarks in the preface to Schütz's collection need to be considered. There is, for example, an obvious discrepancy between the composer's statement that his works are to be performed 'without basso continuo' and the fact that the original print contains an optional continuo part, described somewhat mysteriously on the title-page as having been included 'according to advice and desire, but not from necessity' (Worbey der Bassus Generalis, auff Gutachten und Begehren / nicht aber aus Nothwendigkeit / zugleich auch zu befinden ist). The likelihood is that the part was provided by the publisher, Johann Klemm, possibly without the composer's knowledge or consent, as a means perhaps of providing support to less skilled performers, or of giving the collection a more 'up-to-date' appearance. Certainly Schütz can have had no hand in the figuring of the bass line which is amateurish in the extreme. At the same time various comments in the preface seem to indicate the composer's willingness to accept some instrumental participation. In a reference to the different styles found generally in church music without continuo, he distinguishes between those 'proper to the pulpit' in which 'solo voices' are

[3] *GBS*, No. 71, 194: 'Allermassen dann auch in Italien / als auff der rechten Musicalische hohen Schule (als in meiner Jugend ich erstmhals mein Fundamenta in dieser Profession zulegen anfangen) der Gebrauch gewesen / das die Anfahenden jedesmahl derogleichen Geist- oder Welltlich Wercklein / ohne den Bassum Continuum, zu erst recht ausgearbeitet . . .'

[4] *GBS*, No. 71, 194: '. . . auch allbereit hievon in etwas Nachrichtung habe / das ein / mir wohlbekandter / so wohl in Theoriâ als Praxi hocherfahrner Musicus / hiernechst der gleichen Tractat an das Tage-Liecht werde kommen lassen / der hierzu / insonderheit uns Deutschen auch sehr zuträglich und nutzbar wird seyn können.'

used, and those for 'full choir with both vocal and instrumental parts, split for better effect into separate groups'. Both these styles, he adds, 'may be found in my present work'. He seems here to be indicating that in certain motets in his 'second style', instruments may for good effect double or, more particularly, replace, some of the vocal lines; or it may, on the other hand, be simply that he is referring to the scoring used in some of the last works in the collection where, in support of one or two solo voices, accompaniment by several unspecified instruments is actually prescribed. Amongst several less obvious contexts where instruments might be used one could cite the motets No. 18, 'Die Himmel erzählen die Ehre Gottes' (The heavens declare the glory of God), SWV 386, and No. 25, 'Ich weiss, dass mein Erlöser lebt' (I know that my redeemer liveth), SWV 393, for six and seven voices, respectively. In the former there are three identical tutti passages, the first two set to recurrences of the opening line of the text and the third to the second half of the doxology setting from 'Wie es war im Anfang' (as it was in the beginning) which, occurring like grand refrains at spaced intervals, seem to cry out for instrumental enrichment, particularly, perhaps, by cornetts and trombones; and in the latter there is an unusually prolonged succession of lightly and fully scored passages, the typical 'verse and chorus' effect of which could well be underlined by contrasted instrumental support, with the thinly-scored sections gaining as much enhancement as the most grandiose.

In the final paragraph of his preface Schütz observes, less ambiguously, that any organist who so chooses may without compunction write a supporting organ score or tablature, 'since in this style of music the desired effect may then be the more readily achieved'.[5] This again is hardly likely to have been suggested simply as a makeshift way of supporting inexperienced choralists; more probably it was intended to show how, for some works and in some particular performance venues, organ support could provide warmth and colour to the significant benefit of the music. Such a procedure would provide a perfectly rational offshoot from the *basso seguente* type of organ support, commonly adopted in the performance of vocal polyphony in earlier times. Although the modern concept of a pure 'a cappella' manner of presentation is undoubtedly beautiful in effect, it has no unassailable foundation in historical practice.

The range of styles within the collection suggests that it may well contain works composed over an extended period. Clearly different in origin from the main body of the compositions are five of the last six settings (Nos. 24 and 26–9) which, although they cannot each be dated with certainty, appear to form a kind of 'instructional appendix', with which the composer seeks to illustrate the type of study to which he was committed during his first visit to Venice. Four of the works (Nos. 24, 26, 28, and 29) are for one or two solo voices, supported by a group of unspecified

[5] 'Sondern auch diese Art der Music desto mehr ihren gewünschten Effect erreichen werde'.

instruments, and characterized by contrapuntal interplay of a severely traditionalist type; and the other (described earlier on p. 14) is a German-texted version (in seven parts, some vocal, some instrumental) of a Christmas motet, 'Angelus ad pastores', by Andrea Gabrieli, possibly included in the collection by an oversight. Other settings which may, on stylistic grounds, be judged of early origin include No. 16, 'Ein Kind ist uns geboren' (Unto us a child is born), SWV 384, and No. 25, 'Ich weiss, dass mein Erlöser lebt' (I know that my redeemer liveth), SWV 393, neither of which displays the same degree of contrapuntal finesse and harmonic variety as the main body of works. There is, however, only one work of early origin which can be dated with certainty—No. 20 'Das ist je gewisslich wahr' (This is a true saying and worthy of all acceptation), SWV 388, for six voices (SSATTB), which was originally composed in 1630 as a memorial on the death of Schein. Distinctive in structure, the work not only provides scope for several solo and tutti contrasts, but also contains within its first fifty bars a larger than usual amount of repetition, with four matching sections of music, alternately in ¢ and 3/2 time, allied to successive text fragments. Apart from the addition of one-and-a-half bars at bar 73, the revision in 1648 involved a replacement of the original, very elaborate, 'Amen' setting with one of a simpler, more dignified character, crowned by a majestic plagal cadence.

It is likely that an important incentive to Schütz to compile his collection was provided by the example of Schein's *Israelsbrünnlein*, a volume of twenty-six settings of German sacred texts, which had been published in 1623. Markedly innovative for its time, Schein's collection—aptly described on its title-page as written 'in a strange and curious Italian-madrigal style' (auf eine sonderbar anmutige italien-madrigalische Manier)—forms a landmark as significant in the unfolding history of the German motet as does, in its turn, Schütz's later set. Apart from a final work for six voices, Schein restricts himself to five-voice textures and, unlike Schütz, employs more Old Testament and Apocrypha texts than New Testament ones. Both sets, however, were dedicated to the Leipzig Council, both were clearly designed to show their authors' skill as contrapuntists, and both contain settings appropriate to a wide range of liturgical occasions, including a substantial proportion suitable to weddings and funerals. There is, however, only one text, 'Die mit Tränen säen' (They that sow in tears shall reap in joy), on Psalm 126: 5–6, which is common to both collections. Schein's version[6] is well-known for its powerful chromatic opening, depicting the mourners' tears, a *locus classicus* of early-baroque expressionism (see Ex. 39a). Schütz makes no attempt to emulate this, but starts instead with a three-voice (SST) setting of sombre Dorian phrases in close-linked imitation. The brighter mood of the second half of the first sentence ('shall reap in joy') evokes, however, a similarly vivid response from each composer,

[6] *J. H. Schein: Neue Ausgabe sämtlicher Werke*, ed. A. Adrio (Kassel, 1963–) Vol. 1, 15; also in *Das Chorwerk*, 14.

Ex. 39

(a) Schein

Die mit Trä - - - - - nen sä - - -

- - - - - - - en

(b)

wer - den mit Freu - den, mit Freu - den, mit Freu - den, mit Freu - den ern - ten

(a) Schütz

Die ___ mit Trä - nen sä - - - -

Die ___ mit Trä - - nen sä - -

- - - - - - - - en

en

(b)

wer - den mit Freu - den, mit Freu - den ern - ten

lively dactylic patterns from Schein and lightly scored trio sections in triple
metre from Schütz, set in both cases at high pitch (see Ex. 39b). Where the
methods of the two composers diverge most significantly is in their handling of the final words of the text, where Schein's 'madrigalian' flourish on
'Garben' (the 'sheaves' brought back with rejoicing) stands in striking contrast to Schütz's largely syllabic, more calmly meditative, ending.

It is amongst his six-voice settings—Nos. 13 to 24 in the collection—that
the majesty of Schütz's writing is most clearly in evidence. Based on short
plastic themes, shaped by the spoken rhythms and pitch inflections of
their German texts, the motets achieve structural grandeur by juxtaposing
sections in imitative polyphony and chordal homophony, by frequent

129

interchanges between separate groups of voices, by the use of cross-rhythms, syncopation, and variations in metre and tempo, and by short-and long-range repetitions of central thematic material. Also within the constraints of a largely syllabic style, they provide many instances of colourful text illustration. Two of the motets—No. 15, 'Ich bin eine rufende Stimme in der Wüsten' (I am the voice of one crying in the wilderness), SWV 383, from John 1: 23, and 26–7, and No. 21, 'Ich bin ein rechter Weinstock' (I am the true vine), SWV 389, from John 15: 1–2, 5, 4—show how, for the purposes of symmetry, a central varied reprise is matched to a gapped or re-ordered text. In No. 15, by omitting verses 24 and 25, Schütz is able to highlight the two grandly oratorical statements of John—beginning 'I am the voice' (Ich bin eine rufende Stimme) and 'I baptise with water' (Ich taufe mit Wasser)—and by setting them to matching melodic patterns, the second of which (in a long-range reprise at bar 44) is an elegant variation of the first, to achieve a fine formal balance, both musical and textual. In No. 21 a similar, equally effective pattern is adopted in which, by again changing the verse order of his text (to 1, 2, 5, and 4) the composer is able to ensure the recurrence (at bar 42) of the original 'true vine' metaphor, and to underline its importance by setting it (in a similar manner to No. 15) to a graceful variant of its original theme (see Ex. 40a and b).

In some cases Schütz appears to have chosen his texts as much for their pictorial qualities—and thus for the scope they provide for musical illus-

Ex. 40

tration—as for their religious significance. In No. 14, a six-voice setting of 'Tröstet, tröstet mein Volk' (Comfort ye, comfort ye, my people), SWV 382, from Isaiah 40: 1–5, an extended *tripla* section from bar 42 embraces a range of symbolic text-and-music patterns, which are almost as meaningful to the eye of the score-reader as to the ear of the listener. At bar 52, in an antiphonal exchange between low- and high-voice trio groups, the 'smooth way (ebene Bahn) made straight in the desert', is symbolized by a unison passage for all three voices in each group, based on a single note and rhythm; and from bar 61, 'every valley' (alle Tal) is depicted by a descending melodic curve in the upper voices (*a' f' c#' d' e'*) the deepest point of which is given extra intensity by falling a diminished fourth; and lastly, the 'smoothing of the rough places' ('und was hökkerig [höckerig] ist', literally 'and what is humpy') is portrayed by a splendid complex of cross-rhythms in a tightly woven three-voice (SSA) texture (see Ex. 41). In No. 15, 'Ich bin eine rufende Stimme' (mentioned earlier for its structural ingenuity), powerful realism of effect is achieved by contrasts between adjacent sections. At bar 20, for example, a barren line of falling semibreves and minims, for 'in the wilderness' (in der Wüsten), is overtaken suddenly by a finely chiselled imitative passage in shorter note-values for 'make straight the way of the Lord' (Richtet den Weg des Herren), with the word 'Weg' coloured at each appearance by an extended rising melisma in dotted rhythms. Most deeply moving in this work, however, is the simplest device of all. At bar 57, for the words 'but there standeth one among you', a sudden stillness is created by a declamatory passage (a type of measured *falsobordone*) on a tonic chord for the full ensemble (with the first tenors anticipating by half a bar), which falls away abruptly to a trio texture (TTB) at deep pitch for the words 'whom ye know not'. The picture vividly created is of the crowd surrounding John suddenly gripped by the significance of his words, and glancing uneasily about them for the one they have failed to notice.

Amongst the texts used in the *Geistliche Chor-Music* are some which are found also in other works by Schütz: the chorale stanzas of Nos. 4 and 5, 'Verleih uns freiden' and 'Gib unser Fürsten', for example, in *Symphoniae sacrae* II, and the funeral texts of Nos. 11, 12, 22, 23, and 25, at various points in the *Musikalische Exequien*. However in one case only, that of the Advent Collect, 'O lieber Herre Gott', SWV 381 (set as No. 13 in the motet

Ex. 41

collection and as SWV 287 in the *Kleine geistliche Konzerte* I), is it possible
to trace any significant relationship between the parallel settings. Both
works are in G minor (Dorian transposed) and both contain lively contrasted sections in 3/2 time for the words 'to receive him [the Son of God]
with joy'. But the most striking similarity occurs between the actual themes
used to set the final words of the text, 'durch denselbigen deinen lieben
Sohn' (through thy same dear Son) and 'Jesum Christum', and the way in
which, in both cases, they are linked in invertible counterpoint. The principal difference is that the concerto version incorporates a separate motif for
'Amen', while the six-voice motet setting introduces the word only in the
last two bars, set as the final cadence. (see Ex. 42 and compare Ex. 27 on
p. 94).

Ex. 42

Two of the motets (Nos. 2 and 19), described by Schütz as 'arias', are
more homophonic in style and involve many exact sectional repeats; they
thus form a separate category. No. 12 is a funeral anthem for five voices
(SATTB) on the text, from John 3: 16, 'Also hat Gott die Welt geliebt' (For
God so loved the world, that he gave his only begotten Son, that whosoever
believeth in him should . . . have everlasting life). Although simply set, in
four-square harmony, the work reveals most impressively the composer's
mastery of the flexible declamatory style—for example in bars 10 to 14,
where repeated trochaic patterns, for soprano and second tenor, on 'einge-
bornen' (only begotten [Son]), are set aslant the prevailing 4/4 time, and
conflict gently (weak against strong) with a similar figure, entering in bar
11, in the first tenor part. The other aria, also appropriate to funeral usage,
is a setting of the chorale text 'Herzlich lieb hab ich dich, o Herr' (Heartfelt
love have I for thee, O Lord). Scored for six voices (SSATTB), it again is
largely homophonic in style but, with varying combinations of voices,
involves a number of trio and quartet groups interspersed between sections
for the full ensemble. A large number of repeats, dictated mainly by the Bar

form (A–A1–B) characteristic of chorales, and here disguised frequently by exchanges between the vocal lines, make for a work of considerable magnitude. But, as so often with Schütz, only the slightest hint of the original chorale melody is to be found.

The late 1640s, one of the most fertile periods of the composer's career, were crowned by the third and last set of his *Symphoniae sacrae*, a collection of twenty-one German concertos, published in Dresden in 1650, and dedicated to the elector Johann Georg. On a larger scale and more richly scored than any of his works since the *Psalmen Davids* of 1619, these settings involve from three to six (solo) vocal parts, two treble instruments (designated by the composer 'violins or other similar instruments'), and continuo, together with (in sixteen out of the twenty-one concertos) one or more 'complementi', tutti groups with supporting functions similar to those of the 'Capelle' in the *Psalmen Davids*. In some rare cases where six principal voices are combined with two four-voice complementi, two violins, and continuo (examples include SWV 415 'Saul, Saul, was verfolgst du mich?' and SWV 417 ('Komm heiliger Geist') there results a texture of sixteen at least partially independent parts. In his preface 'to the gracious reader' the composer declares that the complementi should be used *ad beneplacitum* (meaning 'at the approval' or 'discretion' of the performers), and underlines their optional status by requiring that the organ be registered according to whether or not they are used. However, the importance he attaches to them is none the less made clear in a further sentence where he proposes that the four complementi part-books might be re-copied, so as to provide yet another chorus which, in combination with its partners, could supply both 'vocal and instrumental' resource. When one takes into account the important formal functions of these tutti choruses—the highlighting of new text sections, the strengthening of refrains, the creation of antiphonal effects, and the reinforcement of climaxes—it is hard to see how, in most cases, they could be omitted without damage to the whole concept of their associated settings. The *ad libitum* proposal is therefore probably best regarded as a makeshift option, forced upon Schütz, no doubt, by the uncertain performance conditions of the time.

The texts of the collection are drawn from a variety of biblical and other sources: psalms, gospels, and epistles, together with verses from the Apocrypha, chorale stanzas, and some German translations of Latin writing by Bernard of Clairvaux; and as in the *Geistliche Chor-Music*, passages from the New Testament predominate. Amongst a number of works known to be based on earlier compositions are two psalm settings: No. 5, 'O Herr hilf' and No. 15 'Siehe, wie fein und lieblich ists'. The former is an expanded version of SWV 297, on the same text, in the *Kleine geistliche Konzerte* I of 1636. The revision includes the addition, at the beginning and the end, of an identical twelve-bar symphonia for two violins and continuo, an enlargement of the central triple-time section ('Praised is he that cometh in the name of the Lord') from twenty-two to thirty bars, with various readjustments to the voice-parts, and the inclusion, from the start of the tripla section, of integral accompaniments for the strings. From even earlier origins is No. 15, a splendidly effective reworking of the wedding anthem, on Psalm 133 ('Behold, how good and pleasant a thing it is for brethren to dwell together in unity'), which Schütz composed in 1619 for the marriage of his brother Georg to Anna Gross. In addition to its lively instrumental writing, particularly in the countersubjects of its opening fugal prelude, the work in its revised form contains textures of unusual richness, including a vivid antiphonal double-chorus setting of 'Wie fein und lieblich' at the opening, and effective slow choral entries during the instrumental introduction to the *secunda pars*.

Linked by their texts are No. 8, 'O süsser Jesu Christ, wer an dich recht gedenket' (O sweet Jesu Christ, whosoever thinks aright of thee, his heart is filled at once with joy) and No. 9, with its opening phrase of similar meaning, 'O Jesu süss, wer dein gedenkt, sein Herz mit Freunde wird überschwenkt'. Both works are based on translations of the famous *Jubilus*, 'Jesu dulcis memoria', of Bernard of Clairvaux. In No. 8 Schütz takes the first five strophes (out of a total of fifty) of a German version by Johann Heermann and sets them for SSAT 'favoriti', two violins, a four-part complementum (optional, but with both voices and instruments specified), and continuo. The setting reflects the rapturous character of the text, not only in its use of high voices for the solo ensemble, but also by the overall delicacy of its vocal textures. In each of the first four strophes, for example, extended openings are provided by pairs of solo voices, S/S, S/S, S.1/T, and S.2/A, respectively; only in the final stanza—for the text 'No hand can write, no heart speak of what Jesus's love is'—are the full forces, including the additional voices and instruments, employed. The other work, No. 9, is based on stanzas 1, 2, 4, and 6 of a different German translation of Bernard's hymn. Supposedly by Conrad Vetter, this was included in Johann Arndt's *Paradies Gärtlein*, a renowned anthology of devotional writings originally published at Magdeburg in 1612. Schütz's setting—for two sopranos, two tenors, two violins, and continuo—is derived, as a form of parody, from a similarly scored Marian motet, 'Lilia convallium' (Lilies of the valley), by Alessandro Grandi, first published in Venice in 1625 in his *Motetti a 1, 2, et 4 voci con Sinfonie d'Istromenti*.[7] Apart from various changes made necessary by its new text-underlay, it is the distinctively national traits of the German concerto that most markedly differentiate it from its Italian model. Where Grandi keeps his voices and instruments severely apart, using the latter solely in independent sinfonias, Schütz blends the two to achieve a typically teutonic richness of texture; and where the Italian provides bare melodic lines to allow for improvised decoration, the German composer, aware that many of his performers will lack experience of the latest techniques, writes into his score many of the embellish-

---

[7] See Jerome Roche, 'What Schütz learnt from Grandi in 1629', *The Musical Times*, 113 (1972), 1074.

ments he regards as essential. With the insertion of this contrafactum of Grandi into his volume, Schütz completed a whole series of such 'borrowings', each (apart from the first one listed) located in one of his major German language collections: Marenzio in the *madrigale spirituale* 'Ach Herr, du Schöpfer aller Ding'; Giovanni Gabrieli in the *Psalmen Davids* (No. 13); Viadana in the *Kleine geistliche Konzerte* II (No. 9), Monteverdi in the *Symphoniae sacrae* II, (No. 17); and Andrea Gabrieli in the *Geistliche Chor-Music* (No. 27). No doubt he regarded this as the most fitting way in which he could pay tribute to the Italian composers who throughout his career had provided his most consistent sources of inspiration.

A small number of the concertos are based on familiar dramatic scenes recorded in the gospels, which necessarily involve passages of narration, dialogue, and direct speech. Their texts, more usually set in terms of solo voices with limited forms of accompaniment, may well have presented Schütz, in the context of his grander settings of 1650, with considerable compositional problems. In order to maintain the large-scale structures and rich textures characteristic of the collection as a whole, the composer, it appears, was forced to adopt Procrustean methods, sometimes seeking expansion, by means of an unusually large amount of repetition (of short phrases, or of whole sections in different scoring) or by the addition of extra text material, and sometimes contraction, by a carefully judged curtailment of the accounts. In the case of No. 4, 'Mein Sohn, warum hast du uns das getan', based on the record (from Luke 2: 48–9) of the twelve-year-old Jesus debating with the doctors in the temple, three solo voices (a choirboy treble, a mezzo-soprano, and a bass), representing the child and his parents, engage in an elaborate type of dialogue which, as a means of enlarging the structure, is designedly more repetitive than realistic. In the absence of a gospel text for Joseph, a simple imitative part is invented for him, and the parental protestations are given largely in duet form, with continuo accompaniment only. The role of the child Jesus, on the other hand, long and equally repetitive, is constantly enriched by accompaniments and interludes for the two violins. In order to support the slender text material, extra substance is provided by a solemn opening symphonia (intended perhaps to portray the seriousness of the child's debate), and by the addition of a majestic, fully scored, setting of part of Psalm 84: 1, 2, and 4 (How lovely are thy dwellings, O Lord of Hosts), the relevance of which appears to lie only in the connection between the 'Lord's dwellings' and the temple visited by the boy Jesus. Similar structural concerns may well have been raised by the text of No. 6, 'Siehe, es erschien der Engel des Herren'. Presumably for the sake of brevity the familiar Christmas story (from Matthew 2: 13–15) of the appearance of an angel to Joseph in a dream, urging him to escape with Mary and the infant Jesus to Egypt, is cut short at the end of verse 15 with words of the prophet, 'Out of Egypt have I called my son'; and as a result the account is left curiously incomplete, not least when compared with the full version of the story, provided mainly in recitative, in Schütz's *Christmas History* of 1665. In the concerto, however, as a solution to the problem of balance, the composer ingeniously contrasts the solo-voice utterances of the angel with powerful tutti settings of the narrative passages, many of them with complementum support, and thus succeeds in projecting structural grandeur in place of realistic descriptive detail.

Dialogue, narration, and instrumental pictorialism are managed with great skill in No. 17, 'Meister, wir wissen, dass du wahrhaftig bist', a setting of the story (from Luke 20: 21–5) of Christ and the tribute money. At the opening, substance is provided by a fourteen-bar sinfonia, in which short melodic patterns on violins and continuo, with repeated rhythms and chromatic ascents at various levels, create a vividly conspiratorial aura, aptly expressive of the duplicity of the questioning spies (see Ex. 43). Subsequently, in the course of a largely continuous vocal polyphonic texture, interrupted solely by short string passages, the Favorito ensemble (SSATB), in dialogue with a solo tenor representing Christ, functions both as the deceitful questioners and, with more tenuous scoring, as the narrator. Christ's famous response is represented in two halves, each with continuo accompaniment only, the manner of which again suggest an idealized rather than a realistic conception. Whereas 'Render unto Caesar the things which are Caesar's' is treated quite succinctly, with declamatory phrases in

Ex. 43

C time, the ensuing passage, 'and unto God the things that are God's', attracts a twenty-bar arioso passage in triple time, in which sections of 4, 4, 6, and 6 bars (the second an improvised 'echo' for continuo alone) cadence, in turn, in C major, G minor, D minor, and G minor (the home tonic). Finally, abandoning all sense of dramatic realism, both halves of Christ's response are re-set as a grand chorus for the total forces, with the complementum, not previously used, lending added weight to a climax of impressive sonority.

It would be unreasonable to suppose that Schütz adopted these relatively 'intractable' texts for his large-scale settings in any way capriciously. His object may well have been to effect a deeper penetration than usual beneath the literal surface of the various accounts, and in the process to create, through a projection of colour and perspective, a musical parallel to the religious canvases of the Italian Renaissance artists, whose work he must surely have admired during his two extended visits to Venice. The success which crowned his efforts is nowhere more clearly apparent than in No. 18, 'Saul, Saul, was verfolgst du mich?', the most widely renowned of all his works, in which the account (from Acts 9: 1–9) of St Paul's conversion on the road to Damascus is presented in a skeletal but none the less intensely dramatic form.[8] The text consists solely of Christ's utterances: 'Saul, Saul, why persecutest thou me?' (from verse 4) and 'It is hard for thee to kick against the pricks' (from verse 5). None of the accompanying narrative is set, nor any of Saul's questioning words, so that the focus is placed entirely upon his intense personal experience, recreated for the listener with awesome vividness. Set in Dorian D minor, the work is scored for SSATBB favoriti, two violins, two four-part complementi (to include instruments as well as voices) and continuo, and thus deploys one of the largest forces found in the collection. For the opening phrase, four summoning cries of 'Saul', separated by rests, rise from the depths in the two bass parts and lead on to a falling cadential figure for 'why persecutest thou me?', the calmer style of which at once implies a gentle form of reproach. This pattern is then repeated four times, at different pitch levels: by the alto and tenor (cadencing on the dominant), the two sopranos (cadencing on the mediant), the two violins (returning to the tonic), and finally by the full ensemble, with the initial chordal cries duplicated in antiphonal echoes between the three 'choral' bodies, and with tapered dynamics and contracted rhythms to create an added sense of mystery. A notable feature of the setting is the flexibility of its rhythms. The composer's original time-signature ¢3/1 indicates three breves to a bar, each divisible into two semibreves (Time perfect, Prolation imperfect), which in modern notation is normally represented by a 3/2 signature, with the original note-values halved and bar-lines added to provide for three minims to each measure. However, the word-rhythms in the opening statement—in which the most natural stresses fall on the

[8] It is noteworthy that this work was included in a concert given in 1864 by the Vienna *Singakademie* under the direction of Brahms, a constant supporter of Schütz's music.

second cry of 'Saul' in bar 1 and on the second syllable of 'verfolgst' in bar 2—imply, initially, alternate bars with two and three *tactus* (in modern terms, with 6/4 and 3/2 signatures); and similarly the contracted patterns for 'was verfolgst du mich?' (from bar 21) suggest a repeated phrase set within two 6/8 bars, where the 'new' quaver equals the quaver of the previous section. The whole rhythmic complex, together with the somewhat changed form which it takes, from bar 34, under a plain **c** signature may be seen in Example 44 where, for simplicity's sake, the bar-lines and time-signatures are placed in accordance with the word-stresses.

Ex. 44

For the second text-fragment Schütz provides a single phrase, initially for solo tenor, which embraces contrasted ideas—one for 'Es wird dir schwer werden' (It is hard for thee) and the other for 'wider der Stachel zu löcken' (to kick against the pricks). These are treated increasingly in isolation and, after separate development in a variety of contrapuntal groupings, combine eventually with a fully scored version of the original 'Saul, Saul' motif. Supremely imaginative is the treatment of the final section of the work. From bar 66, in the tenor line of the favorito group, marked *forte*, the single word 'Saul' is continually repeated in emphatic long notes, with enhanced urgency created every two bars by a stepwise ascent in whole tones from c' to e'; and against this the other five favorito voices, in three successive sections, sing 'was verfolgst du mich?' three times, with a rise in pitch each time to match that in the tenor line. And, to provide further expressive colour, each utterance is enhanced by a succession of tapered dynamics—*forte*, *mezzo piano* and *pianissimo*—with both complementi providing a powerful impact at each *forte* entry. This pattern persists until the penultimate bar where, following a final series of decreasing dynamic levels, the vocal texture is suddenly reduced to the alto and tenor lines only for a last murmured statement of 'verfolgst du mich?' In the process there is created not only a vivid depiction of the gradual fading of the mysterious voice, and of the 'light from heaven', but also a new, even milder sense of sorrowful reproach for Christ's words. It is interesting to compare with this work the arresting portrayal (Rome, 1601) of the same scene by Caravaggio, a painter renowned for his skill in capturing moments of violent action through vivid contrasts of light and shade and a masterly use of perspective. In the artist's version the apostle's horse, with its white mane gleaming and right foreleg menacingly raised, dominates the scene, while Saul, flung from its back, lies prostrate on the ground, with both arms raised, apparently in anguished supplication. His physical distress is obvious; but his mental state remains, almost inevitably by the nature of the medium, hardly at all disclosed. By contrast, in Schütz's setting, it is precisely this missing element—the imaginative penetration of the subject's thoughts and feelings—that, through the relentlessly unfolding character of the music, is so memorably restored. Ideally, of course, the fullest interpretation of the scene could be achieved by combining the visual and aural elements and thus allowing the richly conceived vision of each artist to complement that of the other.

Finally, attention may be called to two works more closely related to the liturgy: No. 14 'Vater unser, der du bist im Himmel' (the German Lord's Prayer) and No. 20 based on the famous Pentecostal hymn, 'Komm, heiliger Geist'. An unusual feature of the Lord's Prayer setting is the manner in which the composer prefaces each of the nine principal clauses of the text with the word 'Vater', set to a two-note figure, initially a falling minor third. As a means of attaining unity this compares interestingly with the system adopted by Schein in his setting of the prayer (No. 18 in the second volume of his *Opella nova* of 1626), in which the main body of the text, scored as a duet for countertenor and bass soloists, with continuo, is interrupted seven times by a Capella setting (for five-part 'chorus and instruments') of the text's final sentence: 'Denn dein ist das Reich und die Kraft und die Herrlichkeit' (For thine is the kingdom the power and the glory), the last of which broadens out into a climactic interpretation of 'von Ewigkeit. Amen' (for ever and ever. Amen). In both works chromaticism is used to enhance the solemnity of the opening phrase of the text—by Schein with a melodic ascent from g to c' for baritone and d' to g' in semitones for countertenor, and by Schütz, even more weightily, with two pairs of slow-moving root-position chords (for ATTB) with chromatic harmonies over roots a third apart: E flat major to C major, and F major to D major (see Ex. 45a and b).

The text of 'Komm, heiliger Geist', is drawn from a hymn by Luther, composed probably in May 1524, which was based on the ancient Latin antiphon, (*In vigilia pentecostes*), 'Veni sancte spiritus, reple tuorum corda fidelium' (Come Holy Spirit, fill the hearts of thy faithful people), which in German became 'Komm, heiliger Geist, Herre Gott, erfüll mit deiner Gnäden gut deiner Gläubigen Herz'. Luther's hymn consists of a more or less literal translation of the Latin antiphon (of which he remarked in one of his Table Talks[9] that 'both the words and music were composed by the

---

[9] *D. Martin Luthers Werke*, Tischreden (Weimar, 1912–21) 4, 334, No. 4478.

Ex. 45

(a)   Schein

(b)   Schütz

Holy Ghost himself'), together with two further stanzas of his own composition. In Schütz's setting (in Ionian C major and scored for SMez-S-TTBarB, two violins, two SATB complementi, and continuo) the three stanzas are set to different music, with varied voice-groupings (TTBarB/ SMez-SB/ and the full Favorito ensemble), and with the identical tutti versions of 'Alleluja', each of sixteen bars, interspersed. By adopting throughout the work, apart from the last eight bars, a (Trinitarian) triple metre and a strikingly lithe melodic style, a setting of fully dance-like character is achieved, in which the lightness and grace of the principal sections is precisely counterbalanced by the grand sonority of the 'Alleluja' choruses. Notable features include the use of a tiny head-motive for the opening words of stanzas two and three—respectively 'Du heiliges Licht' and 'Du heilige Brunst'—and the presence, at the centrepoint of the first two stanzas, of a colourful chord sequence—C major, 6#/3 on A, and E major, (with E minor, G major, and C major added in the third stanza)—set in different vocal groupings to 'o, o, o [o Herr]', the emotive style of which recalls bars 42–5 ('o, o, o Jesu miserere') of the solo tenor concerto, 'O misericordissime Jesu', SWV 309, in *Kleine geistliche Konzerte* II. The rich harmony of these tiny interventions returns, characteristically, during the last eight bars of the work, where a chord progression embracing E, A, D, G, and C majors leads to a final plagal cadence, in which the obbligato violins and all fourteen of the vocal lines participate, to create an impression of immense power.

12

The final years of achievement, 1657–70

With the accession of Johann Georg II, many of Schütz's former causes of concern, in particular his desire to be granted some form of retirement, were considerably eased. In 1657 new arrangements were drawn up whereby the two existing Kapelle (those of the former elector and of his successor) were amalgamated and placed under the control of the two most prominent Italian musicians at the court, Giovanni Andrea Bontempi, who had joined the Dresden Kapelle in 1650 after service as a singer at St Mark's, Venice, and Vincenzo Albrici, who had arrived in Dresden as recently as 1654, together with his brother Bartolomeo and at least five other Italian musicians, after service at the court of Queen Christina in Stockholm. Meanwhile Schütz, in recognition of his long service, was accorded the honorary title of Senior Kapellmeister, granted an annual pension of some 400 thalers, and at last given permission to take retirement and leave Dresden. It is clear, however, that his services continued to be keenly sought as an advisor to the Dresden court on musical matters, and as a provider of new compositions for important occasions there. Furthermore, as is made clear in a travel pass issued on his behalf by the elector in April 1658, it was expected that he would be present and give service in Dresden 'some three or four times each year and . . . [be] furnished each time with two fresh horses at each exchange point'.[1] The special favour showed to Italian musicians at this time, under the new dispensation of Johann Georg II, became increasingly a matter of dismay amongst the Germans at the Dresden court. Not only were the foreigners in receipt of larger salaries than their German colleagues, but also in several cases, were preferred to them in elections to senior posts. In 1663, for example, Marco Gioseppe Peranda was chosen to succeed Albrici as Kapellmeister in preference to Schütz's protégé, Christoph Bernhard, whose claims to the position were at least equally good. Also, German music began quite rapidly to lose place to Italian works, and the inclusion of masses and motets by Albrici, Peranda, and others, together with the Catholic practices of several of the 'intruders', inevitably caused outrage amongst many devout

---

[1] Spagn., Doc. 12, 163 and 174: '. . . Jahrlichen 3 biß 4. mahl . . . undt ihn mit Vorspannung mit zweÿ Pferden von Ambte zu Ambte jedes mahl wollen versehen wissen'.

9. Schütz: engraving by Christian Romstet from a painting by an unknown artist

INDEX.

FINIS.

10. Index of the *Kleine geistliche Konzerte* II, from vox primus partbook, 1639

11. 'Ich will den Herren loben': *Kleine geistliche Konzerte* II,
vox primus part-book, 1639

SYMPHONIARUM SACRARUM

SECUNDA PARS

Worinnen zubefinden sind

Deutsche

CONCERTEN

Mit 3. 4. 5. Nehmlich einer/ zwo/ dreyen
Vocal, und zweyen Instrumental- Stimmen/
Alß Violinen; oder dergleichen

Sambt beygefügtem geduppelten BASSO CONTINUO
Den einen für den Organisten, den andern
für den Violon

In die Music versätzt
Durch

Heinrich Schützen/

Churfürstl. Sächß. Capelmeister.

SECUNDA VOX.

Mit Römischer Keyserl. Majest. Freyheit.

M.DC.   XLVII.

Opus Decimum.

Gedruckt zu Dreßden bey Gimel Bergens/ Churfürstl. Sächß.
Hof-Buchdruckers/ Sel. Erben/ In Verlegung Johann Klemmens
Hof-Organistens daselbst/ und Alexander Herings
Organisten zu Budissin.

12. Title-page of *Symphoniae sacrae* II, secunda vox, 1647

13. 'Es steh Gott auf' from *Symphoniae sacrae* II, vox primus part book

14. Johann Georg II: engraving by an unknown artist

15. The electoral palace at Dresden: engraving from *Wechsen Chronik*, Nuremberg, 1679

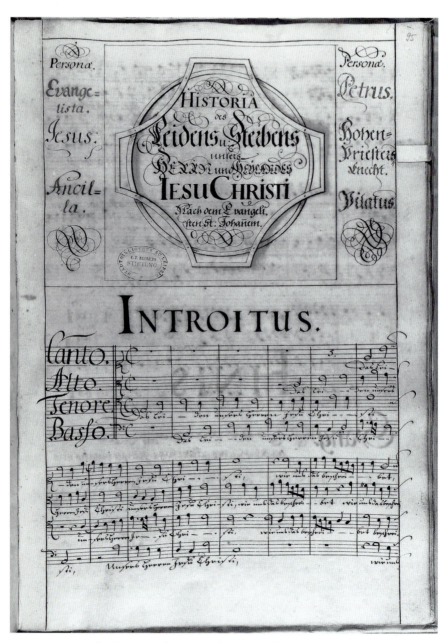

16. St John Passion: title-page and opening of Introit in manuscript of
Zacharias Grundig

Lutherans. Happily Schütz who, as we have noted earlier (p. 106), had suffered unwarranted accusations in 1653 over the growing Italianization of the Kapelle, was able to remain, in his new circumstances, relatively aloof from these latest problems.

Shortly after the funeral of the late elector, Schütz sold his house in Dresden and appears—on the evidence of a prefatory epistle, written from there in September 1657, in support of Christian Dedkind's famous collection of solo songs *Aelbianische Musenlust*[2]—to have taken up residence again in Weissenfels. During the following months he was fully occupied with his revision of the *Becker Psalter* (see pp. 60–2 for discussion of the original version), which included a final enlargement by fifty-six further settings. The work was completed in Dresden, where from August 1660 Schütz had to remain for several months at the elector's command, and publication followed in April 1661. For a time, with the keen support of the elector, the Psalter gained acceptance in public worship in many parts of Saxony, despite some reservations about the literary quality of its texts; but in the long run, its subtleties of rhythm and its modal style lost favour with congregations, and it proved unable to compete with the several other collections of the period, with their metrical tunes and regular harmonic tread. In his preface Schütz declared, 'I would have preferred (truth to tell) to have spent the remaining short period of my life in the revision and completion of various . . . more ingenious creations I have embarked upon'.[3] It may, however, be indicative of the value he set upon the work that in April 1661 he sent presentation copies of it to his admired patron, Duke August of Brunswick and Lüneburg (for his wife and himself), and in the later 1660s dispatched a further two copies, bound in gold, to Duke Moritz of Saxe-Zeitz.[4]

A further major undertaking of the period, in which, curiously, the composer appears not to have been directly involved, was the publication in 1657 of his *Zwölff geistliche Gesänge* (Twelve sacred songs) Op. 13, under the supervision of Christoph Kittel, the Dresden court organist. Like many earlier Lutheran anthologies, this volume contains a range of polyphonic pieces designed both for church and school use, including liturgical settings with a purity of line and suppleness of texture which recall the styles of late-Renaissance polyphony, and various 'choirboy' songs—a mealtime grace and benediction, a German Lord's Prayer, and a Latin hymn of thanks. Apart from two double-choir works ('O süsser Jesu Christ', SWV 427, on the *Jubilus* of St Bernard, and 'Christe fac ut sapiam', SWV 431), the settings are for four voices (SATB) with in each case an optional continuo part. The church pieces, for morning services, include German-language versions of the Kyrie, Gloria, and Credo, a setting of the Words of

[2] Spagn., Doc. 11, 169 and 171.
[3] '. . . der Ich sonst (der Wahrheit zu bekennen) meiner übrige kurtze Lebens-zeit / lieber mit Revidirung undt complirung etlicher / . . . mehr Sinnreichen Inventionen / hätte anwenden wollen'.
[4] Spagn., Doc. 44, 344 and 347.

Institution, and a motet for performance during the distribution of the elements at Holy Communion; and for Vespers, a German Magnificat ('Meine Seele erhebt den Herren') set, as are all the other pieces, in a restrained, largely syllabic style, but crafted with exquisite skill. In the first two church settings links with tradition are preserved by the use of chant paraphrase. Thus the Kyrie adaptation is based on the ancient Latin troped plainsong, 'Kyrie fons bonitatis pater ingenite' which in its free German form becomes 'Kyrie Gott Vater in Ewigkeit, gross ist dein Barmherzigkeit'; while the Gloria employs the text of a rhymed version by Luther, 'All Ehr und Lob soll gottes sein', and its associated melody which in turn is derived from a *Gloria tempore paschali* chant of the Roman rite. The Credo, based on a literal German translation of the Nicene Creed, and free from any pre-existent melodic material, is conceived, despite its conciseness, in deeply expressive terms, and strikingly reveals the composer's mastery of word-setting in polyphony of a most intensely concentrated type. Amongst the shorter items there are two, No. 10 'Aller Augen warten auf dich' and No. 11 'Danket dem Herren, denn er ist freundlich' (each in three *partes* with a central *Pater noster* in common) which are simplified, German-texted versions of the final motets, Nos. 36–40, in the *Cantiones sacrae* of 1625. Intended as a Grace and Benediction for use before and after meals, they include such appropriate text-lines as 'thou givest them their meat in due season' (Ps. 145: 15) and 'who giveth food to all flesh' (Ps. 136: 25). When all three *partes* of the Grace were sung, some guests at the royal table may well have felt that the charm of pre-prandial counterpoint hardly compensated for so long a delay to the start of their meal.

An entry in the Dresden court diaries for 1660 records the performance at Vespers on Christmas Day of a 'History of the birth of Christ in recitative style'. This almost certainly refers to the composition by Schütz (to be considered in more detail in the next chapter), since no other setting 'in recitative style' is known to have existed at that period. Later, an apparently fixed place for *Christmas History* performances was given in the new elector's Chapel Order of *c*.1662, in which, amongst details of the liturgy for the whole Church Year, an entry for Christmas Day Vespers includes *Die Geburt unsers Herrn und Heilandes Jesu Christe, figuraliter*.[5] In this case, however, since the term 'figuraliter' normally indicates a concertato style, as opposed to plainchant or simple polyphony, rather than one specifically involving recitative, the entry could well apply to settings by composers other than Schütz, such as Peranda, Nicolaus Strungk, and Tobias Zeutschner, each of whom is known to have based works on the Christmas story. Indeed, in the late 1660s, as Wolfram Steude has shown, Schütz's Christmas setting was rivalled, and after his death superseded, at Dresden, by a similar work by Peranda.[6]

[5] Spagn., Doc. 13, 180 and 198.
[6] Wolfram Steude, 'Die Markuspassion in der Leipziger Passionen-Handschrift des Johann Zacharias Grundig' *Deutsche Jahrbuch der Musikwissenschaft*, 14 (1969), 103.

In April 1661, following publication of the revised and enlarged *Becker Psalter*, Schütz returned to Weissenfels and appears to have remained there for most of the following eighteen months. Throughout this period, major renovations were being undertaken at the palace church in Dresden, and in the meantime services were transferred to the Sophienkirche and other venues in the city. The work was completed by September 1662 and on the 28th of that month a service of consecration of the restored building was held. Most of the music for the occasion was specially composed by Albrici and given under his direction. Schütz, it seems, was not present, but in the court diary a performance is recorded of a setting by him of Psalm 100, now identified as SWV 493, for double chorus and continuo,[7] which was later incorporated into his so-called 'Swan-song' (to be discussed in chapter 14). Shortly afterwards the composer is noted as having been in Dresden for the wedding of Erdmuth Sophia, the elector's daughter, to Ernst Christian, Margrave of Brandenburg-Bayreuth. The associated celebrations, which lasted from 18 October to 13 November, embraced a number of musical events, most notably a performance of Bontempi's opera *Il Paride*—his 'erotopegno musicale' (musical pledge of love) as he called it—a work of major importance, since it provided one of the main foundations for a last-ing operatic tradition in Germany and at Dresden in particular. No works by Schütz are reported as having been performed, but it is possible that the motet 'Aquae tuae Domine', first given in Dresden in June 1662, but now lost, may have been presented.

In 1663 Duke Moritz of Saxe-Zeitz, the youngest son of Johann Georg I, moved from his existing seat in Naumburg and set up his official residence in Zeitz where, in addition to commanding the rebuilding of the palace and its church, he engaged Schütz as his honorary Kapellmeister, to give advice on his principal musical requirements. The earliest documentary evidence of this is contained in a letter to the Duke, of 14 July 1663, in which the composer refers to the training of choirboys for the new Kapelle, to the need for a *positif* as well as a main organ in the church, and to the probable cost of various instruments—a bass viol, a violone, and a spinet—then under construction in Dresden.[8] It is not unlikely, however, though the evi-dence is slender, that an association between the two men, and the first stages of planning, may have begun some six years earlier, when Moritz and Schütz are known both to have been present in Weimar at an assembly to elect a successor to the Emperor Ferdinand III. Later correspondence (following the letter of July 1663) suggests that relations between the two were not always entirely harmonious. Although the Duke seems to have been happy to accept Schütz's proposal of 1663, that Johann Jacob Löwe von Eisenach should be appointed as Kapellmeister, and Clemens Thieme as concert-master, he appears to have ignored several of his other recom-mendations and, in the composer's opinion, to have made inadequate

---

[7] See W. Steude, *NSA*, 39, xvii.   [8] Spagn., Doc. 41, 329 and 332.

arrangements for the proper care of a number of compositions he had provided for the court.[9] The renovated church was eventually consecrated on 1 May 1664. Whether Schütz was present for the occasion, or whether any of his music was performed, is uncertain; but it is likely that the setting of Psalm 100, specified in the service book, was a revised version of the one (SWV 493) used two years earlier for the consecration service at Dresden.

Evidence of the close relationship which Schütz continued to enjoy with the court at Wolfenbüttel is contained in a letter of 10 January 1664 from the composer to Duke August. As a token of thanks for the many kindnesses he has received from him over the years, he writes that he is sending his patron as many of his compositions as he can assemble; and at the same time expresses his deep gratitude for 'the high honour your royal highness has agreed to bestow on them by granting them a little space in your royal library, renowned throughout Europe'.[10] Although it is now no longer certain which works the composer presented on this occasion, there has survived a catalogue, written on the same type of paper as the letter, in which all of Schütz's published collections, from Op. 1 to Op. 14, are listed, with asterisks placed opposite those 'sent to Wolfenbüttel';[11] and significantly, all the ones so marked are still to be found, in the composer's own handwritten copies, in the renowned Herzog-August-Bibliothek in Wolfenbüttel. Later in the letter he remarks that there are several, even better, compositions which he would have wished to send, but which, because of poverty, he had been unable to publish; amongst these must certainly have been the first version of the St John Passion, SWV 481a, which the composer did in fact send to Wolfenbüttel in April of the following year, as a birthday gift for the Duke. To end his letter of January 1664, Schütz, in a diplomatically convoluted sentence, refers to his 'meagre income' (meines sparsamen Einkommens) and his difficulty in 'eking out his existence' (wo nicht mich sonst unterweilen kümmerlich behelfen und hinbringen) and goes on to suggest, without actually mentioning money, that in response to his 'most humble reminder', there might be made to him 'all possible most modest amends' (hirmit mich auch zu aller mir möglichen unterthngsten vergeltung).

The court diaries provide valuable information about performances of Schütz's works in Dresden during the 1660s. In addition to the account (noted above) of 'a Christmas History in recitative style' in 1660, details are provided about the presentation of all the composer's Passion settings. Thus, the first version of the St John passion was given on Good Friday, 24 March 1665, and in the following year the full traditional series was performed: the St Matthew on Passion (Judica) Sunday, 1 April; the St Luke on

---

[9] Spagn., Doc. 44, 343 and 346.
[10] Spagn., Doc. 38, 317 and 319: '. . . das solcher meiner geringen arbeit, Sie gnädigst gesonnen, die Ehre und hohe gnade zu erweisen, undt deroselben auff dero fürstl. undt durch gantz Europa höchsberumbten Bibliotheck noch Ein räumlein gnädigst zu gönnen . . .'.
[11] Spagn., Doc. 39, 321 and 324.

Palm Sunday, 8 April; and the St John (no doubt in its revised version) on Good Friday, 13 April. That Passion composition of a strictly liturgical character should have featured so late in Schütz's career may in part be attributable to the new and detailed plan for worship at the palace church set out in the Chapel Order of Johann Georg II, mentioned above. A significant entry—the fifth, on folio 5v—requires that 'the Passion shall be sung on Judica Sunday, Palm Sunday and Good Friday', and furthermore that the music for each of the Sundays in Lent 'shall be sung in cappella',[12] indicating that no instruments, not even the organ, should be used. At a time when Passion composers in north Germany were venturing, ever more boldly, to evolve new types of setting, in which instrumental accompaniments and reflective commentary in the form of chorales and arias, were prominent features, Schütz, at the end of his career, clearly welcomed the chance to develop, in conformity with the Dresden Order, his concept of the severely traditional pattern. And as we shall see in the next chapter, the uncluttered a cappella style proved for him, as much for artistic as for liturgical purposes, an ideal medium through which to present with deepest meaning the sombre events of Passiontide.

Although, during the last years of the decade, Schütz's activities were increasingly restricted by failing health, he was able in July 1665 to attend, as godfather, the baptism of Augustus, the newly-born son of his former colleague, David Pohle. Then Kapellmeister in Halle, Pohle had been employed at Dresden from the early 1650s as an instrumentalist in the electoral ensemble, and later served as Kapellmeister both at Zeitz and Merseburg. On 15 October 1665, at a service to celebrate the birthday of the elector's wife, a performance is recorded in the court diary of Psalm 100, 'Make a joyful noise unto the Lord'; although the work is described as 'newly composed by Kapellmeister Schütz', it is probable that the entry refers to yet another airing of the setting originally written for the renovation of the palace church in May 1662—but no doubt in some further revised form. Whether or not Schütz was present on this occasion is uncertain, but unlikely. From 1667 the composer lived mainly in Weissenfels, and during that year undertook to give tuition to the twenty-one-year-old Johann Theile, the last of his long succession of pupils, who was later to achieve renown with his St Matthew Passion (1673), one of the earliest to include reflective commentary, and his opera *Adam und Eva* with which the new opera house in the Gänsemarkt at Hamburg was inaugurated in 1678. Finally, towards the end of the 1660s, when money was perhaps of less consequence to him than formerly, the composer was granted (in line with a general rise in pay for the Kapelle) a large increase in his retirement salary, the new amount of which, 800 thalers per annum, was double what he had been accustomed to receive when in full-time service to the former elector. And in 1669 he was presented by Johann Georg II, the man to whom, as a

[12] Spagn., Doc. 13, 178 and 196.

young prince, he had dedicated his first set of *Symphoniae sacrae* in 1629, and whose musical talent he had never failed to acknowledge,[13] with a gilded cup, in recognition of the lifetime of service he had so faithfully rendered to Saxony in general and to the Dresden court in particular.

[13] See chapter 6, n. 6, for the title of one of Johann Georg II's most important compositions.

The late biblical dramas: the *Christmas History* and the three Passions

When in 1664 the *Christmas History*[1] was published, Schütz (or his unidentified publisher) departed somewhat strangely from the usual practice, by releasing its main component parts separately and in different forms. The only portions issued in print were the role of the Evangelist(marked *Chor des Evangelisten*) and its associated continuo parts for organ and violone, together with a title-page which names the new elector, Johann Georg II, as the work's 'gracious instigator', and a publisher's preface which provides useful insights into the composer's intentions. The remainder of the work (marked *Chor der Concerten*), comprising ten items—the opening and closing choruses, and eight so-called Intermedia, in which the reported speech of the main characters in the story is delivered by solo voices in the form of arias and ensembles, with obbligato instrumental support—was left in manuscript, with instructions (also given in the preface) 'that it could be obtained at moderate cost, together with the printed copies of the Evangelist's part, either from the Kantor in Leipzig [Sebastian Knüpfer] or Alexander Hering, organist of the Kreuzkirche in Dresden'[2]—the latter very probably the anonymous publisher concerned.

The reason behind this apparently somewhat cavalier procedure is made plain in the preface, where the composer is quoted as saying that 'his work would hardly be likely to achieve its proper effect except in well-established princely chapels, where the necessary resources would be available for its performance';[3] and that any choirmaster who so wished might 'rearrange the concerted items to suit the resources available to him, or even employ someone else to set their texts'.[4] Clearly Schütz feared that, if the work (already of proven popularity) were to be made too readily available, a

---

[1] *Historia der freuden- und gnadenreichen Geburth Gottes und Marien Sohnes, Jesu Christi* (Dresden, 1664), NSA, 1.

[2] '. . . deßwegen entweder in Leipzig bey selbigen Cantor oder zu Dresden bey Alexander Hering Organisten in der Creuz Kirchen, sich anzumelden, worselbst mit Authoris Bewilligung dieselbigen, nebenst diesen Dreyen Abdrücken zu den Chor des Evangelisten, umb eine billige Gebühr zu erlangen seyn würden.'

[3] '. . . daß außer fürstlichen wohlbestälten Capelle, solche seine Inventionen schwerlich ihren gebuhrenden effect anderswo erreichen würden.'

[4] 'Auff die ihnen beliebende Manier und verhandenes Corpus Musicum, gar auffs neue anders selbst aufzusetzen, oder durch andere componieren zu lassen.'

number of the smaller German courts without adequate facilities might be tempted to mount performances of it and almost certainly with unfortunate results. Further difficulties, though less serious ones, warranting prefatory advice only, were anticipated with the narrative passages in recitative; 'these', it was said, 'are of a type not printed previously in German sacred works', and need to be sung 'in a clear narrative style by a tenor with a good light voice, who is able to match the music to the natural rhythm (Mensur) of the words, without the control of a rigid (hand-given) *tactus*'.[5] And 'in view of their novelty', it is suggested, 'they may be replaced at will by the older style of mock-plainchant intonation without organ accompaniment, similar to that used in our churches for the role of the Evangelist in the Passion or other sacred histories'.[6]

Much though one may applaud the composer's protective stance towards his great *Historia*, the somewhat piecemeal manner of its original publication in 1664 inevitably placed its long-term survival, as a unified work, in some jeopardy. When in 1885 Philipp Spitta issued the first volume of his Schütz edition (a volume devoted to the *Historiae* and Passions) the only section of the Christmas work still available to him was the setting of the Evangelist's role from the 1664 print, and this he relegated to an appendix. Subsequently, however, a series of fortunate discoveries made possible the assembly of an almost complete and unquestionably authentic version of the work. The first and most important of these was made in 1908 by Arnold Schering, who unearthed, in the Düben collection at Upsala,[7] a largely complete setting, contained in several manuscript partbooks. Since this source contains what is clearly a more primitive setting of the Evangelist's role, it has been confidently assumed to be the earliest version of the work—the 'History of the birth of Christ, in recitative style', a performance of which was reported (without naming the composer) at Christmas 1660 by the Dresden court diarist (see p. 144). Almost complete, this Swedish source lacks only the opening chorus, apart from its continuo figured bass (by means of which an editorial reconstruction of the whole texture has been greatly facilitated), and the second trombone part in the fifth Intermedium. In 1909 this setting, with both versions of the Evangelist's part, was included in volume 17 of Spitta's edition. Then in 1933, yet another version, again far from complete, with instrumental incipits only for the Intermedia, was found in Berlin by Max Schneider.[8] This source contains revisions to the 1664 setting of the Evangelist's part—believed by Schneider to be the composer's final corrections of 1671—and purports to restore also the first fifteen

---

[5] '. . . eine gute, helle Tenor-Stimme zu erwehlen und gebrauchen wissen, von welche die Worte (ohne einige Tactgebung mit der Hand) nur nach der Mensur einer vernehmlichen Rede abgesungen werden mogen.'

[6] 'Worinnen die Evangelisten in der Passion oder auch andern geistlichen Geschichten, bisher in unsern Kirchen ohne Orgel pflegen abgesungen zu werden.'

[7] Universitetsbibliothek Upsala, Vok. mus. i hdsk. Caps. 71.

[8] Max Schneider, 'Zum Weihnachtsoratorium von Heinrich Schütz', *Theodore Kroyer: Festschrift zum 60. Geburtstage* (Regensburg, 1933), 140.

bars of the missing trombone part in Intermedium 5. Since, however, it has no author attribution, this version is now believed to have insufficient authority to be taken as a wholly reliable guide to the composer's intentions.[9] Especially unconvincing is the restored second trombone section, partly because its imitative opening peters out uncharacteristically after only two bars, and partly because, in bar 11, it provides ungainly parallel fifths with the presumably authentic first trombone part. The uncertain nature of some of the revisions made to the Evangelist's part, and its continuo line, following the earliest known setting in the Upsala source, means that no version of the work can yet be identified as fully definitive. But the very large body of material which remains is sufficient to provide a unified and wholly idiomatic composition; one which, in numerous modern performances, has proved to be amongst the most vividly effective of all the composer's works.

More varied in scoring than any of his other works, the *Christmas History* has a 'cast' comprising a tenor Evangelist (with his separate continuo line); twelve soloists (S, 3A, 3T, 4B, Bar.) who represent the principal characters in the story; a chorus of six voices (SSATTB) for the 'heavenly host' in Intermedium 2, and one of four voices (SATB) for the *Beschluss* (the final chorus), in each case with an optional 'complementum' of viols; and a large group of obbligato instruments—2 violins, 2 violettas (alto *viole da braccio*), viola da gamba, 2 recorders, bassoon, 2 clarini/cornettini, 2 trombones, and organ and violone ('Bass-Geige') continuo—whose principal function is to enhance characterization by the provision of apt sonorities: violettas for the angel, recorders for the shepherds, trombones for the high priests, clarini for Herod, and so on. The text is formed by two linked sections of gospel narrative—from Luke 2: 1–21 and Matthew 2: 1–23—the first of which tells of the birth of Jesus, the shepherds' visit to the manger, and the infant's circumcision; and the second, the search by the Wise Men for Jesus's dwelling-place in Bethlehem, Herod's plot to kill the child, the holy family's flight into Egypt, and their eventual return to Galilee.

In order to achieve a balance between the lengthy sections of narrative in recitative and the concerted items, Schütz forms each of the latter into a well-rounded dramatic scene of considerable length, in which elaborate vocal and instrumental patterns contribute to word-illustration and characterization, and lively contrapuntal writing to a sense of vigorous activity. The order of presentation, and details of scoring, of the Intermedia are as follows:

Fig. 5

(1) The Angel greets the shepherds: S, 2 violette and b.c.
     'Fürchtet euch nicht' (Fear not)

(2) The heavenly host: Chorus (SSATTB), viol
     'Ehre sei Gott' (Glory be to God)   complementum (ad lib), 2 vn. and b.c.

[9] See Eva Linfield, 'A New Look at the Sources of Schütz's Christmas History', *SJB*, 4/5 (1982/83), 19, for a full survey of the background to the work.

(3) The Shepherds: 'Lasset uns nun gehen' (Let us now go to Bethlehem)	3 A, 2 recorders, bn. and b.c.
(4) The Magi: 'Wo is der neugeborne König?' (Where is the newborn king?)	3 T, 2 vn. (or ?clarino horns),[10] bn. and b.c.
(5) The high priests: 'Zu Bethlehem' (At Bethlehem)	4 B, 2 tbn. and b.c.
(6) Herod: 'Ziehet hin und förschet' (Go and search diligently)	Bar., 2 clarini/cornettini and b.c.
(7) The Angel appearing to Joseph: 'Stehe auf, Joseph' (Arise, Joseph)	S, 2 violette and b.c.
(8) The Angel appearing to Joseph: 'Stehe auf, Joseph'	(as in 7)

The vividness of Schütz's biblical scenes parallels that found in numerous religious paintings of the period, such as *The Adoration of the Shepherds* (1650) by José de Ribera ('Lo Spagnoletto' as they called him in Italy), the *Adoration of the Magi* (1619) by Diego Velázquez, and *The Flight into Egypt* (1604) by Annibale Carracci of Bologna. In Lutheran circles, a reluctance to admit visual religious art, with its deeply-rooted Catholic associations, as an everyday medium for spiritual enlightenment, had engendered a reliance on the association between the textual imagery of the bible and music, as the most effective alternative form of religious stimulus for their followers. Significantly, in the *Christmas History*, Schütz was able, by embedding his musical tableaux within a continuously unfolding narrative, to benefit from a dynamic, quasi-theatrical dimension, largely unavailable to the pictorial artists, and one wholly consistent with central Lutheran ideology.

The narrative setting is normally syllabic in style, limited in compass (from *f* to *d'* in the tenor range), and objective in expression; but some rare exceptions to each of these features can be found. A tiny melisma, for example, provides colour for the phrase 'und wikkelt ihn in Windeln' (and wrapped him in swaddling clothes) in the first section of the account; and a vividly telling 'twinkling' pattern symbolizes the Bethlehem 'Star' (Stern),

---

[10] The idea that parts for horns should replace those for the violins, originally specified, was initiated by Klaus Hofmann in 'Zwei Abhandlungen zur Weihnachshistorie von Heinrich Schütz', *Musik und Kirche* (1970), 325, on the grounds that the instrumental characterization, so typical of the work in general, would thus be better served—a not unreasonable proposition since violin timbres seem ill-fitted to the context. More recently, however, Eva Linfield (op. cit., 31–2) has expressed doubts about the ability of horns of the period to cope with the music of Intermedium 4, and has suggested cornetts or clarini as better alternatives, both on technical and characterization grounds. One basic, and not altogether convincing, supposition underlying the proposal to alter the scoring is that 'a mistake might have crept into Hering's publication, either through his own oversight or possibly that of a scribe' (Linfield, op. cit., 32).

both when the Wise Men are innocently seeking Jesus's birthplace, in Intermedium 4, and, with obvious irony, when Herod, with murder in his heart, is enquiring about the time that the star appears, in the narrative section before Intermedium 6. Extensions above and below the normal pitch-range depict contrasts of mood between exaltation and deep sorrow. A striking example occurs in the section before Intermedium 7 where, in detailing the Magi's gifts, the words 'und Myrrhen' (and myrrh) are set gravely to the notes *d–f–e* (see Ex. 46), with a sombre colouring surely intended to

Ex. 46

express anguished foreboding of the soldiers' offer of myrrh to dull Christ's pain at his Crucifixion (Mark 15: 23) and its use to anoint his body before burial (John 19: 39)—in Milton's words 'the Babe yet lies in smiling infancy that on the bitter cross must redeem our loss, so both himself and us to glorify'.[11] Few other instances are found where the detached style of the narration gives way to an expression of feeling; but one of particular note occurs in the description of Herod's massacre of the children 'from two years and under' where, at the prophetic words (from Jeremiah 31: 15) 'much lamentation and weeping, and great mourning, Rachel weeping for her children, and would not be comforted, because they are not', the Evangelist's normal mask of objectivity seems suddenly to fall away, to allow, with a poignant use of chromaticism, his real emotional response to be revealed (see Ex. 47).

In contrast each of the Intermedia provides consistent scope for detailed characterization and pictorial effect. The three scenes (Nos. 1, 7, and 8) portraying the Angel messenger are linked not only by their scoring, but also by the use of a one-bar ostinato pattern at different pitch-levels in the bass, depicting (as Schütz is careful to specify in each case) the 'rocking of the Christ-child's cradle'. This was probably a traditional, and no doubt well-loved feature of Christmas music of the period. One example, to which Moser[12] calls attention, occurs in an anonymous *Historia nativitatis Christi*, of 1638/9, from Breslau, in which bass patterns are found with such slightly mysterious directions as 'Orgelwiegen' (organ rocking) and 'Wiegen zum Chor', *pian'* (rocking softly in the choir) attached. The seventh and eighth

---

[11] *On the Morning of Christ's Nativity* (1629), stanza xvi.   [12] Mos/Pf., 716.

Ex. 47

utterances of the angelic messenger, solicitous and stately in turn, involve passages of a vividly dramatic character: in No. 7 a giant melisma of forty-two notes on the word 'fleuch' (flee), which provides ones of the most extravagant vocal passages in the work; and in No. 8, for the text 'Arise, and take the young child and his mother, and go into the land of Israel: for they are dead that sought the child's life', urgent vocal repetitions, supported by independent string parts over swiftly-changing chordal patterns on the continuo, by which sections of accompanied recitative are provided, of a forward-looking, quasi-operatic nature (see Ex. 48).

In the portrayal of the shepherds a charming sense of rustic simplicity is created, partly by the pastoral 'piping' of recorders and bassoon in the opening sinfonia and partly by the playful manner in which the opening instrumental theme is taken up in inversion by the voices at their first entry (see Ex. 49). The imitative textures, a consistent feature of the Intermedia, have a lightness of style in the shepherd's trio which is conspicuously wanting in the gruff setting in Intermedium 5—for four basses supported by two trombones (with the second part missing, as noted above) and continuo—of the words of the chief priests and scribes. So marked is the contrast that it is tempting to suppose that, with the ponderous counterpoint he assigns to them, Schütz

Ex. 48

Ex. 49

may have intended secretly to cast scorn on the priests, not least because of the baneful role they were later to play in Christ's life. Even more striking is the characterization achieved in Intermedium 6, where the tawdry majesty of Herod is immediately demonstrated by the use of two high (clarino) trumpets in close imitation in the opening sinfonia. As with many of Schütz's bass solos, strenuous demands are made not only on the singer's technique but also on his powers of theatrical presentation. Within a vocal compass extending over a thirteenth, from F to d', numerous repetitions of short rising and falling motifs set to 'ziehet hin' (go forth) and 'dass ich auch kommen' (that I may also come) are deployed to signify the king's ill-suppressed rage; and in a final blustering melisma of nineteen notes on ' und es angebeten' (and worship him) the basic insincerity of the tyrant's words is unmistakably revealed (see Ex. 50).

Ex. 50

Marked differences of style distinguish the two surviving choruses. In the six-voice setting of the words of the angelic host, 'Ehre sei Gott in der Höhe' (Glory to God in the highest), the assembled singers—'trailing clouds of glory'—provide a texture suffused with imitative counterpoint; while in the final chorus (the *Beschluss*), a German setting—'Dank sagen wir alle Gott' (Now thank we all our God)—of the ancient Christmas Sequence 'Grates nunc omnes', is set in a largely chordal style which provides continually for sonorous antiphony between the four-voice choir and the supporting instrumental group (in which, incidentally, the trombone parts given in some editions are certainly spurious). In the angelic chorus Schütz uses two contrasted melismatic patterns, a winding 'corkscrew' figure for 'Ehre' (glory) and an ascending convex shape for Wohlgefallen (goodwill), and by linking them with adjacent text/theme sections brings brilliant colour to the whole choral complex. Despite the many repetitions made necessary by the brevity of the text, the composer is able, by shifts in scoring and a varied 'key' scheme—from F major through intermediate cadences in B flat, D minor, and G minor—to provide a grandly structured movement of no less than ninety-three bars. Particularly impressive is the shaping of the final section, in which repetitions of the 'Wohlgefallen' motif rise stepwise in the upper voices, over a major seventh from *f′* to *e″*, to generate an ever-increasing sense of exaltation. In the other chorus, the *Beschluss*, Schütz uses the natural rhythm of the words, together with numerous 'hemiola' cross-rhythms at cadences, to achieve a delightful sense of freedom within his apparently rigid triple-time framework. Ex. 51, from bar 27, shows how varied the music looks when the bar-lines are adjusted to match the normal word accentuation. It is, however, principally from the use of persistent rhythmic groups, embracing more-or-less exact antiphonal echoes by the instrumental ensemble, that the movement's wonderful sense of joyousness results. The radiance we have noted at the end of the angels' chorus is in this final movement aptly paralleled by a pounding chordal pattern, of compelling emotional force, which is set repeatedly, from bar 59, to the words 'Singen, singen: Preis sei Gott' (Sing, sing praise to God)—a phrase hardly to be bettered as an epitome of the composer's life and purpose.

Ex. 51

und uns er - lö - set hat mit sei-nem   Blu - te von des   Teu - fels Ge - walt.

At a time when Passion composers were beginning increasingly to include in their works instrumental accompaniments, and arias and choruses based on non-gospel texts, Schütz, during the mid-1660s, with his St Matthew, St Luke, and St John Passions, maintained a striking allegiance to the principles of the traditional Lutheran *Historia*. This ancient form involved recitation in mock-plainchant for the words of the Evangelist, Jesus, and each of the individual characters, and short, usually four-voice (SATB or ATTB), choruses for the utterances of the crowd groups (the so-called *turbae*). No instrumental accompaniment was permitted, not even the organ (traditionally silent during Holy Week), and apart from an *Exordium* (an opening chorus announcing the gospel authorship) and a *Gratiarum actio* (a final chorus of thanksgiving), non-biblical material (with the occasional exception of chorale stanzas indicated by cues at focal points in the text) was entirely excluded. And since the plainsong reciting-notes from the earliest times were *f, c′* and *f′* respectively for Jesus, the Evangelist, and the other characters, the Lydian mode (or the Ionian form of F major) was used for the individual sayings and harmonized *turba* utterances in virtually all subsequent settings of this type. Schütz, himself, adopted the Lydian mode for his St Luke Passion; but in order to emphasize the individuality of his other two works, he took the unusual step of using the Phrygian mode (with the notes F and D only rarely sharpened) for the St John, and Dorian G minor for the St Matthew.

One essentially Lutheran outcome of the restrained type of presentation fundamental to the *Historia* concept, was to enable congregations, unburdened by exegetical interventions, to enter in imagination into vivid and immediate contact with the events described in first-century Judaea. Schütz, with deep insight, clearly recognized the importance of this aspect; and while accepting the general conventions of the traditional form, he imbued each of its fundamental elements with entirely new life, providing by his emphasis on imagery and drama a culmination to the genre as impressive in its necessarily more restricted way as that achieved some sixty-four years later by J. S. Bach in the realm of the oratorio Passion.

On the evidence of the court diaries (see pp. 146–7) the first of Schütz's three Passions to be performed at Dresden was the St John setting, on 4 March 1665. Described at the time as 'newly composed', this was the first version of the work, a manuscript copy of which Schütz had sent to Wolfenbüttel in the same year for inclusion in the library of Duke August. Shortly afterwards the composer revised the Passion, and in its altered form[13] it was given again at Dresden on Good Friday, 13 April 1666, together with the other two Passions (as previously noted on p. 147) on the normal preceding occasions, the St Luke on Palm Sunday, 8 April, and the St Matthew on Judica Sunday, 1 April. Thus, with one lingering doubt, it may be assumed that composition of all three works followed almost immediately upon the completion of the *Christmas History*. The 'lingering doubt' concerns the St Luke Passion which, although described in the diaries, in 1666, as 'newly composed', displays features of style—the more limited nature of its recitation, for example, and the lack of key variety in its *turba* choruses—to suggest that it may have been written earlier than the other two. Some commentators have suggested the mid-1650s as a possible period of origin, and attempted to trace a link with a St Luke Passion, of 1653, by the Delitzsch cantor, Christoph Schultze; but the evidence for this is not entirely convincing.[14] Also it is noteworthy that, together with its more primitive features, the work contains others, notably in its choral writing, which are equally as advanced in style and technique as those of its fellow settings. It is not impossible, therefore that, like the emended version of the St John Passion, the surviving work may be a revision of an earlier setting, now lost.

That the three Passions were left unpublished in Schütz's lifetime should not perhaps surprise us. No doubt the usual practical difficulties were encountered; but it is not unlikely also that the composer regarded the works as too intensely personal a contribution to the Dresden repertory to be thought suitable for wider circulation. Their eventual survival resulted from the production, more than twenty years after the composer's death, of a beautifully clear handwritten copy by Zacharias Grundig, who had joined the Dresden *Hofkapelle* in 1692. Only the St Matthew setting, the first in the volume, is positively ascribed to Schütz, but there can be no doubt about the

---

[13] The revision concerns mainly the role of the Evangelist. Previous omissions are rectified, numerous minor emendations are made to the melodic line, and in order to provide for clearer articulation, additional 'punctuation' notes of greater length are inserted.

[14] H. Kretschmar, *Führer durch den Konzertsaal*, Part 2, Vol. 1, *Kirchliche Werke* (Leipzig, 1921), 34: and Mos/Pf., 668.

authenticity of the other two: the St John, since it is a typically Schützian revision of the fully verified earlier version, and the St Luke because of its overall style. However, the presence in Grundig's volume of an anonymous St Mark Passion in a mock-Schützian style (included no doubt to complete the full range of gospel accounts) has presented a problem over which, until quite recently, generations of scholars have puzzled. The Passion is scored for the same forces as the other settings and is exactly similar to them in general structure; but on various stylistic grounds—its frequent use of rhetorical silences, its often somewhat stilted imitative counterpoint, its lack of modal influence—it is clearly not by Schütz. Nowadays, following more extensive research into the court diaries, the work can be attributed with confidence to Schütz's Dresden colleague, Marco Gioseppe Peranda.[15] The setting contains passages of effective dramatic writing, but suffers, by comparison with Schütz's taut forms of expression, from a damaging prolixity, through which the natural flow of the drama is often weakened. It is hard to escape the impression that, in attempting, not unreasonably, to match the other works in Grundig's volume, Peranda was often forced into an uneasy compromise between his own style and that of Schütz. Some idea of the differences involved may be gained from Ex. 52, in which the opening sections of the 'Prophesy' choruses from Peranda (St Mark) and Schütz (St Matthew) are set side by side for comparison. Immediately obvious is the way in which Peranda's expansive fugal opening, with its wandering melismatic theme, lacks the dramatic impact of Schütz's tightly-packed stretto treatment. And though not evident from the samples given, it may be noticed that Schütz's setting, of a considerably *longer* text, is actually two bars shorter than Peranda's.

Within the limits imposed by the nature of the genre, Schütz achieves a wide range of text interpretation. For the narrative sections of the Evangelist and the words of the 'speaking' characters, he adopts normal plainchant practice by providing pitch notation only, and by allowing the rhythm and tempo to flow naturally from the singers' instinct for word-accentuation and interpretation. But this by no means precludes the possibility of pointed responses to emotions expressed in the text. Naturally closest to the detached narrative style of liturgical chant is the lengthy role of the tenor Evangelist; but as we have seen earlier in the *Christmas History*, it is not unusual for the composer occasionally to allow the story-teller's emotional reaction to come vividly to the surface. A notable instance, in the St Matthew setting, occurs in the description of Peter's remorse over his denial of Jesus, where the narrator exploits both extremes of his compass, reaching up to *f'* for the words 'Ehe der Hahn krähen wird' (before the cock crow) and down to *d* (a tenth lower) for his account, with paired notes in drooping descent, of Peter's 'bitter weeping'. In natural contrast, the part of Christ (a bass by tradition) is invariably moulded with grace and dignity, using short

[15] See Wolfram Steude, 'Die Markuspassion in der Leipziger Passionen-Handschrift des Johann Zacharias Grundig', *Deutsches Jahrbuch der Musikwissenschaft*, 14 (1969), 96.

Schütz

Ex. 52

(a) Peranda

(b) Schütz

160

melismas and flowing melodic patterns, balanced by rising and falling curves, to impart an aura of calmness and nobility to his words, even under the stress of his trial. In the case of the minor figures in the drama, already vividly delineated in the gospels, added weight is provided by a host of adroit musical details. Striking portrayals in the Matthew Passion include, the greed and duplicity of Judas (an alto), captured by a repeated phrase, ascending in sequence, for his words 'Was wollt ihr mir geben?' (What will ye give me, and I will deliver him unto you?); the conflicting evidence of the false witnesses (two tenors) graphically symbolized by the use of canon at the second; the hectoring style of Caiaphas (a bass) when denouncing Christ's 'blasphemy', evident in a pattern of frenzied upward- and downward-leaping fifths; and the fatal indecisiveness of Pilate (a tenor), shown by a serpentine phrase, for the words 'I am guiltless of the blood of this just person, see ye to it', which stretches up to *e'* flat on 'Blut' (blood) and down by a gradual descent to *f* (a minor seventh lower) on the last syllable of 'Gerechten' (just person)—see Example 53.

Ex. 53

(a)

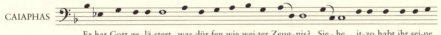

(b)

In place of the simple chordal responses adopted by his predecessors for the crowd choruses, Schütz employs a range of tightly-organized settings (some as little as three bars in length) in which word-illustration and pervasive imitation of a broadly madrigalian character contribute to a powerful type of tone-painting. By means of apt variations in style he contrives to differentiate between the calm, sometimes apparently bewildered, sayings of the assembled disciples in the earlier part of the drama, and the raging of the Jewish mob during the trial scene before Pilate, vividly portraying in the latter, by means of overlapping imitations, the effect of unsynchronized crowd voices. In the St Luke Passion a consistently modal style (Lydian, with B flats used only sparingly), affecting both the separate vocal lines and the resultant harmony, is linked with particularly effective imitative writing. A fine example is the miniature chorus 'Herr, sollen wir mit dem Schwert dreinschlagen?' (Lord, shall we smite with the sword?) where, in a passage peculiar to St Luke's gospel, the disciples offer armed resistance to those who have come to arrest Jesus. In response to the martial nature of the text Schütz leans, uniquely in the Passion choruses, towards the Monteverdian *stile concitato*, colouring his scene with typical repeated notes, pounding rhythms, and fanfare-like motifs (see Example 54).

The trial scene in St John's account, much extended by Pilate's obduracy in face of the crowd's demands, provides for no less than ten short choruses of commanding vigour. When the governor, seeking to save Jesus by invok-

Ex. 54

ing the leniency customarily offered during Passover, asks whether he should release to them their king, the mob's venomous response, 'Nicht diesen, sondern Barrabam' (Not this man, but Barabbas), is set to two tiny motifs (marked *x* and *y* in Example 55) which, by jointly permeating the whole texture, create an eleven-bar complex of singular intensity; and when Pilate declares further his belief in the innocence of Jesus, the frenzied reaction of the mob, in two 'Crucify' choruses, is underlined by the use of triple time, with its concomitant indication of increased speed, and by *prestissimo* and *presto* markings added, respectively, to the last four bars of the two settings.

Ex. 55

In the St Matthew Passion Schütz displays, by his use of an altogether richer tonal palette, increased assurance in his handling of the medium. In many cases the choruses begin and end in different 'keys', and by the variety of their intervening cadences, introduce colourful 'key-areas' away from the central mode. These features, when linked smoothly with the modal pattern of the adjacent passages of recitation, provide, in many cases, for a sustained modulatory scheme. One short example (which is best followed through in the score) will serve to illustrate the basic procedure. After the soldier's cry 'Er rufet den Elias' (He calleth for Elias), centred on D Dorian, the Evangelist's description (of the offering to Christ of a sponge filled with vinegar) moves from G Dorian through brief F Ionian and B flat Ionian passages to an ending in F. Then the ensuing chorus, 'Halt, lass sehen' (Let be, let us see whether Elias will come and save him), begins in F and passes through intermediate cadences on the dominant of D minor (bar 3), C major (bar 6), D minor (bar 10), B flat (bar 12) to conclude in the original G minor. And in the ensuing narrative passage the central mode (G Dorian) is continually modified by short subsidiary sections which show leanings towards the F Ionian, Dorian, B flat Ionian, and C Ionian modes. In the process it is not only the overall musical pattern, but also the frequently changing expressive content of the text which is enriched by the variety of modal colouring. The chorus, 'Halt, lass sehen', at the centre of this section, it may be further remarked, provides a wholly unusual example of the realistic effect which alternating rests and silences can create.

To end each of the Passions Schütz provides a polyphonic setting of a chorale stanza: in the St Luke, 'Wer Gottes Marter in Ehren hat' (He who holds God's suffering in honour), the ninth verse of Böschenstein's 'Da Jesus an dem Kreuze stund', the hymn he had already drawn on so effectively for the *Seven Words from the Cross*; in the St John, 'O hilf, Christe, Gottes Sohn' (O help us, Christ, Son of God), the eighth stanza of Michael Weisse's 'Christus der uns selig macht' (Christ who makes us blessed), taken from the ancient verse, 'Patris sapientia, veritas divina), a version of which, SWV 295, for two tenors and continuo he had previously included in the first part of his *Kleine geistliche Konzerte*; and in the St Matthew, 'Ehre sei dir, Christe, der du littest Not' (Glory be to thee, Christ, who has suffered anguish), the final verse of Hermann Bonn's 'Ach wir armen Sünder' (Ah, we miserable sinners). The St John chorus is designed as a chorale motet, in which the eight sections of the original Phrygian melody provide, in recognizable outlines, for a succession of imitative 'points'; the St Luke setting, on the other hand, has only shadowy features of the original melody, which is almost totally disguised by the composer's attempt to embed its Phrygian characteristics within a chorus in the Lydian mode. The remarkable final chorus of the St Matthew, freely composed with no apparent reference to pre-existent thematic material, is as notable for the boldness of its technique—its treatment of dissonant passing-notes, for example, and its use of inverted secondary seventh chords—as for its grave beauty. Moser, in 1936, was among the first to comment on this, when he wrote in reference to the last section—the Kyrie, Christe, Kyrie eleison—that 'Schütz [here] has had the courage to present modernisms he never previously employed';[16] and indeed it is by no means beyond comprehension that, at the start of his ninth decade, the composer retained still the adventurousness to explore new techniques. More recently, however, the idea has been advanced that, because of his intense preoccupation at the time with his *Opus ultimum* (his setting of Psalm 119, to be discussed in the next chapter), Schütz may have allowed the Passion's final

---

[16] Mos/Pf., 679.

chorus to be completed, or even fully composed, by his colleague Peranda.[17] Nothing certain can be proved; but if one is prepared to accept this idea, it may be expedient to suggest further (in view of the remarkable artistry of the piece) that, like Mozart entrusting the completion of his Requiem to Süssmayr, Schütz may have indicated his general conception to Peranda and left him simply to supply a number of the details, some of which now, not altogether surprisingly, betray stylistic discrepancies. Whatever the truth of the matter, it can hardly be denied that this eloquent chorus provides, with its tranquil contemplation of the spiritual significance of the bitter agonies of the Crucifixion scene, a wonderfully appropriate conclusion, not only to the St Matthew setting, but also to the whole impressive sequence of the composer's Passions.

[17] See Wolfram Steude, foreword to *Heinrich Schütz, Marco-Gioseppe Peranda Passionsmusiken nach dem Evangelisten, Matthäus, Lukas, Johannes und Markus*, Facsimile edn. (Leipziger: Zentralantiquariat der DDR, 1981), 8.

14

Swan-song, 1670–2. Psalm 119: *Opus ultimum*

During 1670, with his health gradually declining, and aware that death was unlikely to be long delayed, the eighty-five-year-old Schütz decided to leave his home in Weissenfels and move to rented accommodation near the electoral palace in Dresden. Once resettled, he was compelled by bodily infirmity to remain for much of his time quietly at home, and (as Geier reported) 'compensated for the religious services he could not longer attend by the reading of Holy Scripture and other books by learned theologians.'[1] In thoughtful anticipation of his demise he chose Psalm 119: 54, 'Thy statutes have been my songs in the house of my pilgrimage', as the text for his funeral sermon, and invited his much esteemed pupil, Christoph Bernhard, to compose, for performance at his funeral, a motet for five voices 'in the style of Palestrina', based on the Vulgate version of the same words ('Cantabiles mihi erant justificationes tuae in loco peregrinationis meae'). The work was completed and won warm approval from the ailing composer. 'My son', he wrote to Bernhard, 'you have done me much kindness in sending me the motet which I requested. I know not how to improve a single note of it'.[2] Unhappily, however, the composition has not survived.

In his choice of a funeral text—one of particular aptness to his natural cast of mind—Schütz's thoughts were guided no doubt by the intensive study he had made of Psalm 119 during his final years, while engaged on the monumental setting of it which forms part of his so-called 'Swan-song'.[3] In its entirety this work (his *Opus ultimum*, a 'personal and spiritual testament'), SWV 482–92, comprises settings for two choruses (each SATB), with organ *basso seguente*, of the whole of Psalm 119, together with Psalm 100, 'Jauchet dem Herren, alle Welt' (Make a joyful noise unto the Lord, all ye lands), SWV 493, and his third and final setting of the German Magnificat, SWV 494. The autograph score is no longer extant; but the discovery in 1900, at the principal church in Guben, of six part-books (now

---

[1] Robin A. Leaver, *Music in the Service of the Church: the Funeral Sermon for Heinrich Schütz (1585–1672)* (St Louis, Concordia, 1985), 61.

[2] From Johann Mattheson, *Grundlage einer Ehren-Pforte* (1740), ed. Max Schneider (Graz: Akademisch Druck- und Verlangsanstalt, 1969), 323.

[3] Wolfram Steude, ed., *Der Königs und Propheten Davids 119, Psalm / in elf Stücken / nebst einem Anhang des 100. Psalms / und eines deutschen Magnificats*, SWV 482–94, NSA, 39.

preserved in Dresden), and a separate organ part (also from Guben and now in the British Library in London), has ensured the survival of a major part of the work. The other two part-books, those of the soprano and tenor lines of the second chorus, were destroyed during the Second World War,[4] but by means of editorial restoration (skilfully provided by Wolfram Steude in *NSA* 39) a wholly satisfactory reconstruction has been achieved for the purposes of modern performance. Three sources have been traced for the work's 'Swan-song' title: it was used by the Dresden pastor, Johann Ernst Herzog, in his farewell oration at the deceased composer's home on the day of his funeral; it is found on a copy of an early version of the Magnificat, in the phrase '[completed] in his eighty-sixth year as the conclusion of his Swan-Song'; and it appears, in 1674, in the dedication to Johann Georg II, and his brothers August, Christian, and Moritz, of a further setting of Psalm 119 by Constantin Christian Dedekind who, in a reference to Schütz's work, remarks that 'he entitled it the Swan-Song (doubtless because he knew it would be his last work)'.[5] It is clear from this that the title was Schütz's own, and that there can be no reason for not retaining it.

On the title-page of the original 1671 print of the 'Swan-song' there are various departures from conventional spelling, such as 'Köhre' instead of 'Chöre', and 'Loob' instead of 'Lob', which relate to an ambitious, but doomed, movement current amongst some German poets of the period—most notably Philipp von Zesen—to bring orthography more closely into line with the spoken sound of words. Amongst those anxious to foster this practice was the poet/composer Dedekind who, as we have seen above, had close connections with Schütz and took a special interest in the publication of his *Opus ultimum*. Significantly the wording on the title-page is laid out in the shape of a palm tree, a feature which relates it both to the renowned literary body, *Die Fruchtbringende Gesellschaft*, founded at Weimar in 1617 for the defence of the German language, and to its sister organization, the *Ordre de la Palme d'Or*, established at Amberg in the same year for Calvinist *littérateurs*. Zesen, often called the 'Well-phrasing One', held a position of some prominence in the first of these societies, and it is probable that membership was an honour to which Dedekind aspired.[6] When it was first propounded, the new-fangled system of spelling was received with considerable hostility, and even in some cases ridicule, by the literati of the period, amongst them the clergyman-poet, Johann Rist, who launched a savage attack upon it. There is, however, nothing to suggest that Schütz himself held any strong opinions either for or against it.

---

[4] See Wolfram Steude, 'Das wiedergefundene Opus ultimum von Heinrich Schütz. Bemerkungen zur Quelle und zum Werke', *SJb* 4/5 (1982/3), 9.

[5] From the organ part of *Dedekinds Könige Davids Göldenes Kleinod* (Sächsische Landesbibliothek, Dresden, Mus. Schw. 26). It is interesting to note that in this source Dedekind says also that 'Schütz often reminded me to add instrumental parts to it [the 119th Psalm] *ad libitum*'.

[6] See Wolfram Steude, *NSA* 39, Preface xv–xvi, for a survey of the unusual orthography, and details of Dedekind's special interest in it.

Psalm 119 comprises 176 verses (in sustained praise of God's law), set out in twenty-two stanzas of eight verses each, which are headed in succession with the twenty-two letters of the Hebrew alphabet—from Aleph and Beth to Schin and Tau. Schütz, in his setting, pairs the stanzas to create eleven motets of sixteen verses each, and places the Hebrew letters, also in pairs, above each composition. Whether or not the collection originally had a specific liturgical function is not nowadays easy to determine; but it may well be indicative of such a purpose that each of the psalm settings (including that of Psalm 100) begins with a plainchant altar intonation, and that each composition (including the Magnificat) ends with a setting of the lesser doxology ('Ehre sei dem Vater und dem Sohn'). Also suggestive of a liturgical aim is the fact that all the psalm settings are infused with elements from their related plainsong psalm-tones and their associated modal patterns. By including transposed forms of various of the modes Schütz provides an organic system of 'key-centres', whereby the Aeolian mode—for motets 1 and 2, and for Psalm 100 and the Magnificat—furnishes a tonal framework for the whole 'Opus', and within it embraces, in sequence, settings in the G Dorian, Mixolydian, Phrygian, Dorian, G Dorian, F Ionian, Phrygian, Ionian, and D Aeolian modal centres. The first phrase of each psalm is set in plainchant (as the altar intonation) and leads directly into the first polyphonic section, allotted in each case (apart from motets 8 and 9) to the first chorus alone. The method can be seen in Ex. 56, which shows the elegant opening of the seventh motet, SWV 488, with the words 'Wie habe ich dein Gesetze so lieb! (O how I love thy law!) set to chant, and 'Täglich rede ich davon' (It is my daily meditation) to polyphony. In the doxology settings further use is made of the original chant melody: in the

Ex. 56

opening section, as a prefatory intonation; and in the eight-voice settings of the final section ('wie es war im Anfang, jetzt und immerdar, Amen'), either as a cantus firmus in long notes in the two soprano lines or, in paraphrase as the basis for imitative writing which suffuses the entire texture.

With his 'Swan-song'—a work demanding sustained powers of invention within a relatively restricted area of technique, comparable to those required of Bach by his *Goldberg Variations* or (in worthy parallel) of Milton by the twelve books of his *Paradise Lost*)—Schütz provided a climactic demonstration of his advanced technical skills. The problems presented by the great length of the text are encompassed by means of a large amount of syllabic and chordal writing, with less text-repetition than is usual with the composer. But by establishing continuous reciprocity between the two choruses, with both separate and antiphonal treatment, and by supplying finely moulded plastic rhythms for his melodic lines, the composer is able to create a richly varied panoply of choral polyphony. The essentially contemplative character of the psalm is naturally reflected in the music, but markedly animated sections and examples of word-illustration in the composer's most mature style are by no means lacking. Immediately striking is the passage from the fourth motet at bar 26, which includes verse 54, the one cited above which Schütz chose to epitomize his life's work. After a short imitative setting (bar 21) for the first chorus alone, of verse 53 in which the psalmist's horror at 'the wicked who forsake God's law' is expressed, the famous sentence is given by the full ensemble, with overlapping antiphony between the two choirs and arresting figuration at each appearance of the all-important word 'Lied' (song). A sketch of the whole complex is shown in Ex. 57, in which the two soprano lines stand for their respective choruses, and the figured continuo line indicates the harmony. In one or two places Schütz, not untypically, introduces small additions or alterations to the biblical text. One example occurs in the fifth motet at bar 99, and again at bar 116, where verses 78 and 79—referring to the psalmist's shameful treatment by the proud, and his yearning for those who fear God to turn to him—are each prefaced by repeated cries of 'Ach' (closely paralleling the non-biblical interjections found in several of the composer's monodic works) to be sung alternately by the two choruses. Another instance occurs in the eleventh motet at bar 39 where, in the psalmist's phrase, 'Great peace have they which love thy law' (Grosse Frieden haben die, die dein Gesetz lieben) in verse 165, Schütz substitutes the word 'joy' (Freude) for 'peace' and 'name' (Name) for 'law'. Curiously at this point, for the only time in the complete collection (apart from the final portion of the doxology setting of the ninth motet), there occurs a change to triple time. The reason for the text change is by no means certain; but it is tempting to speculate that it was for purely musical reasons—of structural variety, for example—that triple time was introduced at this juncture; and that it was this metre, with its many buoyant associations, which may in turn have prompted the substitution of 'joy' for 'peace'.

Ex. 57

Although firmly linked with the motets of Psalm 119, both by their scoring and, as we have noted earlier, by their culminating role in the cycle of modal centres, the final two works in the collection explore very different, less introspective, areas of expression. The setting of Psalm 100, SWV 493, is almost certainly the same, though no doubt in a revised form, as that performed on several occasions during the previous nine years:[7] at the services,

---

[7] See pp. 145–6; and Wolfram Steude, 'Das wiedergefundene Opus ultimum', 17 (n. 4, above).

at Dresden in 1662 and (less certainly) at Zeitz in 1664, for the consecration of their renovated palace churches; at a service in 1665 to mark the birthday of the elector's wife; and at Dresden, both in January 1667 and July 1668, on the latter occasion at a service to celebrate the signing of a recent peace treaty. None of the settings used at these performances has survived; but at least one report of the events specifically mentions an Introit, intoned from the altar by the officiating priest, and a response from the choir '(choraliter) in German', a general description which accords well with the final form found in SWV 493. In a diary reference to the performance of 1667, it is noted that 'trumpets and timpani' were used in support of the chorus, a practice which appears wholly consonant with the exultant character of the text, and one that might well be applied to the 1671 version. Comparison with SWV 36, the double-choir setting of the same psalm—included more than fifty years earlier, at the outset of the composer's career, in his *Psalmen Davids* of 1619—shows how far, during the intervening period, his creative range and technical mastery had developed. The works are of nearly equal length, and both are highly effective interpretations of the text; but in place of the plain syllabic style and somewhat mechanical echo effects of SWV 36, the later work displays a majestic sweep, with grandly extended paragraphs, and widely varied choral textures. Vivid colouring of the text is manifested in bars 35–45 where vigorous, closely imitative *passaggi*, taken up by both choruses for the words 'Er hat uns gemacht' (It is he that hath made us), are set in telling contrast to the faltering textures created for 'und nicht wir selbst' (and not we ourselves) which immediately ensue (see Ex. 58).

And equally impressive is the twenty-bar setting (in bars 101–21) of the psalm's final words—'and his truth endureth to all generations' (und seine Gnade Wahrheit für und für)—in which sharply-contoured quaver patterns (with one note to a syllable), distributed between the two choruses, gradually unite and, in a rising pattern of 'tumbling' imitations to suggest a host of eager voices, lead to a resplendent climax.

In the case of the final work in the collection, the German Magnificat SWV 494, the survival (originally at Grimma) of an earlier, non-autograph, version, with a full set of partbooks has largely eliminated the problem of the missing chorus parts in the Guben source, and made possible a reconstruction which is likely to agree very closely (apart from any slight modifications he may have made in the interim) with the composer's final conception. A strange feature of the text, in both versions, is the omission from St Luke's account of verse 50, 'And his mercy is on them that fear him from generation to generation' (Und seine Barmherzigkeit währet immer für und für bei denen die ihn fürchten), an anomaly which parallels the equally curious omission of verse 49 'for he that is mighty hath done to me great things . . .' in the German Magnificat setting, SWV 344, from the second set of *Symphoniae sacrae*. In neither case can any clear reason for the change be adduced, beyond an oversight or some undisclosed (but scarcely

Ex. 58

conceivable) doctrinal or liturgical motive. Typical in its technical restraint of the composer's last-period style, the work involves a great deal of chordal homophonic writing in triple time, parcelled out antiphonally between the two choruses; but by means of contrasted pitch levels for many of the antiphonal 'responses'' and the frequent use of hemiola cross-rhythms, particularly at the cadence points, any impression of harmonic or rhythmic monotony is readily avoided. The work begins with a seven-bar setting, in 2/2 time, of the opening words 'Meine Seele' (My soul), in which the full forces engage in a type of choral canon, with the first chorus providing the *dux* and the second a somewhat free *comes* three bars later.

Although the principal 'key' of the work is A minor, this beginning focuses on F major and D minor, and it is not until the tenth bar of the ensuing triple-time section that a full close (with a Picardy third) on A Aeolian is reached. This major chord then provides the catalyst for a whole sequence of major harmonies, with C, F, and D major chords, almost invariably in root position, creating for verse 47, 'And my spirit hath rejoiced in God my saviour' an aura both of joyousness and powerful spiritual involvement. Apparently unfettered by his relatively simple formal and metrical pattern, Schütz encompasses within the work a wide range of expression. At bar 105, for example, with a section of finely shaped polyphony for the words 'in the imagination of their hearts', for Chorus 1 alone, he provides a wonderfully meditative, 'oasis' of sound amidst vigorous repetitions, in pounding crotchet patterns, of the preceding passage, 'He hath shewed strength with his arm; he hath scattered the proud' (see Ex. 59). Such is the appeal of this section that the composer is unable to resist repeating it, between bars 109 and 121, with a beautiful eight-voice expansion of the 'oasis' passage. Very striking also is the opening of the doxology setting where, in order to enhance structural coherence, F major harmony and duple time are recalled, together with a further freely canonic choral overlap; and in the process there is established, unmistakably, a long-range link with the opening of the whole work, two hundred bars earlier.

Ex. 59

At the end of this, his last work, the composer added to each voice-part the letters of his monogram *HSC, Henricus Sagittarius Capellae Magister*; and below the final line of the second-chorus bass part, wrote in large letters the word FINIS, to indicate, most touchingly, that this was not only the end of his last immense undertaking, but also the conclusion of his entire life's work.

During the months which followed he was afflicted (in Geier's words) 'by occasional serious attacks of apoplexy which he managed to survive with the help of appropriate medicines'.[8] On 6 November 1672, however, just after nine o'clock in the morning, he suffered a more severe stroke and, after falling helpless to the floor, was taken to his bed. His physician was called and provided further treatment, but found that he could do little for him. A father confessor was then summoned to his bedside, to provide spiritual comfort and give him a last blessing. And finally, 'as it struck four, amongst the prayers and songs of those around him, he passed away softly and blissfully [in the eighty-seventh year of his life], without a single tremor'.[9] His funeral took place eleven days later, on 17 November. Early in the morning the clergy, Kapellmeisters, choristers, and other members of the court assembled at the composer's lodgings, No. 10, Moritzstrasse, where hymns were sung, a motet by Schütz was performed, and a farewell address was given by the court pastor, Johann Ernst Herzog.[10] The coffin was then borne in procession to the Frauenkirche for the main funeral service, during which Bernhard's specially-written motet on the chosen funeral text was performed by the Germans of the court ensemble, together with three unspecified works by Schütz 'for voices and instruments'; and a lengthy sermon of immense erudition was delivered by Dr Martin Geier, the senior court preacher.[11] The elector, it appears, did not attend, but was represented by the Dresden privy counsellor, von Wolfframbsdorff. Finally, to the accompaniment of a further unnamed work by Schütz, the coffin was carried to the entrance porch of the church and buried there 'beside his wife' (according to Moser).[12] A slab of black marble was placed over his tomb with, engraved upon it on a bronze plaque, the epitaph: 'Heinrichus Schützius / Asaph Christianus / Exterorum Delicium, Germaniae Lumen / Sereniss. Saxoniae Elect. / Joh. Georg I et II Capellae / cui LVII annos praefuit / immortale decus / Quod caducum habuit / sub hoc monumento Electorali / munificentia extructo deposuit / Aetatis suae / Anno LXXXVII / aerae nostrae / MDCLXXII /. (Heinrich Schütz, Christian Asaph, a joy for foreigners, a light for Germans, [master] of the chapel of their Serene

---

[8] Robin A. Leaver, op. cit (from the biographical section), 61.

[9] Ibid., 62.   [10] Ibid., 10.

[11] In addition to praising the achievements of the deceased, Geier took the opportunity to inveigh against the 'unspiritual, dance-like, yea, even ridiculous, modes of song' which he believed to characterize much of the latest church music. His target, it appears, was not only the increasingly Italianate (and Catholic) domination of the music at court, but also—since he spoke of 'those who for their voice's sake have been emasculated'—the presiding Italian Kapellmeister, Giovanni Bontempi.   [12] Mos/Pf., 224.

Highnesses, the Electors Johann Georg I and II, over which he presided for fifty-seven years: what in him was mortal is laid here, in the eighty-seventh year of his life, beneath this monument, erected by the munificence of the Elector in the year 1672 of our era).[13]

During the last years of his life, as an inevitable penalty of longevity, Schütz had become increasingly isolated. Most of his old friends and colleagues, together with many members of his family, had preceded him to the grave; and progressive changes in musical and religious thought had signalled the likelihood that his achievements would soon suffer a rapid eclipse. At Dresden, the importation over the years of Italian musicians had brought about a sharp increase in operatic activity. Following the success of Bontempi's *Il Paride* in 1662, the opening of the Kurfürstliches Opernhaus in 1667—with a performance of *Teseo* by Pietro Andrea Ziani—and the subsequent production there of works by Carlo Pallavicino—most notably his *Gierusalemme liberata* in a splendidly lavish performance in 1687—the foundations were laid at the Saxon court from which the city was to develop into one of the most important centres for opera in Germany, a centre which in due course was to come successively under the directorial influence of Weber and Wagner. At this stage, however, it is entirely unlikely that it would have occurred to anyone to look back to Schütz's *Dafne* as the seed, however small, from which this final grand development had grown.

In the religious sphere, population movement from country to town, resulting from the ravages of the Thirty Years War, confronted the large civic churches with greatly increased congregations; and in order to provide for a wide spectrum of intellectual perception, and to discourage any dangerous leanings towards rationalism, the resident clergy were driven to adopt observances of a severely formal kind, together with a rigid adherence to orthodox teaching. Sermons, which remained, at least in theory, of central importance in Lutheran worship, frequently became the pretext for a display of abstruse, and often tiresomely irrelevant, learning. As one contemporary observer acidly remarked: 'The sermon is for most preachers an oration, or an artificial, rhetorical speech, pieced together from the Bible, one paragraph after another. The preacher dare not stop at one thing but must rush on to pile up more and more (it is strange to find there are such inquisitive people). He must adorn every detail, taking up an hour or more before he finishes; and this is supposed to be the planting of the words of truth in our hearts.[14] In deeply thoughtful reaction, there developed, under

[13] The grave was destroyed in 1721, when the church was rebuilt, but a description of it is included amongst a number of epitaphs and memorial inscriptions assembled in 1714 by the sexton, J. G. Michaelis. The items described include an emblem showing an open book, with the words 'Vitabit libitinam' (from Horace, *Odes* 3, xxx, 7) inscribed on it. The words 'Christian Asaph' on the plaque 'erected through the munificence of the elector' refer to the 'psalm-singer, appointed to sound with cymbals of brass', whose description is contained in I Chronicles 15: 19.

[14] From Theophilus Grossgebauer, *Drei geistliche Schriften*, (Frankfurt, 1682), 34. A similar viewpoint was expressed more succinctly by Herder who wrote: 'Every leaf of the tree of

the leadership of P. J. Spener, the movement known as Pietism, which attempted with marked success to throw off the shackles of scholasticism and emphasize instead the centrality of sensitive biblical study, the devotional life, and more direct and emotional forms of evangelism—in effect to achieve a return to basic Lutheranism.

Church music, at the same time, also underwent significant change. The 'concerto', as the primary service music of Schütz's time, was gradually superseded from the mid-1660s by the so-called 'church cantata', the principal new features of which were the integration of freely composed religious verse with biblical and chorale texts, the adoption of a wide range of musical forms, including operatic recitative and aria at one extreme and complex choruses, often fugal or canonic, and often on a chorale basis, at the other, and the provision of richer types of orchestral support. Prominent amongst those involved in the initial development of the new form were the Schütz pupils, Weckmann and Bernhard, together with Johann Philipp Krieger at Weissenfels, Johann Kuhnau at Leipzig, and the renowned organist of the Marienkirche in Lübeck, Diderik Buxtehude. For these and numerous other 'cantata' composers the worship of God was thought to be best served through music in which grandeur of structure was matched with richness of texture and intricacy of technical detail. Like medieval craftsmen engaged upon the building and ornamenting of a cathedral, it was, they believed, their solemn duty to use to the utmost the skills with which they were endowed. The Pietists, on the other hand, concerned particularly for the interests of the average church-goers of the time—whose reaction to elaborate church music was often one of incomprehension or even resentment—advocated that public and private worship should be expressed solely in terms of hymns and simple religious songs. Except for the influence of some of its more fanatical supporters, Pietism, with its emphasis on personal expression, warmth of feeling, and a new popular lyricism, was by no means entirely without benefit to the development of artistic church music; but an inevitable clash of viewpoints, which often were only half understood by those involved, led at times to conflict—not least, as in the case of J. S. Bach at St Blasius in Mühlhausen, when an ambitious church composer came under the supervision of a clerical incumbent of inflexible Pietist views.

It is not surprising that, against this background of change and controversy, the music of Schütz and his contemporaries faded quite soon from living memory. Copies of Schütz's works would naturally have been preserved in several of the most important libraries of northern Germany—not only at Dresden and Wolfenbüttel, but also at Leipzig, Lüneburg, and Hamburg—and may well have come to the attention of visiting scholars. Indeed, it is not unlikely that the library at Lüneburg, a particularly grand

life was so dissected and anatomised that the dryads wept for mercy' (Quoted in A. Tholuck, *Der Geist des lutherischen Theologen Wittenbergs im Verlauf des 17. Jahrhunderts* (Hamburg, 1852), 247.

one founded in the sixteenth century, may have been consulted by the teenage Bach during his time as a pupil at the Michaelisschule there from 1700. The library possessed a rich collection of sacred polyphony both of the Renaissance masters and of the greatest of the seventeenth-century Germans, including Schütz, Schein, and Scheidt; and if, as a mere school-boy, Bach was allowed to use its facilities, he can hardly have failed to learn something of the methods of composition common in Schütz's day.

Direct links between Schütz and Bach are not, however, easy to trace. Apart from the striking coincidence that both their birth-dates and their first formative encounters with Italian music (Schütz at Venice in 1610–13 and Bach at Weimar in 1711–13) are separated by almost exactly a hundred years, it is through their commitment to orthodox Lutheranism, and to the biblical and hymn texts upon which its tenets firmly rest, that they are most closely interconnected. In purely musical terms the nearest stylistic parallel is probably to be found between the larger settings in Schütz's *Geistliche Chor-Music* and various of Bach's motets, with their common exclusion of free poetic texts and integrated instrumental support (apart possibly from the continuo), and their broadly similar liturgical aims, particularly for funerals and other, primarily commemorative, occasions. But this apart, the gulf between the two composers, though negligible in terms of years, is all but unbridgeable in regard to style and technique. By the early eighteenth century developments in the fields of opera (the extended *da capo* arias of the Neapolitans), instrumental music (the grand ritornello forms of the Italian concerto composers), and orchestral writing (the disciplined string and wind ensembles of the French court), each of which was to prove profoundly influential on both the sacred and secular music of Bach, had so greatly changed the face of European music that an immense and inevitable watershed was formed between the two centuries with their divergent stylistic aims. None of this should be taken to suggest, however, that Schütz was no more than a 'forerunner' to Bach, destined always to remain under the shadow of his great successor. When accepted on his own terms, and within the relevant cultural criteria of his time, he soon emerges as an equally inspiring creative artist whose work, given the exercise of a responsive historical mind, can amply repay in aesthetic pleasure every effort applied to it in serious study.

Appendix A

Calendar

Year	Age	Life	Contemporary musicians and events
1585		Heinrich Schütz born, 8 Oct., at Köstritz. Eldest son of Christoph Schütz and his wife, Euphrosyne, née Bieger. Baptised 9 Oct.	Aichinger c. 21; F. Anerio 25; G. Anerio c. 18; Banchieri 17; J. Bull c. 22; Byrd 42; Caccini 35; Campion 18; Cavalieri c. 35; Croce c. 28; Demantius 16; Donato c. 55; Eccard 32; Farnaby c. 19; A. Ferrabosco (sen.) 42; A. Ferrabosco (jun.) c. 7; M. Franck 6; G. Gabrieli 30; Gagliano 3; Gastoldi c. 30; Gesualdo c. 24; Gibbons 2; Grandi c. 10; Guerrero 57; Handl 35; Hassler 21; India c. 3; Ingegneri c. 38; Lassus c. 53; Lechner c. 32; Le Jeune c. 55; Marenzio c. 32; Merulo 52; R. Michael c. 33; Monte 64; Monteverdi 18; Morley c. 28; Palestrina 60; Peri 24; Porta c. 57; H. Praetorius 25; M. Praetorius 14; Regnart c. 45; Rosseter 10; Rosthius c. 43; Ruffo 77; F. Soriano c. 36; Striggio 45; Usper c. 15; Vecchi c. 35; Viadana c. 25; Victoria 37; Weelkes 9; Wert 50. A. Gabrieli (52) dies; Tallis (80) dies.
1586	1		Schein born, 20 Mar.
1587	2		Scheidt born, 3 Nov.; Ruffo (79) dies, 19 Feb.
1588	3		A. Ferrabosco sen. (45) dies, 12 Aug.
1589	4		

Year	Age	Life	Contemporary musicians and events
1590	5	The Schütz family moves to Weissenfels to the inn 'Zum güldenen Ring' (bequeathed by Albrecht Schütz). Heinrich begins his education at the local school. Probably taught music by the town cantor, Georg Weber, and the organist, Heinrich Colander.	
1591	6		Jacob Handl (Gallus) (41) dies.
1592	7		John Jenkins born.
1593	8		Ingegneri (45) dies, 1 July.
1594	9		Palestrina (69) dies, 2 Feb.; Lassus (*c.* 64) dies, 14 June.
1595	10		
1596	11		H. Lawes born, May; Rovetta born (Venice). Wert (61) dies, 6 May.
1597	12		B. Marini born (Brescia).
1598	13	The Landgrave Moritz of Hessen-Kassel visits the Schütz inn, hears Heinrich sing, and urges him to come to his court at Kassel as a chorister and school pupil.	L. Rossi born (Torremaggiore).
1599	14	He is taken by his father to Kassel to study at the Collegium Mauritianum	Marenzio (46) dies, 22 Aug. Regnart (*c.* 48) dies, 2 Oct.; Guerrero (71) dies, 8 Nov.
1600	15		
1601	16		Cavalli born 14 Feb.; C. Porta (73) dies, 19 May; B. Pallavicino (50) dies, 26 Nov.
1602	17		W. Lawes born, May; Cavalieri (52) dies, 11 Mar.; Morley (45) dies, early Oct.
1603	18		B. Donato (*c.* 76) dies; De Monte (82) dies, 4 July;
1604	19		H. Albert born, 8 July; Merulo (71) dies, 5 May;
1605	20		Carissimi born, 18 Apr.; Benevoli born, 19 Apr.; Vecchi (54) dies, 19 Feb.
1606	21		
1607	22		Luzzaschi (62) dies, 10 Sept.
1608	23	He matriculates at the University of Marburg, intending to study law.	The Protestant States (with the notable exception of Saxony) form a Union, under the Elector Palatinate, to protect their interests.

Year	Age	Life	Contemporary musicians and events
1609	24	The Landgrave Moritz visits Marburg and urges him to go to Venice for study with Giovanni Gabrieli. He leaves for Venice, apparently without parental consent.	A rival alliance, the Catholic League, is formed, headed by Maximilian of Bavaria. The two sides prepare for conflict. Croce (52) dies, 15 May.
1610	25	Marked progress in composition during the year. Sigismund, Margrave of Brandenburg, prompted by Gabrieli, persuades Moritz to allow him a further year of study.	Monteverdi's *Vespers* and 6-part Mass published, and dedicated to Pope Paul V.
1611	26	His *First Book of Italian Madrigals* published with a dedication to Moritz. His stipend is renewed for an extra year's study	Shakespeare's *The Tempest* and *The Winter's Tale* first performed. Victoria (63) dies, 20 Aug. Eccard (58) dies, Autumn.
1612	27	G. Gabrieli dies, aged 59, on 12 Aug. Schütz probably stays in Venice for a fourth year at his parents' expense.	Hammerschmidt born (Brüx); H.L. Hassler (48) dies, 8 June.
1613	28	He returns to Germany and becomes second organist at the Hesse Kapelle.	Gesualdo (52) dies 8 Sept.
1614	29	Elector Johann Georg of Saxony requests Moritz to grant him Schütz's services, briefly, to assist at the baptism of his second son, August, in Dresden. He goes to Dresden in Sept. and returns to Kassel a month later.	Tunder born (Bannesdorf); F. Anerio (54) dies, 26/7 Sept.
1615	30	Johann Georg asks Moritz (in Apr.) to lend him Schütz for a further two years. Moritz reluctantly agrees.	
1616	31	Moritz asks for him to be returned to Kassel; but Johann George demands that he should remain permanently at Dresden.	Froberger born, *c.* 18 May.
1617	32	The elector refuses to compromise with Moritz, and Schütz finally leaves Kassel for Dresden. His initial title is 'provisional Kapellmeister'. On 15 July he provides a	

Year	Age	Life	Contemporary musicians and events
		mythological ballet (text and music) for a visit by the Emperor Matthias and his family; and, in October, music for a grand celebration of the centenary of the Reformation.	
1618	33	Together with Michael Praetorius and Scheidt, he is invited to assist in the reorganization of the Kapelle at Magdeburg cathedral.	In May the 'defenestration of Prague' marks the beginning of the Thirty Years War. Caccini dies (73), 9 Dec.
1619	34	On 1 June, he marries Magdalena Wildeck. The *Psalmen Davids* are published. On 9 Aug. his brother Georg is married in Leipzig; He composes the concerto SWV 48 for the occasion. On 15 Aug. together with Scheidt, Staden, and Praetorius, he visits Bayreuth for the inauguration of a new organ in the Stadtkirche	Emperor Mathias dies; Ferdinand of Bohemia is elected Holy Roman Emperor.
1620	35		Frederick of Bohemia, a Calvinist, is defeated by the imperial forces under General Tilly at the Battle of White Mountain (west of Prague). Cazzati born at Lucera; Campion (53) dies, Feb.
1621	36	He composes ceremonial music (SWV 49 and probably SWV 338) for a meeting at Breslau in Oct. at which Johann Georg receives, on behalf of the Emperor, pledges of loyalty from the Silesian States. Late in the year his elder daughter Anna Justina is born.	M. Praetorius (50) dies, 15 Feb.; Sweelinck (59) dies, 16 Oct.
1622	37		Sebastiani born, 30 Sept.; Gastoldi (*c.* 56) dies.
1623	38	The *Resurrection History* is published. A short elegy, SWV 52, is composed on the death of Johann Georg's mother, the Duchess Sophia.	Cesti born, *c.* 4 Aug.; Byrd (80) dies, 4 July.

Year	Age	Life	Contemporary musicians and events
		His second daughter, Euphrosina, is born, on 28 Nov.	
1624	39		Monteverdi's *Combattimento di Tancredi e Clorinda* published. Bontempi born in Perugia.
1625	40	His *Cantiones sacrae* are published. On 15 Aug. his sister-in-law, Anna Maria Wildeck, dies; and on 6 Sept. his wife, Magdalena dies. He does not remarry, and his daughters are placed in the care of their maternal grandmother.	O. Gibbons (42) dies, 5 June.
1626	41		The forces of Christian IV of Denmark are defeated by Wallenstein in Aug. at the Battle of Lutte. Legrenzi born, *c.* 11 Aug.; Coprario (*c.* 51) dies (London); Dowland (63) dies (London).
1627	42	In the spring, his opera-ballet *Dafne* is performed at Hartenfels castle in Torgau to celebrate the wedding of Johann Georg's daughter, Sophia Eleonora, and Georg II of Hessen-Darmstadt. In October, together with 18 musicians, he accompanies Johann Georg to an electoral assembly at Mühlhausen. The concerto SWV 465 is composed for the occasion.	Kerll born, 9 Apr.; Viadana (*c.* 67) dies, 2 May; Mauduit (70) dies, 21 Aug.
1628	43	His *Becker Psalter* is published in Freiberg. On 11 Aug. he leaves Dresden on a second visit to Venice. Explores the latest operatic styles there, with 'guidance' from Monteverdi.	Cambert born (Paris). A. Ferrabosco jun. (*c.* 50) dies, Mar.
1629	44	His *Symphoniae sacrae* I are published in Venice, and dedicated to Prince Johann Georg, the elector-apparent of Saxony. He arrives home in the autumn.	P. Agostini born, 16 Oct.; India (*c.* 47) dies, 19 Apr.

Year	Age	Life	Contemporary musicians and events
1630	45	He provides music for the wedding of the elector's daughter, Maria Elisabeth, and Friedrich III of Holstein-Gottorf in Feb.; and for the centenary of the Augsburg Confession in June.	Ferdinand II dismisses general Wallenstein and reinstates Tilly. The Catholic princes fear the growth of the Emperor's power. Hostilities are realigned to the territorial powers versus the Emperor rather than Catholics against Protestants. Gustavus Adolphus of Sweden enters the war on the side of the Protestant states. G.F. Anerio (63), dies 12 June; Schein (44) dies, 19 Nov.
1631	46	He publishes the motet 'Das ist je gewisslich wahr', SWV 277, in memory of Schein. In Feb., with his Kapelle, he accompanies the elector to an assembly in Leipzig, at which the question of wartime alliances are considered. In the autumn both his father and his father-in-law die.	The city of Magdeburg is pillaged by forces under Tilly. Saxony enters the war for the first time. At Breitenfeld (near Leipzig) the imperial forces under Tilly are defeated by the Swedes and Saxons.
1632	47	Finances at Dresden are severely drained by Saxony's military involvement. The Kapelle is much reduced in size and musical activities of any elaboration virtually cease.	Tilly is mortally wounded at the Battle of the River Lech. The Emperor recalls Wallenstein; Gustavus Adolphus defeats Wallenstein at Lützen, but is killed in the battle. G.B. Vitali born, 18 Feb.; Lully born, 28 Nov. Monteverdi's *Scherzi Musicali* published. Peri (72) dies, 12 Aug.; Knüpfer born, 6 Sept.
1633	48	He is invited to go to Denmark to direct the music for the wedding of Johann Georg's daughter, Magdalena Sibylla, and the Danish Crown Prince Christian.	
1634	49	The Danish wedding festivities, held during Oct. include a ballet and two comedies, with music (now lost) of his composition.	The Swedes are defeated by the Spanish at the Battle of Nördlingen. Wallenstein is assassinated. A. Krieger born, 7 Jan.; Banchieri (66) dies.
1635	50	In Feb. his mother dies; he leaves Copenhagen in Mar. On 24 June a service is held at	The Peace of Prague is signed to create a united German front against the Swedes. Richelieu

Year	Age	Life	Contemporary musicians and events
		Dresden to mark the Peace of Prague. On 2 Aug. C. Cornet dies; and on 3 Dec. Count Heinrich Posthumus of Reuss dies.	brings French troops into the war against Spain. D'Anglebert born (Paris).
1636	51	At the interment of Heinrich Posthumus, on 4 Feb., a performance is given of his specially-written *Musikalische Exequien*. In the autumn his *Kleine geistliche Konzerte* I are published.	Hopes raised by the Peace of Prague evaporate. France makes an official declaration of War.
1637	52	A second visit to Denmark, which he intended to make, fails to materialize. It appears that Weckmann went in his place. In the late spring his brother Georg dies.	Milton's *Comus* and *Lycidas* written. Emperor Ferdinand II dies. Colonna born, 16 June; Buxtehude born (? Oldesloe).
1638	53	In July Anna Justina, his elder daughter dies (aged 17). In Nov. the opera-ballet *Orpheus* is composed for the wedding of Johann Georg, Crown Prince of Saxony, and Magdalena Sybilla of Brandenburg (music lost).	Wilbye dies, Sept./Nov.; Donati dies, 21 Jan.
1639	54	His *Kleine geistliche Konzerte* II are published. From the autumn he begins a 14-month period as Kapellmeister to Georg of Calenberg.	M. Franck dies, 1 June.
1640	55	He remains in service to Duke Georg, probably living at Hildesheim, the Duke's official place of residence. In Feb. a second edition of the *Becker Psalter* is published.	Monteverdi's *Il ritorno d'Ulisse* premiered. Agazzati born, 10 Apr.; Farnaby dies (*c.* 77) in Nov.
1641	56	In Jan. he returns to Dresden. In a letter in Mar., he recalls having suffered a 'recent severe illness'.	Cavalli's *Didone* premiered.
1642	57	His second visit to Denmark, is at last undertaken, probably from Oct. until the end of Apr., 1644. In Nov. he directs the music for the double wedding of the twin daughters of Christian IV.	The English Civil War begins. Bononcini born in Sept.; Funcke born.

Year	Age	Life	Contemporary musicians and events
1643	58		Monteverdi's *L'Incoronazione di Poppea* premiered. Cavalli's *L'Egisto* premiered. Gagliano (61) dies 25 Feb.; Frescobaldi (60) dies 1 Mar.; Monteverdi (76) dies 29 Nov.
1644	59	Lives mainly in Brunswick. Active at the court of Duke of Brunswick-Lüneburg in Wolfenbüttel. He appears to have collaborated with the Duchess Sophie Elisabeth (a gifted composer) in a musico-dramatic venture.	Cavalli's *L'Ormindo* premiered. Biber born in Aug.; Stradella born, 1 Oct.
1645	60	Plans to retire to live with his sister Dorothea in Weissenfels, but only partial retirement granted. Asked to arbitrate in a dispute about musical technique between Scacchi and Siefert, he reluctantly agrees. This is supposedly the year in which his *Sieben Worte Christi* was composed.	M.A. Charpentier born (Paris, *c*. 1645); W. Lawes (43)dies, 24 Sept.
1646	61	In mid-winter he visits Weimar to share in birthday celebrations for Eleonora Dorothea, wife of Duke Wilhelm of Saxe-Weimar.	Theile born, 29 July.
1647	62	On 1 May his *Symphoniae sacrae* II are published, and dedicated to Prince Christian of Denmark.	Pelham Humfrey born.
1648	63	His daughter Euphrosina marries Christoph Pincker on 28 Jan., at Dresden. His *Geistliche Chor-Music* is published, partly as a response to the Scacchi Siefert dispute.	The Peace of Westphalia signed on 24 Oct. Schelle born in Sept.
1649	64		Charles 1 of England beheaded on 30 Jan. Blow born in Feb.; J. Ph. Krieger born 25 Feb.
1650	65	In July, following the departure of the Swedish forces from Dresden, services of thanksgiving are held to	Cardoso (*c*. 82) dies, 24 Nov.

Year	Age	Life	Contemporary musicians and events
		mark the end of the war. From 14 Nov., festivities are mounted for the double wedding of Christian and Moritz (the elector's youngest sons) with Christiana and Sophia Hedwig, respectively, of Holstein-Glücksburg. The contribution of Schütz may have included the (lost) ballet *Paris und Helena*. In September his *Symphoniae sacrae* III are published, and dedicated to Johann Georg.	
1651	66	On 14 Jan.: He again petitions the elector for permission to retire, but without success. Many of the Kapelle musicians are reported to be suffering desperate financial hardship.	Cavalli's *La Calisto* premiered. H. Albert (47) dies, 6 Oct.
1652	67	In Oct. the marriage takes place of Magdalena Sybilla (widow of the Danish Crown Prince) to Duke Friedrich Wilhelm of Saxe-Altenburg. An intended performance of the ballet-opera, *Der triumphie-renden Amor* (music lost), is cancelled because of a family bereavement.	
1653	68	Proposal by the Crown Prince, that Bontempi should alternate with him in the direction of services, causes him serious affront. Dismay in the Kapelle over the increasing favour accorded to Italian musicians.	Johann Georg divides the electorate of Saxony between his four sons. Corelli born, 17 Feb.; Pachelbel born, Sept.; Ziani born (Venice); L. Rossi (*c.* 56) dies, 20 Feb.
1654	69		Steffani born 25 July; V. Lübeck born, Sept. Scheidt (67) dies, 24 Mar.
1655	70	His daughter Euphrosina dies on 11 Jan. Services in Dresden on 24/5 September (doubtless with Schütz directing) are held to mark the centenary of the Peace of Augsburg.	

187

Year	Age	Life	Contemporary musicians and events
1656	71	The Elector Johann Georg dies on 8 Oct. Elaborate rituals include interment at Freiberg cathedral on 4 Feb. of the following year. Schütz composes two versions of the German Nunc dimittis, SWV 432–3, in tribute.	Tomkins (84) dies, *c.* 8 June.
1657	72	The new Elector, Johann Georg II, appoints Bontempi and Albrici as joint directors of the Kapelle. Schütz retires, as Kapellmeister Emeritus, sells his house in Dresden and moves to Weissenfels. His Twelve Sacred Songs (*Zwölff geistliche Gesänge*) are published in Dresden under the supervision of Christoph Kittel.	Erlebach born, *c.* 24 July
1658	73		Torelli born, 22 Apr.
1659	74		Purcell born.
1660	75	In the spring, he visits Wolfenbüttel, possibly for the birthday of Duke August. A performance of the 'History of the Birth of Christ' (almost certainly Schütz's work) is recorded in the Dresden court diaries for Christmas Vespers.	Restoration of the Church and Monarchy in England; Charles II enthroned. Kuhnau born, 6 Apr.; A. Scarlatti born, 2 May; Campra born, *c.* 3 Dec.
1661	76	Renovations to the palace church at Dresden begin. The third, revised and enlarged, edition of his *Becker Psalter* is published. He sends presentation copies to Wolfenbüttel for Duke August and his wife.	
1662	77	He composes a setting of Psalm 100 for the reopening of the palace church in Dresden on 28 Sept. On 3 Nov. Bontempi's opera *Il Paride* is performed during celebrations at the wedding of Erdmuth Sophia (the new Elector's daughter) and Ernst Christian of Brandenburg-Bayreuth.	Cavalli's *L'Ercole amante* premiered. H. Lawes (66) dies, 21 Oct.

Year	Age	Life	Contemporary musicians and events
1663	78	In July, he advises Duke Moritz (the elector's youngest brother) on the organization of his new Kapelle at Zeitz.	Scheidemann (*c.* 68) dies at Hamburg.
1664	79	In Jan. he sends copies of his printed works to Wolfenbüttel for inclusion in the Duke's library. On 1 May the rebuilt palace church at Zeitz is opened. His *Christmas History* (the role of the Evangelist only) is published in Dresden.	
1665	80	First version of the St John Passion performed on Good Friday, 24 Mar.	Bubonic plague in London. B. Marini (*c.* 76) dies.
1666	81	St Matthew and St Luke Passions are performed in Apr.; and St John (probably in its revised version) on Good Friday, 13 Apr.	The Great Fire of London. A. Krieger (32) dies, 30 June.
1667	82	He resides mainly in Weissenfels, and gives tuition to Johann Theile. A gilded cup is presented to him by the elector 'in gracious remembrance'.	Milton's *Paradise Lost* published. Pepusch born in London; Lotti born; Tunder (53) dies, 5 Nov.
1668	83		F. Couperin born 10 Nov.; Rovetta (*c.* 73) dies, 23 Oct. Cesti's *Il pomo d'oro*.
1669	84		Cesti (46) dies, 14 Oct.
1670	85	Weak and hard of hearing, he moves to rented quarters in Dresden. He invites Christoph Bernhard to compose a funeral motet for him.	Caldara born (Venice).
1671	86	His 'Swan-song', comprising double-choir settings of Psalm 119, Psalm 100, and the German Magnificat, is completed.	Milton's *Paradise Regained* and *Samson Agonistes* completed. Bontempi/Peranda's *Dafne* performed.
1672	87	Following attacks of apoplexy, his death ensues at 4 p.m. on 6 Nov. His funeral is held on 17 Nov. at the Frauenkirche in Dresden. The funeral sermon is preached by Dr	Benevoli (67) dies. Biber 2; Blow 23; Bononcini 30; Bontempi 48; Buxtehude 35; Caldara 2; Cambert 44; Campra 12; Carissimi 67; Cazzati 52; Cesti 49;

Year	Age	Life	Contemporary musicians and events
		Martin Geier, and the music performed includes Christoph Bernhard's specially-written motet and three of his own works. On the memorial tablet erected above his burial-place he is extolled as the greatest composer of his age.	M.A. Charpentier *c.* 27; Colonna 35; Corelli 19; F. Couperin 4; D'Anglebert 37; Erlebach 15; Froberger 56; Funcke 30; Humfrey 25; Kerll 45; Knüpfer 39; A. Krieger 38; J. Ph. Krieger 23; Kuhnau 12; Legrenzi 46; Lotti 5; V. Lübeck 18; Lully 40; Pachelbel 19; Pepusch 5; Purcell 13; A. Scarlatti 12; Schelle 24; Schmelzer 50; Sebastiani 49; Stradella 28; Theile 26; Torelli 14; G.B. Vitali 40; Ziani 19.

Appendix B

List of works

Since the number of individual works by Schütz is very large, it has been necessary to limit the scope of the present list. All of Schütz's extant compositions are recorded here, including some of questionable authenticity; but no details are given of their vocal and instrumental scoring, for which the reader is referred to the worklists in the articles on Schütz, in either the *New Grove Dictionary of Music and Musicians* (London, 1980) or *The New Grove North European Baroque Masters* (London, 1985), both ed. Stanley Sadie. The three modern editions of the composer's works are entered below and identified for convenience by the reference letters, G, N, and S, which correspond to those provided in the *New Grove* sources. And below these again there are given, first, the principal collections of Schütz's work in chronological order, each with its publication date, the catalogue (SWV) numbers of the items it contains, and the letter sign and volume number of the modern editions in which it is located; and second, several major works (similarly annotated) which were not published in the composer's lifetime. Finally an alphabetical key is provided of all the composer's works (with the exception of lost ones, known only by their titles), in the form of text incipits with SWV numbers. By cross-referencing these catalogue numbers to those in the *New Grove* worklists (or for simpler purposes to the principal volumes listed below) much of the excluded information will become available.

MODERN EDITIONS

   (i) *H. Schütz: Sämmtliche Werke*, ed. P. Spitta et al. (Leipzig, 1885–94, 1909, 1927; repr. 1968–73) G;

   (ii) *H. Schütz: Neue Ausgabe sämtlicher Werke*, ed. W. Bittinger, W. Breig, W. Ehmann et al. (Kassel, 1955–) N.

   (iii) *H. Schütz: Sämtliche Werke* (still in progress), ed. G. Graulich et al. (Stuttgart, 1971–) S.

PRINCIPAL COLLECTIONS AND MAJOR WORKS

Il primo libro de madrigali [Op. 1], 1611, SWV 1–19 (G 9, N 22, S 1)
Psalmen Davids [Op. 2], 1619, SWV 22–47 (G 2/3, N 23–6)
Historia der Aufferstehung [Op. 3], 1623, SWV 50 (G 1, N 3, S 4)
Cantiones sacrae [Op. 4], 1625, SWV 53–93 (G 4, N 8–9)
Psalmen Davids (*Becker Psalter*) (Op. 5 & Op. 14), 1628 & 1661, SWV 97–256 (G 16, N 6)
Symphoniae sacrae I [Op. 6], 1629, SWV 257–76 (G 5, N 13/14, S 7)

Musikalische Exequien [Op. 7], 1636, SWV 279–81 (G 12, N 4, S 8)
Kleine geistliche Koncerte I & II [Op. 8 & 9], 1636 & 1639. SWV 282–337 (G 6, N 10–12)
Symphoniae sacrae II [Op. 10], 1647, SWV 341–67 (G 7, N 15–17)
Geistliche Chor-Music [Op. 11], 1648, SWV 369–97 (G 8, N 5)
Symphoniae sacrae III [Op. 12], 1650, SWV 398–418 (G 10–11, N 18–21)
Zwölff geistlich Gesänge [Op. 13], 1657, SWV 420–31 (G 12, N 7, S 15)

Published posthumously
Die sieben Worte Christi, *c.* 1645, SWV 478 (G 1, N 2, S 20, 478)
Historia der Geburth Christi, 1663, SWV 435 (G 1, N 1)
Historia des Leidens und Sterbens . . . Jesu Christi
   (i) St Matthew Passion 1666, SWV 479 (G 1, N 2, S 20, 479)
   (ii) St Luke Passion, 1664 (?), SWV 480, (G 1, N 2, S 20, 480)
   (iii) St John Passion, 1665/rev. 1666, SWV 481a/481 (G 1, N 2, S 20, 481)
Schwanengesang, 1671
   (i)   Psalm 119, SWV 482–92 (N 29)
   (ii)   Psalm 100, Jauchzet dem Herrn alle Welt, SWV 493 (N 39)
   (iii) Meine Seele erhebt den Herren (German Magnificat) SWV 494 (N 39)

ALPHABETICAL KEY

(The letter a (in lower case), appended to an SWV number, indicates an early version of the work cited; and the letter A (in upper case) a work—often of doubtful authenticity—confined to the appendix to the (SWV) Schütz catalogue).

Italian texted

	SWV		*SWV*
Alma afflitta, che fai	4	Mi saluta costei	12
Cosi morir debb'io	5	O dolcezze amarissime	2
Di marmo siete voi	17	O primavera	1
D'orrida selce alpina	6	Quella damma son io	11
Dunque à Dio	15	Ride la primavera	7
Feritevi, ferite	9	Selve beate	3
Fiamma ch'allacia	10	Sospir che del bel petto	14
Fuggi, fuggi, o mio core	8	Tornate, o cari baci	16
Giunto è pur	18	Vasto mar, nel cui seno	19
Io moro	13		

Latin texted

	SWV		*SWV*
Ad dominum cum tribulare	71	Buccinate in neomenia tuba	275
Adjuro vos	264	Calicem salutaris accipiam	60
Adveniunt pascha pleno	338	Cantabo Domino in vita mea	260
Anima mea liquefacta est	263	Cantate Domino canticum	
Aspice, Pater	73	novum	81, 463
Attendite, popule meus	270	Christe Deus adjuva	295
Aufer immensam, Deus	337	Christe fac ut sapiam	431
Ave Maria	334	Confitemini Domino	91
Benedicam Dominum	267, A5	Da pacem, Domine	465
Bone Jesu	313	Deus misereatur nostri	55

	SWV		SWV
Discedite a me	87	O misericordissime Jesu	309
Domine Deus, pater	90	O quam tu pulchra es	265
Domine, labia mea	27	Paratum cor meum	257
Domine, ne in furore	85	Pater noster	89, 92
Domine, non est exaltatum	78	Pro hoc magno mysterio	77
Domini est terra	476	Quando se claudunt lumina	316
Dominus illuminatio mea	A10	Quemadmodum desiderat cervus	336
Dulcissime et benignissime Christe	67	Quid commisisti	56
Ecce advocatus meus	84	Quid detur tibi	72
Ego autem sum	436	Quo, nate Dei	59
Ego dormio	63	Quoniam ad te clamabo	62
Ego enim inique egi	58	Quoniam non est in morte	86
Ego sum tui plaga doloris	57	Reduc, Domine Deus meus	75
En novus Elysiis	49	Rorate coeli desuper	322
Et ne despicias	54	Sicut Moses serpentem	68
Exquisivi Dominum	268	Si non humiliter sentiebam	79
Exultavit cor meum	258	Speret Israel in Domino	80
Fili mi, Absalon	269	Spes mea, Christe Deus	69
Gratias agimus tibi	93	Sumite psalmum	A9
Heu mihi, Domine	65	Supereminet omnem scientiam	76
Hodie Christus natus est	315, 456	Surrexit pastor bonus	469
In lectulo per noctes	272	Te Christe supplex invoco	326
In te, Domine, speravi	66, 259	Teutoniam dudum belli	338
Inter brachia	82	Tulerunt Dominum	499
Invenerunt me	273	Turbabor, sed non perturbabor	70
Jubilate Deo in chordis	276	Veni de Libano	266
Jubilate Deo omnis terra	262, 332	Veni, dilecte mi	274
Magnificat anima mea	468	Veni, Domine	437
Meas dicavi res Deo	305	Veni, Redemptor gentium	301
Nonne hic est	74	Veni, rogo, in cor meum	83
O bone Jesu	471	Veni, Sancte Spiritus	328, 475
O bone, o dulcis	53	Venite ad me	261
Oculi omnium in te sperant	88	Verba mea auribus percipe	61
O Jesu, nomen dulce	308	Verbum caro factum est	314
Oculi omnium in te sperant	88	Vulnerasti cor meum	64

German texted

	SWV		SWV
Ach bleib mit deiner Gnade	445	Ach Herr, mein Gott	102, 102a
Ach Gott, der du vor dieser Zeit	157	Ach Herr, straf mich nicht	24
		Ach Herr, wie lang willt du	109, 109a
Ach Gott vom Himmel	108, 108a	Ach wie gross	99, 99a
Ach Gott, warum verstösst du nun	187, 187a	Ach wie soll ich doch	474
		All Ehr und Lob	421
Ach Herr, du Schöpfer	450, 450a	Allein Gott in der Höh sei Ehr	327
Ach Herr, du Sohn David	A2	Alleluja, lobet den Herren	38
Ach Herr, es ist der Heiden Heer	176, 176a	Aller Augen warten	429, 429a
		Alles was Odem hat	256, 256a

Appendix C

Personalia

Aichinger, Gregor (1564/5–1628), German composer, a pupil of Giovanni Gabrieli. Published sacred works both in polychoral and concerto styles, and in conservative polyphony. From 1584 he became organist to the Fugger family in Augsburg.

Albert, Heinrich (1604–51), German composer, a cousin and one-time pupil of Schütz. From 1630 organist at Königsberg cathedral. He contributed, in collaboration with the poet Simon Dach, to the development of German song, publishing ten books of *Arien oder Lieder* (1638–50).

Albertis, Gaspar de (*c*. 1480–*c*. 1560), Italian composer, *maestro di cappella* of the Santa Maria Maggiore church in Bergamo. His three Passion settings (from before 1541) in a mixed responsorial and polyphonic style provided the model for Scandello in his St John Passion (Dresden *c*. 1560).

Albrici, Vincenzo (1631–96), Italian composer. Widely travelled, he was appointed Kapellmeister at Dresden in *c*. 1656 after service at Rome and at the court of Queen Christina in Stockholm. Subsequently he served also at the Chapel Royal in London and, after conversion to Protestantism, at St Thomas's, Leipzig.

Baryphonus, Henricus (1581–1655), important German theorist who, in his *Pleiades musicae* (1615) and other volumes now lost, advocated an approach to compositional theory based on harmony rather than counterpoint.

Becker, Cornelius (1561–1604), poet and theologian. Author of the *Becker Psalter*, containing rhymed versions of the psalms, which were set by a number of Lutheran composers, including Schütz in 1628.

Belli, Guilio (*c*. 1560–1621), prolific composer of sacred and secular music in modern and traditional styles. *Maestro di cappella* of Imola cathedral and, from 1595, of the Frari church in Venice.

Bernard of Clairvaux, St (1090–1153), founder of the Clairvaux monastery in Champagne, France. Author of religious poems, including the famous *Jubilus* 'Jesu dulcis memoria', parts of which, in two different translations, were set by Schütz in his *Symphoniae sacrae* III.

Bernhard, Christoph (1628–92), German composer and theorist and one of Schütz's favourite pupils. Author of important musical treatises, and composer of a specially commissioned motet for Schütz's funeral. Kapellmeister at Dresden from 1681.

Boehme, Jacob (1575–1624), German mystic, and author of the treatise *Aurora* (1612). Greatly influential on Lutheran religious thought.

Bontempi, Giovanni Andrea (*c*. 1624–1705), Italian composer who became joint Kapellmeister (with Schütz and Albrici) at Dresden in 1656. His festival opera *Il*

Paride (1662) laid the foundations for a continuing operatic tradition at the Dresden court.

Bugenhagen, Johann (early 16th century), German theologian and colleague of Luther. His *Passionsharmonie* (1526) provided texts for Schütz's *Sieben Worte Christi* and for many early Passion settings in motet style.

Burck, Joachim a (1546–1610), German composer noted for his motet-style St John Passion of 1568.

Buxtehude, Diderik (*c.* 1637–1707), Danish/German composer. Organist of the Marienkirche at Lübeck where he restarted *Abendmusik* concerts, for the performance of cantatas and oratorio-style works, mainly ones of his own composition.

Caccini, Guilio (*c.* 1545–1618), Italian composer and singer. A member of Count Bardi's Florentine Camerata. Author of *Le nuove musiche* (1602), a volume of new style madrigals and songs for solo voice and continuo.

Calvisius, Seth (1556–1615), influential German theorist and composer of hymns and psalm settings.

Carracci, Annibale (1560–1609), a leading Italian painter of his time. Included amongst his pioneering landscapes is *The Flight into Egypt* (Rome, 1603).

Caravaggio, Michelangelo Merisi da (1571–1610), one of the most important Italian painters of the seicento. Notable examples of his work include the *Crucifixion of St Peter* and the *Conversion of St Paul* in the Cerasi Chapel of Santa Maria del Popolo, Rome.

Colander, Heinrich (b. *c.* 1540), organist and sometime burgomaster at Weissenfels. Almost certainly a teacher of Schütz during his boyhood. He was married to the widow of Schütz's uncle Matthes.

Cornet, Christoph (d. 1635), musician and student friend of Schütz during his schooldays at Kassel. In 1618 he succeeded Georg Otto as Kapellmeister to the Kassel court. For his funeral in 1635 Schütz provided a specially-composed German Nunc dimittis, SWV 352.

Crüger, Johannes (1598–1662), German composer and theorist. Important contributor to the development of the Protestant chorale, most notably with his *Praxis pietatis melica* collection, published in 1648.

Dedekind, Constantin Christian (1628–1715), composer and poet. He joined the Dresden Kapelle as a bass in 1654 and later became director of the court orchestra. He is best remembered for his *Aelbanische Musen-Lust*, a collection of 146 solo songs with continuo, sacred and secular.

Donatello (Donato di Niccolo) (1386–1466), Florentine sculptor of the early Renaissance. Notable amongst his works are a bronze statue of David, a St George, and a stone relief Annunciation scene at Santa Croce, Florence.

Donati, Ignazio (*c.* 1575–1638), Italian composer who contributed significantly to the development of the small-scale sacred motet in concertato style.

Dowland, John (1563–1626), English composer and lutanist who travelled extensively in Europe. Amongst the courts he visited was that of the Landgrave Moritz of Hessen-Kassel who composed a pavane for lute in his honour.

Dulichius, Philipp (1562–1631), German composer. Nicknamed 'the Pomeranian Lassus', his liturgical works, in twelve volumes, reveal Netherlandish and Venetian influences.

Eggenburg, Hans Ulrich von, a Protestant aristocrat who converted to Catholicism in 1615 and became chancellor to the court of the Emperor Matthias in Vienna. Schütz dedicated his *Cantiones sacrae* to him in 1625.

Fromm, Andreas (1621–83), Cantor at the Marienkirche in Stettin. Noted for his *Lazarus* (1649), an *Actus musicus* designed for quasi-theatrical performance in church.

Gabrieli, Andrea (1533–85), Italian composer. Organist, from 1566, of St Mark's, Venice. Cultivated ceremonial music, much of it involving spaced choirs (*cori spezzati*).

Gabrieli, Giovanni (*c.* 1553–1612), Italian composer, nephew of Andrea Gabrieli. Renowned for his polychoral concertato works designed, with choirs of voices and instruments, to exploit the architecture of St Mark's, Venice. Schütz was his pupil from 1609.

Gagliano, Marco da (1582–1643), Italian composer, *maestro di cappella* of Florence cathedral from 1608. His opera *Dafne* (on Rinuccini's text) was staged at Mantua in 1608.

Geier, Martin (1614–80), senior court preacher at Dresden at the time of Schütz's death in 1672. Preached the sermon at the composer's funeral, and left a valuable short account of his life.

Glarean, Heinrich (1488–1563), Swiss theorist, renowned for his exposition of modal theory in his *Dodecachordon* of 1547.

Grandi, Alessandro (*c.* 1587–1630), Italian composer who made important contributions to the new style of concertato church music.

Gryphius, Andreas (1616–64), a leading figure in German seventeenth-century literature, both as a poet and a dramatist.

Guarini, Giovanni Battista (1537–1612), Italian poet, author of the pastoral drama *Il pastor fido* (1583).

Gustavus Adolphus (1594–1632), King of Sweden from 1611. A major champion of the Protestant cause during the Thirty Years War.

Hainhofer, Philipp (d. 1647), Augsburg patron of the arts and agent to Duke August of Wolfenbüttel. A friend and valued advisor to Schütz.

Hassler, Hans Leo (1564–1612), German composer. Chamber musician to the Fugger family in Augsburg, and organist at the Dresden court chapel from 1608.

Hoënegg, Matthias Hoë von (1580–1645), senior court preacher during Schütz's early years at Dresden. Socially exclusive and an unyielding opponent of Calvinism, he was often derided as the 'Hoëpriester'.

India, Sigismondo d' (*c.* 1582–1629), Italian composer of madrigals and chamber monodies, which frequently display an expressive use of chromaticism.

Janequin, Clément (*c.* 1485–1558), French composer who cultivated the Parisian *chanson* and made a speciality of programmatic pieces, descriptive of birdsong, a battle, a hunt, and other scenes.

Johann Georg I (1585–1656), ruler of the Saxon electorate from 1611 until his death in 1656. Although much devoted to the pleasures of the table and the hunt, he was a man of pious disposition and a skilled diplomat.

Johann Georg II (1613–80), succeeded his father as Elector of Saxony in 1656. Deeply interested in music, and himself something of a composer, he gave strong support to Schütz.

Kittel, Caspar (1603–39), pupil and colleague of Schütz at Dresden, who studied in Italy and introduced the term 'cantata' into Germany.

Kittel, Christoph (d. 1680), the son of Caspar, a minor composer, noted for his set of 12 keyboard preludes in successive keys.

Klemm, Johann (*c.* 1595–post 1651), court organist at Dresden from 1625. Remembered as a composer for his *Partitura seu Tablatura italica* (1631), comprising two- to four-part fugues for organ and other instruments, and as a music-publisher for having issued at least two of Schütz's collections, the *Symphoniae sacrae* II and the *Geistliche Chor-Music*.

Knüpfer, Sebastian (1633–76), German composer, cantor of St Thomas's, Leipzig from 1657. Produced numerous church works in the vocal concerto style, often with elaborate orchestration.

Krieger, Adam (1634–66), German composer renowned for his contribution to the development of German song.

Krieger, Johann Philipp (1649–1725), prolific German composer who played a major part in the early development of the church cantata, producing over 2000 specimens.

Lechner, Leonhard (*c.* 1553–1606), German composer, a follower of Lassus. Known for his German motet Passion of 1593, and his numerous lieder and song motets.

Le Maistre, Matthaeus (*c.* 1505–77), a Netherlander, he served as Kapellmeister at Dresden from 1554 to 1568. His most notable contributions comprise German sacred and secular songs.

Lobwasser (*fl.* 1573), author of the Lobwasser Psalter (1573), a German translation, for Lutheran use, of the Marot–de Bèze Genevan Psalter.

Longueval, Antoine de (*fl.* 1507–22), French composer, whose St Matthew Passion (*c.* 1510) is probably the earliest extant setting in motet style.

Löwe von Eisenach, Johann Jakob (1629–1703), German composer, a pupil of Schütz at Dresden, who became Kapellmeister at Wolfenbüttel in 1655 and Zeitz in 1663.

Luzzaschi, Luzzasco (*c.* 1545–1607), a prominent musician at Ferrara during the later 16th century, renowned for his madrigals, several of which are in *moderno* style with solo voices and keyboard.

Marenzio, Luca (1553–99), Italian composer, one of the most celebrated and prolific madrigalists of his time, noted for his skill in mood- and word-painting.

Marino, Giambattista (1569–1625), a leading Italian lyric poet, many of whose verses were set by madrigalists of the period, including Schütz in his Op. 1 set of 1611.

Marot, Clément (1496–1544), French poet who provided 50 psalm translations for the first Calvinist psalter. After his death the work was completed by Théodore de Bèze.

Martinengo, Giulio Cesare (d. 1613), *maestro di cappella* of St Mark's, Venice, during Schütz's first visit from 1609.

Michael, Rogier (*c.* 1552–*c.* 1619), Schütz's immediate predecessor as Kapellmeister at the Dresden court. A prolific composer of sacred vocal music.

Michael, Tobias (1592–1657), the son of Rogier Michael, who became Kantor of St Thomas's, Leipzig, in 1631 succession to Schein.

Moritz, Landgrave of Hessen-Kassel (1572–1632), the first of Schütz's influential patrons. A ruler of wide learning and distinguished musical abilities.

Moritz, Duke of Saxe-Zeitz (b. *c.* 1618), fourth son of Johann Georg I of Saxony. Records show that he sought Schütz's advice in establishing the Kapelle at his court.

Musculus, Andreas (1514–81), Lutheran author of a book of *Precationes* from which Schütz derived a number of the texts for his *Cantiones sacrae* of 1625.

Nauwach, Johann (*c.* 1595–*c.* 1630), a pupil of Schütz who, after study in Italy, brought the Italian monodic style to Germany for the first time with his *Arie passeggiate* of 1623.

Opitz, Martin (1597–1639), the leading German poet of his generation who reformed versification largely by reducing metrics to iambic and trochaic patterns. He provided the translation of Rinuccini's *Dafne* for Schütz's opera of that name.

Otto, Georg (1550–1618), German composer. *Hofkapellmeister* at Hessen-Kassel from 1586, and teacher both of the future Landgrave Moritz and the young Schütz. The *Ottoneum* theatre in Kassel was named after him.

Peranda, Marco Gioseppe (*c.* 1625–75), Italian composer who worked with Schütz at the Dresden Kapelle and eventually succeeded to the post of *Hofkapellmeister*. His St Mark Passion was formerly attributed to Schütz.

\Peri, Jacopo (1561–1633), Italian composer and singer whose operas *Dafne* and *Euridice* are usually recognized as the first in the history of the genre.

Pfleger, Augustin (*c.* 1635–86), German composer important for his numerous sacred works, including a *Sieben Worte Jesu Christ am Kreuz* (1670).

Porta, Costanzo (*c.* 1528–1601), Italian composer who, in addition to a large body of church music, published five important books of madrigals (1555–86).

Posthumus, Count Heinrich (1572–1635), sovereign of Gera, Schütz's birth-region. A close friend of the composer, the count invited him to provide a work of exceptional elaboration—the *Musikalische Exequien*—for his funeral.

Praetorius, Michael (*c.* 1571–1621), German composer and theorist who was closely associated with Schütz at Dresden during 1613–16. Adapted Protestant liturgical music to the Venetian style of the period, and provided with his *Syntagma musicum* (1614–20) a vast compendium of information about contemporary musical practice.

Priuli, Giovanni (*c.* 1575–1629), a pupil of Giovanni Gabrieli who served at Graz as Kapellmeister to the Archduke Ferdinand, both before and after he became emperor in 1619.

Reincken, Johann Adam (1623–1722), German composer and organist. A pupil of Scheidemann whom he succeeded as organist at St Catherine's, Hamburg, in 1658.

Ribera, José de (1591–1652), Spanish artist renowned for the expressive power of his paintings, vigorous in his *Martyrdom of St Bartholomeo* (*c.* 1630) and exquisitely tender in his *Adoration of the Shepherds* (1650).

Rinuccini, Ottavio (1562–1621), Italian librettist and poet. Author of texts for the earliest operas, including Peri's *Dafne* (1598) and *Euridice* (1602), and Monteverdi's *Arianna* (1608).

Rist, Johann (1607–67), German poet and hymn writer, and a faithful follower of the reforms of Opitz. In 1658 he founded a literary society, the Order of Elbe Swans.

Rosthius, Nikolaus (*c.* 1542–1622), German composer, remembered for his *Resurrection History* (1598), modelled on the setting, from *c.* 1570, by Antonio Scandello.

Rovetta, Giovanni (1595–1668), Italian composer whose entire career was spent at St Mark's Venice where he became *maestro di cappella*, in succession to Monteverdi, in 1644.

Scacchi, Marco (*c.* 1600–81), Italian composer who served as choirmaster to the Polish court in Warsaw for over 20 years. He became involved in a dispute over musical styles with Paul Siefert (q.v.), with which Schütz became uneasily involved as an arbiter.

Scandello, Antonio (1517–80), Italian composer who was employed from 1549 at the Dresden court and 19 years later, after conversion to Protestantism, was elected Kapellmeister. Famous for his St John Passion of 1561 and *Resurrection History* of *c*. 1570.

Scheidemann, Heinrich (*c*. 1595–1663), organist of the church of St Catharine, Hamburg, from 1629, and an eventual founder of the North German organ school. His pupils included J. A. Reincken (q.v.).

Scheidt, Samuel (1587–1654), distinguished German composer and organist, noted for his *Tablatura nova* (1624), organ works in three volumes, and large output of sacred choral music. He held posts at Halle as court Kapellmeister and city music director, but his activities were frequently curtailed by the Thirty Years War. A friend both of Schütz and Schein.

Schein, Johann Hermann (1586–1630), German composer and poet, and a close friend of Schütz. During the last 15 years of his life he was Cantor at St Thomas's, Leipzig. Principal compositions include his *Opella nova*, settings of chorales in the small concertato style, his *Israelsbrünnlein*, motets for 5 and 6 voices, and his *Diletti pastorali*, madrigals to texts of his own composition.

Schultze, Christoph (1606–83), a pupil of Schein at Leipzig, he became cantor at Delitzsch in 1633. His St Luke Passion (1653) anticipates several features of Schütz's settings.

Selle, Thomas (1599–1663), German composer who became, in 1641, civic director of music at Hamburg. His St John Passion (1643) was the first to incorporate independent instrumental accompaniments and non-gospel insertions.

Siefert, Paul (1586–1666), German organist and composer, a pupil of Sweelinck, who became involved in a bitter dispute with Marco Scacchi (q.v.) about differing styles in sacred music. Schütz, amongst others, was called upon to adjudicate on the issue.

Sophie Elisabeth, Duchess of Wolfenbüttel (1613–76), wife of Duke August. A founder member of the famous Fruit-Bearing Society (*Fruchbringende Gesellschaft*), she was widely recognized for her abilities as an author and composer. Surviving correspondence indicates that she received tuition in composition from Schütz and took part with him in creating a joint musico-dramatic work.

Spener, Jacob (1635–1705), theologian and author of the reform document *Pia desideria* (1675) which led to the establishment of the evangelical 'Pietist' movement in Germany.

Striggio, Alessandro (*c*. 1540–92), Italian composer who served the Medici court at Florence form the 1560s. A major madrigalist, and composer of several stage works (*intermedi*), now lost.

Strunck, Nikolaus Adam (1640–1700), German composer who, in 1688 joined the electoral Kapelle at Dresden and in 1692 became Kapellmeister. Chiefly important are the operas he composed for Hamburg, notably *Esther* (1680) and *Semiramis* (1681).

Theile, Johann (1646–1724), a pupil of Schütz, he became Kapellmeister at Gottorf in 1673 and moved to Hamburg two years later. He is primarily important for his St Matthew Passion (1673), one of the first to introduce commentary arias, and for his opera *Adam und Eva* with which the theatre in the Gänsemarkt in Hamburg was inaugurated.

Tilly, Count von (1559–1632). Flemish commander of the imperial forces during the Thirty Years War. Defeated by Gustavus Adolphus at the battle of Breitenfeld in 1631.

Tasso, Torquato (1544–95), Italian poet, author of the epic romantic poem of the First Crusade, *Gerusalemme Liberata* (1574).

Usper [Sponga], Francesco (*c.* 1570–1641), Italian composer, a pupil of Andrea Gabrieli, who held various appointments in Venice, including that of organist at S. Salvatore from 1614. He is specially noted for the formal coherence of his instrumental works.

Vicentino, Nicola (1511–*c.* 1576), Italian composer and theorist, author of *L'antica musica ridotta alla moderna prattica* (1555), in which he explored new ideas about the functions of chromaticism and, less rewardingly, about ways of using microtones in music of his time.

Velàzquez, Diego Rodriguez de Sylva y (1599–1660), the outstanding Spanish painter of his time. His religious works, such as the *Adoration of the Magi* (1619), reveal an aura of mystery and spirituality, their figures portrayed with expressive realism, in striking contrast to the impersonal 'types' of the existing tradition.

Viadana, Lodovico (*c.* 1560–1627), Italian composer, renowned for his *Cento concerti ecclesiastici*, one hundred small-scale sacred concertos for from one to four solo voices and continuo (1602).

Wallenstein, Albrecht Eusebius Wenzel von (1583–1634), a general of the Habsburg army during the Thirty Years War. He was dismissed in favour of Tilly in 1630, but recalled two years later, following the latter's death in battle. He was defeated by Gustavus Adolphus at Lützen in 1632, and assassinated in 1634.

Walter, Johann (1496–1570), the chief musical associate of Luther, and compiler of the first significant chorale collection, his *Geystliches gesangk Buchleyn* of 1524. Also important are the two pioneering German passions (St Matthew and St John), attributed to him, which date from *c.* 1550.

Weckmann, Matthias (*c.* 1619–74), German composer, a favourite pupil of Schütz, who became organist of the Dresden Kapelle in 1637 and subsequently of the Jacobikirche in Hamburg. He wrote many instrumentally-accompanied sacred works in an extension of the early style of Schütz.

Zesen, Philipp von (1619–89), German poet and novelist who was involved with others in a misguided seventeenth-century attempt to regulate spelling according to speech patterns—some slight evidence of which is to be found on the title-page of Schütz's final work, his 'Swan-song' of 1671.

Ziani, Pietro Andrea (1616–84), Italian composer, active in opera from 1654. His *Teseo* was mounted in Dresden in 1666–7 (the first production at the new Kurfürstliches Opernhaus) on the occasion of the wedding of the princess Anna Sophia.

Appendix D

Select bibliography

Abraham, G., 'Passion Music from Schütz to Bach', *Monthly Musical Record* 84 (1954) 115 and 152.

Adrio, A., 'Heinrich Schütz und Italien', *Bekenntnis zu Heinrich Schütz* (Kassel, 1954), 9.

Agey, C. B., *A Study of the Kleine geistliche Konzerte and Geistliche Chormusik of Heinrich Schütz* (diss., Florida State Univ., 1955).

Aikin, J. P., 'Heinrich Schütz's *Die Bußfertige Magdalena* (1636), *SJb*, 14 (1992), 9.

Arnold, D., 'Schütz's Venetian Psalms', *The Musical Times*, 113 (1972), 1071.

Berner, A., 'Die Musikinstrumente zur Zeit Heinrich Schützens', *Sagittarius*, 1 (1966), 30.

Bittinger, W., *Schütz-Werke-Verzeichnis, Kleine Ausgabe* (Bärenreiter, Kassel, 1960). Supplement by Werner Breig 'Schützfunde und zuschreibungen seit 1960— Auf dem Wege zur Grossen Ausgabe des Schütz-Werke-Verzeichnis', *SJb*, 1 (1979), 63.

Blankenburg, W., 'Die Dialogkompositionen von Heinrich Schütz', *Musik und Kirche*, 42 (1972), 121.

—— 'Heinrich Schütz 1672–1972', *Musik und Kirche*, 42 (1972), 3.

—— 'Heinrich Schütz und der protestantische Choral', *Musik und Kirche*, 7 (1935), 219.

—— 'Schütz und Bach', *Musik und Kirche*, 42 (1972), 219.

—— 'Zur Bedeutung der Andachtstexte im Werke von Heinrich Schütz', *SJb*, 6 (1984), 62.

Blume, F., *Protestant Church Music*, London, 1975.

—— 'Geistliche Musik am Hofe des Landgrafen Moritz von Hessen', *Zeitschrift des Vereins für hessische Geschichte und Landeskunde*, lxviii (1957), 131.

—— 'Heinrich Schütz nach 300 Jahren', *Syntagma musicologicum*, ii (Kassel) 1976, 139. Eng. trans. in M. Benn *Studies in Musik* [Australia], 7 (1973), 1.

Braun, W., *Die Musik des 17. Jahrhunderts*. Vol. 4 of *Neues Handbuch der Musikwissenschaft*, ed. Carl Dalhaus (Wiesbaden, 1981).

Bray, R., 'The *Cantiones sacrae* of Heinrich Schütz Re-examined', *Music & Letters*, 52 (1971), 299.

Breig, W., 'Heinrich Schütz' "Musikalischen Exequien": Überlegungen zur Werkgeschichte und zur textlich-musikalischen Konzeption', *SJb*, 11 (1989), 53.

—— 'Höfische Festmusik im Werk von Heinrich Schütz', *Daphnis: Zeitschrift für mittlere deutsche Literatur*, 10 (1981), 711.

—— 'Neue Schütz-Funde', *AMw*, xxvii (1970), 49.

Brennecke, W. and Engelbrecht, C., 'Kassel', *MGG*.

Brodde, O., *Heinrich Schütz. Weg und Werk* (Bärenreiter, Kassel, 1972).

Buelow, G., *A Schütz Reader, Documents of Performance Practice. Journal of the American Choral Foundation, Inc.* 27, No. 4 (October, 1985).

Carapezza, P. E., 'Schützens Italienische Madrigale: Textwahl und stilistische Beziehungen', *SJb*, 1, 44.

Chrysander, F., 'Geschichte der Braunschweig-Wolfenbüttelschen Capelle und Oper vom 16. bis zum 18. Jahrhundert', *Jahrbuch für musikalische Wissenschaft*, i (1863), 147.

Donington, R., *A Performer's Guide to Baroque Music* (London, 1974).

Drebes, G., 'Schütz, Monteverdi und die "Volkommenheit der Musik"—*Es steh Gott auf* aus den *Symphoniae sacrae II* (1647)', *SJb*, 14 (1992), 25.

Drude, H., *Heinrich Schütz als musiker der evangelischen Kirche* (diss., Univ. of Göttingen, 1969).

Ehmann, W., 'Die geistliche Chormusik von Heinrich Schütz in ihrer musikalischen Darstellung', *Kirchenmusik*, ed. W. Ehmann (Eberstadt, nr. Darmstadt, 1958), 75.

—— 'Die Kleine geistliche Konzerten und unsere musikalische Praxis', *Musik und Kirche*, 33 (1963), 9.

Engländer, R., 'Die erste italienische Oper in Dresden: Bontempis *Il Paride in Musica* (1662) *Svensk Tidskrift för Musikforskning* 43 (1961), 119.

Faulkner, Q., *The 'Symphoniae sacrae' of Heinrich Schütz: a Manual for Performance* (New York, 1975).

Fechner, J.-U., 'Zur literaturgeschichtlichen Situation in Dresden 1627. Überlegungen im Hinblick auf die "Dafne" Oper von Schütz und Opitz, *SJb*, 10 (1988), 5.

Fischer, K., 'Die Passionhistorie von Heinrich Schütz und ihre geschichtliche Voraussetzungen', *Musik und Gottesdienst*, 20 (1966), 48.

—— *Die Passion. Musik zwischen Kunst und Kirche*, (Stuttgart, Metzler, 1997).

Forchert, A., 'Heinrich Schütz als Komponist evangelischer Kirchenliedtexte', *SJb*, 4/5 (1982/3), 57.

Geier, M., *Kurtze Beschreibung des . . . Herrn Heinrich Schützens Lebens-Lauff* (Dresden, 1672; repr. 1935/R 1972).

Gerber, R., *Das Passionsrezitativ bei Heinrich Schütz und seine stilgeschichtlichen Grundlagen* (Gütersloh, 1929).

Gregor-Delin, M., *Heinrich Schütz: sein Leben, sein Werk, seine Zeit* (Munich, 1984).

Gudewill, K., 'Heinrich Schütz und Italien', *Heinrich Schütz e il suo tempo* (Rome, 1981), 19.

Haack, H., 'Heinrich Schütz und Lodovico Viadana', *Die Musikforschung*, 19 (1966), 28.

Haase, H., *Heinrich Schütz (1585–1672) in seinen Beziehungen zum Wolfenbüttel Hof.* Catalogue of Herzog-August-Bibliothek, No. 8: A. Schlaeger, 1972.

Heller, A., 'Heinrich Schütz in seinen italienischen Madrigalen', *Gustav Becking zum Gedächtnis* (Tutzing, 1975), 373.

Henning, R., 'Zur Textfrage der "Musicalischen Exequien" von Heinrich Schütz', *Sagittarius*, 4 (1973), 44.

Herrmann, M., 'Bemerkungen zur Schütz Rezeption im 17. Jahrhundert am Beispiel der "Breslauer Varianten" der Auferstehungshistorie SWV 50', *SJb*, 12 (1990), 83.

Huber, W. S., *Motivsymbolik bei Heinrich Schütz* (Basle, 1961).

Jung, H. R., 'Neues zum Thema "Heinrich Schütz und Weimar" ', *SJb*, 9 (1987), 105.

Just, M., 'Rhythmus und Klang als Formfactorem in den "Kleinen geistlichen Konzerten" von Heinrich Schütz', *SJb*, 9 (1987), 44.

Kirchner, G., *Der Generalbass bei Heinrich Schütz*, (Bärenreiter, Kassel, 1960).

Kirwan-Mott, A., *The Small-scale Sacred Concertato in the Early Seventeenth Century* (Ann Arbor, 1981).

Köhler, S., *Heinrich Schütz; Anmerkung zu Leben und Werk* (VEB Deutscher Verlag für Musik, Leipzig, 1885).

—— 'Heinrich Schütz in Venedig: die Bedeutung der musikalischer Renaissance für sein Werk', in *Heinrich Schütz und seine Zeit* (Berlin, 1972), 26.

Kreidler, W., *Heinrich Schütz und der Stile concitato von Claudio Monteverdi* (Kassel, 1934).

Krummacher, F., *Die Choralbearbeitung in der protestantischen Figuralmusik zwischen Praetorius und Bach* (Kassel, 1978).

Kunze, S., 'Instrumentalität und Sprachvertonung in der Musik von Heinrich Schütz', *SJb*, 1 (1979), 9.

Larsen, J. P., 'Schütz und Dänemark', *Sagittarius*, 2 (1969), 9.

Leaver, R. A., 'Heinrich Schütz as a Biblical Interpreter' *Bach* 4/3 (1973), 3.

—— 'The Funeral Sermon for Heinrich Schütz', *Bach* 4/4 (1973), 3; 5/1 (1974), 9; 5/2 (1974), 22; 5/3 (1974), 13.

Linfield, E., 'A New Look at the Sources of Schütz's *Christmas History*', *SJb*, 4/5 (1982/83), 19.

McCulloch, D., 'Heinrich Schütz (1585–1672) and Venice', *Church Music*, 2 (1967) No. 20, 8 and No. 21, 4.

Moser, H. J., *Heinrich Schütz: sein Leben und Werk* (Bärenreiter, Kassel, 1936; rev. 1954). Eng. trans., Carl Pfatteicher (St Louis Concordia, 1959).

Müller, E. H. (ed.), *Heinrich Schütz: Gesammelte Briefe und Schriften* (Regensburg, 1931; repr. Hildesheim, Olms, 1976).

Müller-Blattau, J. M., *Die Kompositionslehre Heinrich Schützens in der Fassung seines Schülers Christoph Bernhard* (Leipzig, 1926; 2/1963).

Osthoff, W., 'Monteverdi's *Combattimento* in deutscher Sprache und Heinrich Schütz', *Festschrift Helmuth Osthoff* (Tutzing, 1961), 195.

Parker, G. (ed.), *The Thirty Years War* (London, 1984).

Petzoldt, R. and Berke, D., *Heinrich Schütz und seine Zeit in Bildern* (Kassel, 1972).

Pirro, A., *Schütz* (Paris, 1913; 2/1924; repr. 1975).

Reitter, L., *Doppelchortechnik bei Heinrich Schütz* (Derendingen, 1937).

Rifkin, J., 'Towards a New Image of Heinrich Schütz', *The Musical Times* 126, nos. 1713 (Nov. 1985), 651; and 1714 (Dec. 1985), 716.

Rifkin, J. and Timms, C., 'Schütz, Heinrich', *The New Grove North European Baroque Masters* (London, 1985), 1.

Roche, J., 'What Schütz learnt from Grandi in 1629', *The Musical Times*, 113 (1972), 1074.

Salmen, W., 'Der Tanz im Denken und Wirken von Heinrich Schütz', *SJb*, 15 (1993), 25.

Schmid, M. H., 'Trompetchor und Sprachvertonung bei Heinrich Schütz', *SJb*, 13 (1991), 28.

Schmidt, E., *Der Gottesdienst am Kurfürstlichen Hofe zu Dresden*. Vol. 12 of *Veröffentlichungen der Evangelischen Gesellschaft für Liturgieforschung* (Göttingen, 1961).

Schmiedecke, A., 'Heinrich Schütz' Beziehungen zu Köstrich, Gera, Weissenfels und Zeitz', *Heinrich Schütz 1585–1672: Festtage 1972*, ed. W. Siegmund-Schultze (Gera, 1972), 24.

Schrade, L., *Das musikalische Werk von Heinrich Schütz in der protestantischen Liturgie* (Basle, 1961).

—— 'Heinrich Schütz and Johann Sebastian Bach in the Protestant Liturgy', *The musical Heritage of the Church*, vol. 4 (St Louis Concordia, 1954), 43.

Skei, A. B., *Heinrich Schütz: a Guide to Research* (Garland, New York and London, 1981).

Smallman, B., *The Background of Passion Music: J. S. Bach and his Predecessors* (2nd ed. New York, 1970).

—— *The Music of Heinrich Schütz* (Leeds, 1985).

Smither, H., *A History of Oratorio, ii: The oratorio in the Baroque Era: Protestant Germany and England* (Chapel Hill, 1977).

Snyder, K. J., 'Bernhard, Christoph', *New Grove Dictionary of Music and Musicians*, ed. S. Sadie (London, 1980), Vol. 2, 624.

Spagnoli, G., *Letters and Documents of Heinrich Schütz 1656–1672: An Annotated Translation*, (Univ. of Rochester Press, 1990; repr. 1992).

Spitta, P., 'Handel, Bach und Schütz', *Zur Musik* (Berlin, 1892).

Steinitz, P., 'German Church Music', *New Oxford History of Music*, Vol. 5 (Oxford, 1975), 557.

Steude, W., Foreword to Heinrich Schütz, *Der Schwangesang*, NSA 39 (Bärenreiter, Kassel, 1984).

—— 'Das wiedergefunden Opus ultimum von Heinrich Schütz. Beinerkungen zur Quelle und zum Werk', *SJb*, 4/5 (1982/83), 9.

—— 'Die Marcuspassion in der Leipziger Passionen-Handschrift des Johann Zacharias Grundig', *Deutsches Jahrbuch der Musikwissenschaft*, 14 (1969), 96.

—— 'Neue Schütz-Ermittlungen', *Deutsches Jahrbuch der Musikwissenschaft*, 12 (1967), 40.

—— 'Peranda, Marco Gioseppe', *The New Grove Dictionary of Music and Musicians*, ed. S. Sadie (London, 1980), Vol. 14, 96.

—— 'Zum gegenwärtigen Stand der Schütz-Biographik', *SJb*, 12 (1990), 7.

Tellart, R., *Heinrich Schütz: l'homme et son oeuvre* (Paris, 1968).

Timms, C., 'Bontempi, Govanni Andrea', *The New Grove Dictionary of Music and Musicians*, ed. S. Sadie (London, 1980), Vol. 3, 37.

Wade, Maria R., 'Heinrich Schütz and "det Store Bilager" [the Great Wedding] in Copenhagen', *SJb*, 11 (1989), 32.

Watty, A., 'Zu Heinrich Schütz' weltlichen Konzert "Ach wie soll ich doch in Freuden leben" (SWV 474)', *SJb*, 9 (1987), 85.

Wedgwood, V., *The Thirty Years War* (London, 1938).

Wessely, O., 'Zur Frage nach dem Geburtstag von Heinrich Schütz', *Anzeiger der phil.-hist. Klasse der Österreichischen Akademie der Wissenschaften*, xc (1953), 231.

Winterfeld, C. von, *Johannes Gabrieli und sein Zeitalter* (Berlin, 1834; repr. 1965).

Witzenmann, W., 'Tonartenprobleme in den Passionen von Schütz', *SJb*, 2 (1980), 103.

Index

Index

Priuli, Giovanni 15
Purcell, Henry:
  Dido and Aeneas (1689) 25
  verse anthem, 'I will give thanks unto thee,
    O Lord' (*c.* 1685) 118

Reichbrodt, Christian 106
Reincken, Johann Adam 4
Resinarius, Balthazar:
  St John Passion (1543) 110–11
Ribera, José de:
  The Adoration of the Shepherds (1650)
    152
Richter, Christoph 81
Rinuccini, Ottavio 33
Rist, Johann 167
Rosthius, Nikolaus:
  Resurrection History (1598) 44, 48
Rovetta, Giovanni 91
Rückert, Friedrich 3
Ruffo, Vicenzo 14

Scacchi, Marco 103, 126
  Breve discorso sopra la musica moderna
    (1649) 126
  Cribrum musicum ad triticum Siferticum
    (1643) 103
Scandello, Antonio 44–5, 48
  Resurrection History (before 1573) 30, 44
  St John Passion (1561) 30
Scheidemann, Heinrich 4
Scheidt, Samuel 30, 31, 126, 177
  Pars prima concertuum sacrorum (1622)
    31
Schein, Johann Hermann 32, 62, 76, 122–3,
    125, 128–9, 139, 177
  Israelsbrünnlein (1623) 122, 128
  Opella nova (Pt. 1, 1618) 91; (Pt. 2, 1626)
    100–1
Schering, Arnold 150
Schiller, Johann Christoph Friedrich von 3
Schirmer, Christian 103
Schneider, Max 150–1
Schottelius, Justus Georg 90
Schreiber, Dorothea 9
Schubert, Franz 3
Schultes, Anna 30
Schultze, Christian Andreas:
  Resurrection History (1686) 49 n. 11
Schultze, Christoph:
  St Luke Passion (1653) 158
Schumann, Robert 3
Schütz, Albrecht 9, 10
Schütz, Anna Justina 32, 102
Schütz, Benjamin 88
Schütz, Christoph 9, 10
Schütz, Euphrosina, *see* Pincker

Schütz, Euphrosyne (née Bieger) 9, 10, 27 n. 2
Schütz, Georg 10, 38, 88
Schütz, Georg Christoph (the elder) 10
Schütz, Heinrich
WORKS (the principal collections are in
chronological order, with their individual
items listed by their catalogue (SWV)
numbers)

Italian madrigals [Op. 1] 1611: 17–25
  O primavera (SWV 1) 18
  O dolcezze amarissime (SWV 2) 17, 18, 21
  Selve beate (SWV 3) 17, 18
  Alma afflita, che fai? (SWV 4) 19
  Così morir debb'io (SWV 5) 17, 19
  D'orrida selce alpina (SWV 6) 17, 19, 21
  Ride la primavera (SWV 7) 19, 20
  Fuggi, fuggi, o mio core! (SWV 8) 19, 23–4
  Feritevi, ferite (SWV 9) 19
  Fiamma ch'allaccia e laccio sei tu ch'infi-
    amma (SWV 10) 17, 19
  Quella damma son io (SWV 11) 17
  Mi saluta costei (SWV 12) 21
  Io moro (SWV 13) 18
  Sospir, che del petto di Madonna esci fore
    (SWV 14) 22–3
  Dunque addio, care selve (SWV 15) 24–6
  Tornate, o cari baci (SWV 16) 21–2
  Di marmo siete voi (SWV 17) 18
  Vasto mar, nel cui seno (SWV 19) 17

Psalmen Davids [Op. 2] 1619: 35–43, 133
  Ach Herr, straf mich nicht, Psalm 6 (SWV
    24) 39
  Aus der Tiefe ruf ich, Psalm 130 (SWV 25)
    39
  Herr, unser Herrscher, Psalm 8 (SWV 27) 37
  Wohl dem, der nicht wandelt, Psalm 1 (SWV
    28) 38
  Wie lieblich sind deine Wohnungen, Psalm
    84 (SWV 29) 38
  Wohl dem, der den Herren fürchtet, Psalm
    128 (SWV 30) 37
  Ich hebe meine Augen auf, Psalm 121 (SWV
    31) 37
  Der Herr ist mein Hirt, Psalm 23 (SWV 33)
    37
  Ich danke dem Herrn von ganzen Herzen,
    Psalm 111 (SWV 34) 41
  Singet dem Herrn ein neues Lied, Psalm 98
    (SWV 35) 41
  Jauchzet dem Herren, alle Welt, Psalm 100
    (SWV 36) 41, 171
  Alleluja! lobet den Herren, Psalm 150 (SWV
    38) 42
  Ist nicht Ephraim mein teurer Sohn (motet)
    (SWV 40) 37
  Die mit Tränen säen (motet) (SWV 42) 37

214